Computer
Basics

Windows® 10 Edition

ABSOLUTE BEGINNER'S GUIDE

Michael Miller

800 East 96th Street,
Indianapolis, Indiana 46240

Computer Basics Absolute Beginner's Guide, Windows® 10 Edition

ISBN-13: 978-0-7897-5451-6
ISBN-10: 0-7897-5451-7

Library of Congress Control Number: 2015945278

Printed in the United States of America

First Printing: August 2015

Trademarks

All terms mentioned in this book that are known to be trademarks or service marks have been appropriately capitalized. Que Publishing cannot attest to the accuracy of this information. Use of a term in this book should not be regarded as affecting the validity of any trademark or service mark.

Warning and Disclaimer

Every effort has been made to make this book as complete and as accurate as possible, but no warranty or fitness is implied. The information provided is on an "as is" basis. The author and the publisher shall have neither liability nor responsibility to any person or entity with respect to any loss or damages aris-ing from the information contained in this book.

Special Sales

For information about buying this title in bulk quantities, or for special sales opportunities (which may include electronic versions; custom cover designs; and content particular to your business, training goals, marketing focus, or branding interests), please contact our corporate sales department at corp-sales@pearsoned.com or (800) 382-3419.

For government sales inquiries, please contact governmentsales@pearsoned.com.

For questions about sales outside the U.S., please contact international@pearsoned.com.

Associate Publisher
Greg Wiegand

Acquisitions Editor
Michelle Newcomb

Development Editor
William Abner

Managing Editor
Kristy Hart

Project Editor
Andy Beaster

Technical Editor
Vince Averello

Copy Editor
San Dee Phillips

Indexer
Cheryl Lenser

Proofreader
Katie Matejka

Publishing Coordinator
Cindy Teeters

Compositor
Studio Galou

Contents at a Glance

Table of Contents

About the Author

Michael Miller is a successful and prolific author with a reputation for practical advice, technical accuracy, and an unerring empathy for the needs of his readers.

Mr. Miller has written more than 150 best-selling books over the past 25 years. His books for Que include *Easy Computer Basics*, *My Windows 10 Computer for Seniors*, *My Facebook for Seniors*, *My Pinterest*, and *My Social Media for Seniors*.

He is known for his casual, easy-to-read writing style and his practical, real-world advice—as well as his ability to explain a variety of complex topics to an everyday audience.

Learn more about Mr. Miller at his website, www.millerwriter.com. Follow him on Twitter @molehillgroup.

Dedication

To Sherry—life together is easier.

Acknowledgments

Thanks to the usual suspects at Que, including but not limited to Greg Wiegand, Michelle Newcomb, William Abner, San Dee Phillips, Andy Beaster, and technical editor Vince Averello.

We Want to Hear from You!

As the reader of this book, *you* are our most important critic and commentator. We value your opinion and want to know what we're doing right, what we could do better, what areas you'd like to see us publish in, and any other words of wisdom you're willing to pass our way.

As an associate publisher for Que Publishing, I welcome your comments. You can email or write me directly to let me know what you did or didn't like about this book—as well as what we can do to make our books better.

Please note that I cannot help you with technical problems related to the topic of this book. We do have a User Services group, however, where I will forward specific technical questions related to the book.

When you write, please be sure to include this book's title and author as well as your name, email address, and phone number. I will carefully review your comments and share them with the author and editors who worked on the book.

Email: feedback@quepublishing.com

Mail: Greg Wiegand
        Associate Publisher
        Que Publishing
        800 East 96th Street
        Indianapolis, IN 46240 USA

Reader Services

Visit our website and register this book at informit.com/register for convenient access to any updates, downloads, or errata that might be available for this book.

INTRODUCTION

Because this book is titled *Computer Basics: Absolute Beginner's Guide*, let's start at the absolute beginning, which is this:

Computers aren't supposed to be scary. Intimidating? Sometimes. Difficult to use? Perhaps. Inherently unreliable? Most definitely. (Although they're much better than they used to be.)

But scary? Definitely not.

Computers aren't scary because there's nothing they can do to hurt you (unless you drop your notebook PC on your foot, that is). And there's not much you can do to hurt them, either. It's kind of a wary coexistence between man and machine, but the relationship has the potential to be beneficial—to you, anyway.

Many people think that they're scared of computers because they're unfamiliar with them. But that isn't really true.

You see, even if you've never actually used a computer before, you've been exposed to computers and all they can do for the past three decades or so. Whenever you make a deposit at your bank, you work with computers. Whenever you make a purchase at a retail store, you work with computers. Whenever you watch a television show, read a newspaper article, or look at a picture in a magazine, you work with computers.

That's because computers are used in all those applications. Somebody, somewhere, works behind the scenes with a computer to manage your bank account and monitor your credit card purchases.

In fact, it's difficult to imagine, here in the 21st century, how we ever got by without all those keyboards, mice, and monitors (or, for that matter, the Internet and social networking).

However, just because computers have been around for a while doesn't mean that everyone knows how to use them. It's not unusual to feel a little trepidation the first time you sit down in front of that intimidating display and keyboard. Which keys should you press? What do people mean by double-clicking the mouse? And what are all those little pictures onscreen?

As foreign as all this might seem at first, computers really aren't that hard to understand—or use. You have to learn a few basic concepts, of course (all the pressing and clicking and whatnot), and it helps to understand exactly what part of the system does what. But when you get the hang of things, computers are easy to use.

Which, of course, is where this book comes in.

Computer Basics: Absolute Beginner's Guide, Windows 10 Edition, can help you figure out how to use your new computer system. You learn how computers work, how to connect all the pieces and parts (if your computer has pieces and parts, that is; not all do), and how to start using them. You learn about computer hardware and software, about Microsoft's Windows 10 operating system, and about the Internet. And when you're comfortable with the basic concepts (which won't take too long, trust me), you learn how to actually do stuff.

You learn how to do useful stuff, such as writing letters and scheduling appointments; fun stuff, such as listening to music, watching movies and TV shows, and viewing digital photos; online stuff, such as searching for information, sending and receiving email, and keeping up with friends and family via Facebook and other social networks; and essential stuff, such as copying files, troubleshooting problems, and protecting against malware and computer attacks.

All you have to do is sit yourself down in front of your computer, try not to be scared (there's nothing to be scared of, really), and work your way through the chapters and activities in this book. And remember that computers aren't difficult to use, they don't break easily, and they let you do all sorts of fun and useful things after you get the hang of them. Really!

How This Book Is Organized

This book is organized into eight main parts, as follows:

- **Part I, "Understanding Computers,"** discusses all the different types of computers available today; describes all the pieces and parts of desktop, all-in-one, and notebook PCs; and talks about how to connect everything to get your new system up and running.

- **Part II, "Using Windows,"** introduces the backbone of your entire system, the Microsoft Windows operating system—in particular, Windows 10. You learn how Windows 10 works, how it's different from previous versions of Windows, and how to navigate your way around the desktop and the Start menu. You'll also learn how to use Windows to perform basic tasks, such as copying and deleting files and folders.

- **Part III, "Setting Up the Rest of Your System,"** talks about all those things you connect to your computer—printers, external hard drives, USB thumb drives, and the like. You also learn how to connect your new PC to other computers and devices in a home network.

- **Part IV, "Using the Internet,"** is all about going online. You discover how to connect to the Internet and surf the Web. You also learn how to search for information, do research, shop, and even sell things online. This is the fun part of the book.

- **Part V, "Communicating Online,"** is all about keeping in touch. You find out how to send and receive email, of course, but also how to get started with social networking, on Facebook, Pinterest, Twitter, and other social networks. It's how everyone's keeps in touch these days.

- **Part VI, "Working with Software Programs,"** tells you everything you need to know about using software programs. (What some people call "apps.") You learn how software programs work, which apps are included in Windows 10, and where to find more apps. (This last bit covers Microsoft's Windows Store, which is where a lot of fun apps can be had.)

- **Part VII, "Doing Fun and Useful Stuff with Your PC,"** brings more fun—and a little work. You learn all about getting productive with Microsoft Office, as well as how to manage your schedule with the Windows Calendar app. You also discover how to use your PC to manage, edit, and view digital photos; listen to music, both on your PC and over the Internet; and watch movies and TV shows online. Like I said, fun and useful stuff.

- **Part VIII, "Keeping Your System Up and Running,"** contains all the boring (but necessary) information you need to know to keep your new PC in tip-top shape. You learn how to protect against Internet threats (including viruses, spyware, and spam), as well as how to perform routine computer maintenance. You even learn how to troubleshoot problems and, if necessary, restore, refresh, or reset your entire system.

Taken together, the 26 chapters in this book can help you progress from absolute beginner to experienced computer user. Just read what you need, and before long you'll be using your computer like a pro!

Which Version of Windows?

This edition of the *Absolute Beginner's Guide to Computer Basics* is written for computers running the latest version of Microsoft's operating system, dubbed Windows 10. If you're running previous versions of Windows, you'll be better off with previous editions of this book. There are editions out there for Windows 8.1, Windows 8, Windows 7, Windows Vista, even Windows XP. If you can't find a particular edition at your local bookstore, look for it online.

Conventions Used in This Book

I hope that this book is easy enough to figure out on its own, without requiring its own instruction manual. As you read through the pages, however, it helps to know precisely how I've presented specific types of information.

Menu Commands

Most computer programs operate via a series of pull-down menus. You use your mouse to pull down a menu and then select an option from that menu. This sort of operation is indicated like this throughout the book:

Select File, Save.

or

Right-click the file and select Properties from the pop-up menu.

All you have to do is follow the instructions in order, using your mouse to click each item in turn. When submenus are tacked onto the main menu, just keep clicking the selections until you come to the last one—which should open the program or activate the command you want!

Shortcut Key Combinations

When you use your computer keyboard, sometimes you have to press two keys at the same time. These two-key combinations are called *shortcut keys* and are shown as the key names joined with a plus sign (+).

For example, Ctrl+W indicates that you should press the W key while holding down the Ctrl key. It's no more complex than that.

Web Page Addresses

This book contains a lot of web page addresses. (That's because you'll probably be spending a lot of time on the Internet.)

Technically, a web page address is supposed to start with http:// (as in http://www.millerwriter.com). Because web browsers automatically insert this piece of the address, however, you don't have to type it—and I haven't included it in any of the addresses in this book.

Special Elements

This book also includes a few special elements that provide additional information not included in the basic text. These elements are designed to supplement the text to make your learning faster, easier, and more efficient.

A *tip* is a piece of advice—a little trick, actually—that helps you use your computer more effectively or maneuver around problems or limitations.

A *note* is designed to provide information that is generally useful but not specifically necessary for what you're doing at the moment. Some are like extended tips—interesting, but not essential.

A *caution* tells you to beware of a potentially dangerous act or situation. In some cases, ignoring a caution could cause you significant problems—so pay attention to them!

There's More Online

If you want to learn more about me and any new books I have in the works, check out my website at www.millerwriter.com. Who knows, you might find some other books there that you would like to read. You can also follow me on Twitter (@molehillgroup), and leave messages to me on my website. I love hearing from readers!

1

HOW PERSONAL COMPUTERS WORK

Chances are you're reading this book because you just bought a new computer, are thinking about buying a new computer, or maybe even had someone give you his old computer. (Nothing wrong with high-tech hand-me-downs!) At this point you might not be totally sure what it is you've gotten yourself into. Just what is this mess of boxes and cables, and what can you—or should you—do with it?

This chapter serves as an introduction to the entire concept of personal computers —what they do, how they work, that sort of thing—and computer hardware in particular. It's a good place to start if you're not that familiar with computers or want a brief refresher course in what all those pieces and parts are and what they do.

Of course, if you want to skip the background and get right to using your computer, that's okay, too. For step-by-step instructions on how to connect and configure a new notebook (portable) PC, go directly to Chapter 2, "Setting Up and Using a Notebook Computer." Or if you have a new desktop or all-in-one PC, go to Chapter 3, "Setting Up and Using a Desktop Computer." Everything you need to know should be in one of those two chapters.

What Your Computer Can Do

What good is a personal computer, anyway?

Everybody has one, you know (including you, now). In fact, it's possible you bought your new computer just so that you wouldn't feel left out. But now that you have your own personal computer, what do you do with it?

Good for Getting Online

Most of what we do on our computers these days is accomplished via the Internet. We find and communicate with our friends online; we find useful information online; we watch movies and listen to music online; we play games online; we even shop and do our banking online. Most of these activities are accomplished by browsing something called the World Wide Web (or just the "Web"), which you do from something called a web browser. Now that you have a new computer and (hopefully) an Internet connection at home, you won't feel left out when people start talking about "double-u double-u double-u" this and "dot-com" that—because you'll be online, too.

NOTE   Learn more about getting online in Chapter 12, "Connecting to the Internet—at Home or Away."

Good for Social Networking

One of the most popular online activities these days involves something called social networking. A *social network* is a website where you can keep informed as to what your friends and family are doing, and they can see what you're up to, too. There are several social networks you can use, but the most popular are Facebook, Pinterest, Instagram, Tumblr, Twitter, and LinkedIn. You can join one or more of these and start sharing your life online.

NOTE   Learn more about Facebook and other social networks in Chapter 16, "Social Networking with Facebook and Other Social Media."

Good for Communicating

Your new computer is also great for one-to-one communication. Want to send a note to a friend? Or keep your family informed of what's new and exciting? It's easy enough to do, thanks to your new computer and the Internet. You can drop a note via email or keep 'em posted via Facebook or some similar social networking site.

 NOTE   Learn more about communicating with email in Chapter 15, "Sending and Receiving Email."

Good for Sharing Photos and Home Movies

You can also use your computer to store and share your favorite photos and home movies. When you upload a picture, your friends can view it online. You can even touch up the photo before you share it. Pretty nifty.

 NOTE   Learn more about digital photos in Chapter 22, "Viewing and Sharing Digital Photos."

Good for Keeping in Touch

There are a number of ways to use your new computer to keep in touch with absent family and friends. You can communicate over the Internet, via email. You can communicate via Facebook and other social networks. You can even participate in video chats in real time, using your computer's webcam and the Skype video chatting service. It's just like being there!

 NOTE   Learn more about online video chats in Chapter 17, "Video Chatting with Friends and Family."

Good for Entertainment

For many people, a personal computer is a hub for all sorts of entertainment. You can use your computer to watch movies on DVDs and listen to music on CDs. You can go online to find even more movies and TV shows on Netflix and other streaming video services, or listen to all the music you want on streaming music services such as Pandora and Spotify.

NOTE   Learn more about watching TV and movies on your PC in Chapter 23, "Watching Movies, TV Shows, and Other Videos." Learn more about listening to music with your PC in Chapter 24, "Playing Music."

Good for Keeping Informed

Entertainment is fun, but it's also important to stay informed. Your computer is a great gateway to tons of information, both old and new. You can search for just about anything you want online or use your computer to browse the latest news headlines, sports scores, and weather reports. All the information you can think of is online somewhere, and you use your computer to find and read it.

NOTE   Learn more about staying informed online in Chapter 13, "Browsing and Searching the Web."

Good for Work

A lot of people use their home PCs for work-related purposes. You can bring your work (reports, spreadsheets, you name it) home from the office and finish it on your home PC. Or, if you work at home, you can use your computer to pretty much run your small business—you can use it to do everything from typing memos and reports to generating invoices and setting budgets.

In short, anything you can do with a normal office PC, you can probably do on your home PC.

NOTE   Learn more about using your computer for office work in Chapter 20, "Doing Office Work."

Good for Play

All work and no play make Jack a dull boy, so there's no reason not to have a little fun with your new PC. There are a lot of cool games online, plus you can purchase all manner of computer games to play, if that's what you're into. There's a lot of fun to be had with your new PC!

NOTE   This book is written for users of relatively new personal computers—in particular, PCs running the Microsoft Windows 10 operating system. If you have an older PC running an older version of Windows, most of the advice here is still good, although not all the step-by-step instructions will apply.

Inside a Personal Computer

As we'll discuss momentarily, there are a lot of different types of personal computers—desktops, notebooks, tablets, and the like. What they all have in common is a core set of components—the computer *hardware*. Unlike computer *software*, which describes the programs and applications you run on your computer, the hardware is composed of those parts of your system you can actually see and touch.

Well, you could see the parts if you opened the case, which you can't always do. Let's take a virtual tour inside a typical PC, so you can get a sense of how the darned thing works.

The Motherboard: Home to Almost Everything

Inside every PC are all manner of computer chips and circuit boards. Most of these parts connect to a big circuit board called a *motherboard*, so named because it's the "mother" for the computer's microprocessor and memory chips, as well as for all other internal components that enable your system to function. On a traditional desktop PC, the motherboard is located near the base of the computer, as shown in Figure 1.1; on an all-in-one desktop, it's built into the monitor unit; on a notebook PC, it's just under the keyboard; and on a tablet or hybrid model, it's built into the touchscreen display.

On a traditional desktop PC, the motherboard contains several slots, into which you can plug additional *boards* (also called *cards*) that perform specific functions. All-in-one and notebook PC motherboards can't accept additional boards and thus aren't expandable like PCs that have separate system units.

Most traditional desktop PC motherboards contain multiple slots for add-on cards. For example, a video card enables your motherboard to transmit video signals to your monitor. Other available cards enable you to add sound and modem/fax capabilities to your system. (On an all-in-one or notebook PC, these video and audio functions are built into the motherboard, rather than being on separate cards.)

FIGURE 1.1

What a typical desktop PC looks like on the inside—a big motherboard with lots of add-on boards attached.

Microprocessors: The Main Engine

We're not done looking at the motherboard just yet. That's because, buried somewhere on that big motherboard, is a specific chip that controls your entire computer system. This chip is called a *microprocessor* or a *central processing unit (CPU)*.

The microprocessor is the brain inside your system. It processes all the instructions necessary for your computer to perform its duties. The more powerful the microprocessor chip, the faster and more efficiently your system runs.

Microprocessors carry out the various instructions that enable your computer compute. Every input and output device connected to a computer—the keyboard, printer, monitor, and so on—either issues or receives instructions that the microprocessor then processes. Your software programs also issue instructions that must be implemented by the microprocessor. This chip truly is the workhorse of your system; it affects just about everything your computer does.

Different computers have different types of microprocessor chips. Desktop and notebook computers running the Windows operating system use chips manufactured by either Intel or AMD. (Apple Macintosh computers also use Intel chips, although they're different from the chips used in Windows PCs.)

In addition to having different chip manufacturers (and different chip families from the same manufacturer), you'll run into microprocessor chips that run at different speeds. CPU speed today is measured in *gigahertz (GHz)*. A CPU with a speed of 1GHz can run at one *billion* clock ticks per second! The bigger the gigahertz number, the faster the chip runs.

It gets better. Many chips today incorporate so-called *dual-core* or *quad-core* chips. What this means is that a single chip includes the equivalent of two (dual-core) or four (quad-core) CPUs. That's like doubling or quadrupling your processing power! The more cores, the better—especially for processor-intensive tasks, such as editing digital video files.

If you're shopping for a new PC, look for one with the combination of a powerful microprocessor and a high clock speed for best performance. And don't forget to count all the cores; a dual-core chip with two 1.8GHz CPUs is more powerful than a single-core chip with a 2.0GHz CPU.

Computer Memory: Temporary Storage

Before a CPU can process instructions you give it, your instructions must be stored somewhere, in preparation for access by the microprocessor. These instructions— along with other data processed by your system—are temporarily held in the computer's *random access memory (RAM)*. All computers have some amount of memory, which is created by a number of memory chips. The more memory that's available in a machine, the more instructions and data that can be stored at one time.

Memory is measured in terms of *bytes*. One byte is equal to approximately one character in a word processing document. A unit equaling approximately one thousand bytes (1,024, to be exact) is called a *kilobyte (KB)*, and a unit of approximately one thousand (1,024) kilobytes is called a *megabyte (MB)*. A thousand megabytes is a *gigabyte (GB)*.

Most computers today come with at least 4GB of memory, some with much more. To enable your computer to run as many programs as quickly as possible, you need as much memory installed in your system as it can accept—or that you can afford. You can add extra memory to a computer by installing new memory modules, which is as easy as plugging a "stick" directly into a slot on your system's motherboard.

If your computer doesn't possess enough memory, its CPU must constantly retrieve data from permanent storage on its hard disk. This method of data retrieval is slower than retrieving instructions and data from electronic memory. In fact, if your machine doesn't have enough memory, some programs will run very slowly (or you might experience random system crashes), and other programs won't run at all!

Hard Disk Drives: Long-Term Storage

Another important physical component inside your system unit is the *hard disk drive*. The hard disk permanently stores all your important data. Some hard disks today can store up to 6 *terabytes (TB)* of data—that's 6,000GB—and even bigger hard disks are on the way. (Contrast this to your system's RAM, which temporarily stores only a few gigabytes of data.)

A hard disk consists of numerous metallic platters. These platters store data *magnetically*. Special read/write *heads* realign magnetic particles on the platters, much like a recording head records data onto magnetic recording tape.

However, before data can be stored on a disk, including your system's hard disk, that disk must be *formatted*. A disk that has not been formatted cannot accept data. When you format a hard disk, your computer prepares each track and sector of the disk to accept and store data magnetically. Fortunately, hard disks in new PCs are preformatted, so you don't have to worry about this. (And, in most cases, your operating system and key programs are preinstalled.)

 CAUTION   If you try to reformat your hard disk, you'll erase all the programs and data that have been installed—so don't do it!

Solid-State Drives: Faster Long-Term Storage

Not all long-term storage is hard disk-based, however. Many of today's notebook PCs don't have traditional hard disk storage. Instead, they use solid-state flash memory for long-term storage.

A solid-state drive (SSD) has no moving parts. Instead, data is stored electronically on an integrated circuit. This type of storage is both lighter and faster than traditional hard disk storage; data stored on a solid-state drive can be accessed pretty much instantly. Plus, notebooks with solid-state drives are considerably lighter than notebooks with traditional hard drives.

The downside of solid-state storage is that it's more expensive than hard drive storage; although, the price is coming down. What this means is that you typically get a little less storage on an SSD than you would on a similar computer with a traditional hard drive. For example, you might see one ultrabook with a 256GB SSD and another at a similar price with a 500GB or 1TB traditional hard drive. They're not quite on par just yet.

So if it's important for your computer to be fast and lightweight, consider a model with solid-state storage. If you prefer a lower-priced model or need more storage space, stick with a traditional hard disk PC.

CD/DVD Drives: Storage on a Disc

Not all the storage on your PC is inside the system unit. As you can see in Figure 1.2, many PCs feature a combination *CD/DVD drive* that enables you to play audio CDs and movie DVDs, install CD- or DVD-based software programs, and burn music, movies, or data to blank CD or DVD discs.

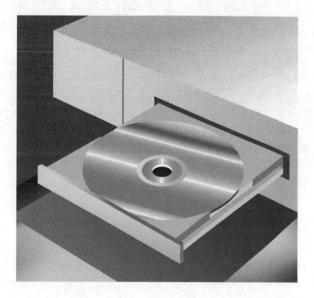

FIGURE 1.2

Store tons of data on a shiny CD or DVD data disc.

Computer CD discs, called CD-ROM discs (the ROM stands for "read-only memory"), look just like the compact discs you play on your audio system. They're also similar in the way they store data (audio data in the case of regular CDs; computer data in the case of CD-ROMs).

NOTE   The *ROM* part of CD-ROM means that you can read data only from the disk; unlike normal hard disks and diskettes, you can't write new data to a standard CD-ROM. However, most PCs include recordable (CD-R) and rewritable (CD-RW) drives that do let you write data to CDs—so you can use your CD drive just like a regular disk drive.

If you need even more storage, consider writing to blank DVD discs. A DVD can contain up to 4.7GB of data (for a single-layer disc) or 8.5GB of data (for a double-layer disc). Compared to 700MB of storage for a typical CD-ROM, this makes DVDs ideally suited for large applications or games that otherwise would require multiple CDs. Similar to standard CD-ROMs, most DVDs are read-only; although, all DVD drives can also read CD-ROMs.

Some high-end PCs do the standard DVD one step better and can read and write high-definition DVDs in the *Blu-ray* format, which enables you store 25GB or more of data on a single disc. Although that storage for PC data might be overkill, it might be nice to play high-definition Blu-ray movies on your PC.

Note that *many* PCs have CD/DVD drives, but not all. That's because many notebook PCs are getting smaller and lighter by leaving out the CD/DVD drives.

Because most software programs these days are downloaded via the Internet (they used to be delivered on CDs and DVDs), you don't need a CD/DVD drive as much as you used to. It's still nice for playing music and movies however, so you can always add an external CD/DVD drive if you want. In most cases, however, you can get by without it if you have a decent Internet connection; just about anything you can find on CD or DVD (including movies and music) is also available online for downloading.

Keyboards: Fingertip Input

Computers receive data by reading it from disk, accepting it electronically over a modem, or receiving input directly from you, the user. You provide your input by way of what's called, in general, an *input device*; the most common input device you use to talk to your computer is the keyboard.

A computer keyboard, similar to the one in Figure 1.3, looks and functions just like an old-fashioned typewriter keyboard, except that computer keyboards have a few more keys. Some of these keys (such as the arrow, Pg Up, Pg Dn, Home, and End keys) enable you to move around within a program or file. Other keys provide access to special program features. When you press a key on your keyboard, it sends an electronic signal to your system unit that tells your machine what you want it to do.

FIGURE 1.3

A keyboard for a desktop PC.

Most keyboards that come with desktop and all-in-one PCs hook up via a cable to the back of your system unit; although, some manufacturers make *wireless* keyboards that connect to your system unit via radio signals—thus eliminating one cable from the back of your system. Keyboards on notebook PCs are built into the main unit, of course, and are typically a little smaller than desktop PC keyboards; many notebook keyboards, for example, lack a separate numeric keypad for entering numbers.

On a Windows PC, there are a few extra keys in addition to the normal letters and numbers and symbols and such. Chief among these is the Windows key (sometimes called the *Winkey*), like the one shown in Figure 1.4, which has a little Windows logo on it. In Windows 10, many operating functions are initiated by pressing the Windows key either by itself or along with another key on the keyboard.

FIGURE 1.4

The Windows key on a computer keyboard.

Mice and Touchpads: Point-and-Click Input Devices

It's a funny name but a necessary device. A computer *mouse*, like the one shown in Figure 1.5, is a small handheld device. Most mice consist of an oblong case with a roller underneath and two or three buttons on top. When you move the mouse along a desktop, an onscreen pointer (called a *cursor*) moves in response. When you click (press and release) a mouse button, this motion initiates an action in your program.

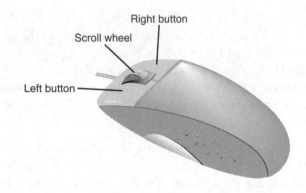

FIGURE 1.5

Roll the mouse back and forth to move the onscreen cursor.

Mice come in all shapes and sizes. Some have wires, and some are wireless. Some are relatively oval in shape, and others are all curvy to better fit in the palm of your hand. Some have the typical roller ball underneath, and others use an optical sensor to determine where and how much you're rolling. Some even have extra buttons that you can program for specific functions or a scroll wheel you can use to scroll through long documents or web pages.

Some newer mice also double as touch input devices. That is, you can tap and squeeze your fingers on a touch mouse much as you can on a touchscreen display. Obviously, you can also use a touch mouse like a traditional rolling and clicking mouse; the touch functionality is just a nice extra.

If you have a notebook PC, you don't have a separate mouse. Instead, most notebooks feature a *touchpad* pointing device that functions like a mouse. You move your fingers around the touchpad to move the onscreen cursor and then click one of the buttons underneath the touchpad the same way you'd click a mouse button.

TIP   If you have a portable PC, you don't have to use the built-in touchpad. Most portables let you attach an external mouse, which you can use in addition to the internal device.

If you use a computer with a touchscreen display, you don't need a mouse at all. Instead, you control your computer by tapping and swiping the screen, using specific motions to perform specific operations. With a touchscreen computer, operation is fairly intuitive.

Network Connections: Getting Connected

If you have more than one computer in your home, you might want to connect them to a home network. A network enables you to share files between multiple computers, as well as connect multiple PCs to a single printer or scanner. In addition, you can use a home network to share a broadband Internet connection so that all your computers connect to the Internet.

You can connect computers via either wired or wireless networks. Most home users prefer a wireless network, as there are no cables to run from one room of your house to another. Fortunately, connecting a wireless network is as easy as buying a wireless router, which functions as the hub of the network, and then connecting wireless adapters to each computer on the network. (And if you have a notebook PC, the wireless adapter is probably built in.)

 NOTE   Learn more about wireless networks in Chapter 11, "Setting Up a Home Network."

Sound Cards and Speakers: Making Noise

Every PC comes with some sort of speaker system. Most traditional desktop systems let you set up separate right and left speakers, sometimes accompanied by a subwoofer for better bass. (Figure 1.6 shows a typical right-left-subwoofer speaker system.) All-in-one desktops and notebook PCs typically come with right and left speakers built in, but with the option of connecting external speakers if you want. You can even get so-called 5.1 surround sound speaker systems, with five satellite speakers (front and rear) and the ".1" subwoofer—great for listening to movie soundtracks or playing explosive-laden video games.

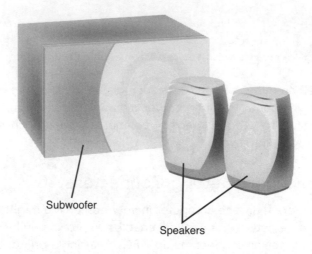

Subwoofer

Speakers

FIGURE 1.6

A typical set of right and left external speakers, complete with subwoofer.

All speaker systems are driven by a sound card or chip that is installed inside your system unit. If you upgrade your speaker system, you also might need to upgrade your sound card accordingly. (You can easily switch sound cards on a traditional desktop PC, but it's really not an option on a notebook or all-in-one.)

Video Cards and Monitors: Getting the Picture

Operating a computer would be difficult if you didn't constantly receive visual feedback showing you what your machine is doing. This vital function is provided by your computer's monitor.

Most computer monitors today are built around an LCD display. On a notebook PC, this display is built into the unit; on a desktop PC, you connect a separate external monitor. You measure the size of a monitor from corner to corner, diagonally. Today's freestanding LCD monitors start at 20" or so and run up to 27" or larger.

A flat-screen LCD display doesn't take up a lot of desk space or use a lot of energy, both of which are good things. Most monitors today come with a widescreen display that has the same 16:9 (or 16:10) aspect ratio used to display widescreen movies—which makes them ideal for viewing or editing movies on your PC.

NOTE   Older computer monitors were built around a cathode ray tube, or CRT, similar to the picture tube found in normal television sets.

Know, however, that your computer monitor doesn't generate the images it displays. Instead, screen images are electronically crafted by a *video card* or chip installed inside your system unit. To work correctly, both the video card and monitor must be matched to display images of the same resolution.

Resolution refers to the size of the images that can be displayed onscreen and is measured in pixels. A *pixel* is a single dot on your screen; a full picture is composed of thousands of pixels. The higher the resolution, the sharper the resolution—which lets you display more (smaller) elements onscreen.

Resolution is expressed in numbers of pixels, in both the horizontal and vertical directions. Most external monitors today can display up to 1920×1080 resolution; notebook PC displays are typically smaller and with slightly lower resolution.

Other Parts of Your Computer System

The computer hardware itself is only part of your overall computer system. A typical PC has additional devices—such as printers—connected to it, and it runs various programs and applications to perform specific tasks.

Providing Additional Functionality with Peripherals

There are lots of other devices, called *peripherals,* you can connect to your computer. These items include

- **Printers**—A printer enables you to make hardcopy printouts of documents and pictures.

- **Scanners**—These devices convert printed documents or pictures to electronic format.

- **Webcams**—These are small cameras (typically with built-in microphones) that enable you to send live video of yourself to friends and family.

- **Joysticks and gamepads**—These are alternatives to mice that enable you play the most challenging computer games.

- **External storage**—These are just like the hard disks inside your computer, but they connect externally to help you back up your precious data.

 NOTE   Learn more about installing peripherals in Chapter 9, "Connecting Other Devices to Your PC—and Your PC to Other Devices." Learn more about using external hard disks in Chapter 10, "Adding Storage and Backup."

You can also hook up all manner of portable devices to your PC, including smartphones, digital cameras, camcorders, and portable music players. You can even add the appropriate devices to connect multiple PCs in a network, which is useful if you have more than one computer in your house.

Fortunately, connecting a new device is as easy as plugging in a single cable. Whether you have a desktop or notebook PC, or even a tablet, most printers connect using a special type of cable called a USB cable. Almost all computers have multiple USB connections (sometimes called *ports*), so you can connect multiple peripherals via USB at the same time.

Doing What You Need to Do with Software and Apps

By themselves, the beige and black boxes that comprise a typical computer system aren't that useful. You can connect them and set them in place, but they won't do anything until you have some software to make things work.

As discussed earlier, computer hardware refers to those things you can touch—the keyboard, monitor, system unit, and the like. Computer *software*, however, is something you *can't* touch because it's nothing more than a bunch of electronic bits and bytes. These bits and bytes, however, combine into computer programs—sometimes called *applications* or just *apps*—that provide specific functionality to your system.

For example, if you want to crunch some numbers, you need a piece of software called a *spreadsheet* program. If you want to write a letter, you need a *word processing* program. If you want to make changes to some pictures you took with your digital camera, you need *graphics editing* software. And if you want to surf the Internet, you need a *web browser*.

In other words, you need separate software for each task you want to do with your computer. Fortunately, most new computer systems come with a lot of this software already installed. You might have to buy a few specific programs, but it shouldn't set you back a lot of money.

 NOTE   Learn more about computer software and apps in Part VI of this book, "Working with Software Programs."

Making Everything Work—with Windows

Whatever program or app you're using at any given point in time, you interface with your computer via a special piece of software called an *operating system*. As the name implies, this program makes your system operate; it's your gateway to the hardware part of your system.

The operating system is also how your application software interfaces with your computer hardware. When you want to print a document from your word processor, that software works with the operating system to send the document to your printer.

Most computers today ship with an operating system called *Microsoft Windows*. This operating system has been around in one form or another for 30 years or so and is published by Microsoft Corporation.

Windows isn't the only operating system around, however. Computers manufactured by Apple Computing use a different operating system, called *OS X*. Therefore, computers running Windows and computers by Apple aren't totally compatible with each other. Google's *Chrome OS* runs on many low-cost Chromebook computers, popular with schools across the country. Then there's *Linux*, which is compatible with most PCs sold today, but it's used primarily by über-techie types; it's not an operating system I would recommend for general users.

But let's get back to Windows, of which there have been several different versions over the years. The newest version is called *Microsoft Windows 10*. If you've just purchased a brand-new PC, this is probably the version you're using. If your PC is a little older, you might be running *Windows 8* or *8.1*, the immediate predecessors to Windows 10 (they skipped the number 9), or maybe even *Windows 7*, *Windows Vista*, or *Windows XP*, all of which are much older.

To some degree, Windows is Windows is Windows; all the different versions do pretty much the same things. Windows 10, however, is much improved over the previous Windows 8/8.1, which lacked some essential features common in older versions of the operating system. Windows 10 corrects all the mistakes Microsoft made with Windows 8 and gives you the user experience people have come to expect. (Which is why I expect a lot of older users will be upgrading directly from Windows 7 to Windows 10, having bypassed Windows 8.)

In any case, you use Windows—whichever version you have installed—to launch specific programs and to perform various system maintenance functions, such as copying files and turning off your computer.

 NOTE   You can learn more about Windows 10 in Part II of this book, "Using Windows."

Different Types of Computers

Although all computers consist of pretty much the same components and work in pretty much the same way, there are several different types to choose from. You can go with a traditional desktop computer, a smaller, more portable notebook model, a touchscreen tablet—or one that combines some or all these features.

Let's look at the different types of computers you can choose from.

Desktop PCs

A *desktop PC* is one with a separate monitor that's designed to sit on your desktop, along with a separate keyboard and mouse. This type of PC is stationary; you can't take it with you. It sits on your desktop, perfect for doing the requisite office work.

Although all desktop PCs sit on your desktop, there are actually two different types of desktop units:

- **Traditional desktops**—A traditional desktop system, like the one shown in Figure 1.7, has a separate system unit that sits either on the floor or beside the monitor.

- **All-in-one desktops**—This newer type of desktop PC builds the system unit into the monitor for a more compact system, like the one shown in Figure 1.8. Some of these all-in-one PCs feature touchscreen monitors, so you can control them by tapping and swiping the monitor screen.

FIGURE 1.7

A traditional desktop PC, complete with monitor, keyboard, mouse, and separate system unit. (Photo courtesy Acer.)

FIGURE 1.8

An all-in-one desktop system, with the system unit and speakers built into the monitor. (Photo courtesy Lenovo.)

A lot of folks like the easier setup (no system unit or speakers to connect) and smaller space requirements of all-in-one systems. The only drawbacks to these all-in-one desktops are the price (they're typically a bit more costly than traditional desktop PCs) and the fact that if one component goes bad, the whole system is out of commission. It's a lot easier to replace a single component than an entire system!

 **NOTE**   Learn more about desktop PCs in Chapter 3.

Notebook PCs

A *notebook PC*, sometimes called a *laptop*, combines a monitor, keyboard, and system unit in a single, compact case. This type of portable PC, like the one shown in Figure 1.9, can operate via normal electrical power or via a built-in battery; when using battery power, a notebook can be taken with you and used just about anywhere you choose to go.

FIGURE 1.9

A typical notebook PC. (Photo courtesy Toshiba.)

Just as there are several types of desktop PCs, there are several types of notebooks, including the following:

- **Traditional notebooks**—These units have screens that run in the 14" to 16" range (15.4" is common) and include decent-sized hard drives (500GB and up) and sometimes a combo CD/DVD drive. These are typically the least expensive notebooks because there's a lot of competition; this category is the most popular.

- **Desktop-replacement notebooks**—These are larger notebooks, with screens in the 17" range. They're not only bigger; they're also heavier, and the batteries don't last as long. As such, these notebooks really aren't designed for true portable use, but rather they replace traditional desktop PCs. Plus, these desktop-replacement models typically cost a bit more than traditional notebooks.

- **Ultrabooks**—An ultrabook is a smaller, thinner, and lighter notebook. Most ultrabooks have screens in the 12" to 14" range, don't have CD/DVD drives, and use solid-state flash storage instead of hard disk storage. All this makes an ultrabook very fast and very easy to carry around without necessarily sacrificing computing power and functionality. However, all this new technology means ultrabooks cost a bit more than more traditional notebooks.

 **NOTE**   Learn more about notebook computers in Chapter 2.

With all these choices available, which type of notebook should you buy? It all depends.

Most users choose traditional notebooks because they do everything you need them to do at a reasonable price. If you need more computing power but don't plan on taking your PC out of the house, then a desktop-replacement model might make sense. If you're a die-hard road warrior who likes to travel light, consider a more expensive but lighter weight ultrabook.

Tablet PCs

A tablet PC is a self-contained computer you can hold in one hand. Think of a tablet as the real-world equivalent of one of those communication pads you see on *Star Trek*; it doesn't have a separate keyboard, so you operate it by tapping and swiping the screen with your fingers.

No question about it, the most popular tablet today is the Apple iPad; no other model comes close in terms of number of users. The iPad runs Apple's iOS operating system, which is also the engine behind the company's iPhones. Also popular are tablets that run Google's Android operating system.

The iOS and Android operating systems, however, are both incompatible with the billion or so computers that run the Windows operating system. That might not be important if all you do with your tablet is browse the Web, read books, and watch movies, but if you want to do more serious work—or read or work on documents created on a Windows computer—then you need a tablet that runs Windows.

Fortunately, there are a few. A Windows tablet, such as the one in Figure 1.10, runs Windows 10 with a special touchscreen interface; you don't have to connect a mouse or keyboard to operate it. This version of Windows 10 uses a series of tiles on a Start screen, as opposed to the desktop and Start menu you find on the PC-based version of Windows.

FIGURE 1.10

Microsoft's Surface Pro tablet computer, complete with optional external keyboard. (Photo courtesy Microsoft.)

Tablets are great for consuming media and information, and they're pretty good for web-based tasks, but they're not that great if you have to get serious work done; the lack of a true keyboard is a killer when you need to type long pieces of text and enter a lot of numbers. Still, a Windows tablet can easily supplement a more traditional PC for many types of tasks and is a strong competitor to Apple's iPad.

 NOTE Learn more about the touch version of Windows in Chapter 6, "Using Windows 10 on a Touchscreen Device."

Hybrid PCs

A hybrid PC is the newest type of personal computer, a blend of the ultrabook and tablet form factors—literally. Think of a hybrid PC as an ultrabook with a touchscreen, or a tablet with a keyboard.

Most hybrid PCs, like the one in Figure 1.11, come with a swivel or fully removable keyboard, so you can type if you need to or get rid of the keyboard and use the touchscreen display as you would a tablet. Windows 10 is optimized for this new type of PC; depending on how you're using the device, you'll either see the traditional Windows desktop or the newer touch interface.

FIGURE 1.11

A hybrid ultrabook/tablet PC that folds from one form factor to another.
(Photo courtesy Lenovo.)

With a hybrid PC, you use it like a touchscreen tablet when you watch movies or browse the Web, and like a notebook PC when you have office work to do. For many users, it's the best of both worlds.

Which Type of PC Should You Choose?

Which type of PC is best for you? It depends on how you think you'll use your new computer:

- If all you plan to do is check your Facebook feed, view some photos and movies, and maybe send the occasional email, then you don't really need a full keyboard and can make do with a tablet or hybrid PC.

- If you need to do more serious work, then a traditional desktop or notebook PC, complete with keyboard and mouse, is a must.

- If you plan to do all your computing in one spot, such as your home office, then a desktop PC can do the job.

- If you want more flexibility—and the ability to take your computer with you— then a notebook or hybrid model is a necessity.

As you can see, there are a lot of choices, and even within these general types, more specific considerations to make. The price depends a lot on the amount of hard disk storage you get, the size of the display, the amount of internal memory, the speed of the microprocessor, and other technical details. And don't forget the design; make sure you choose a model you can personally live with, in terms of both style and functionality.

Don't Worry, You Can't Screw It Up—Much

I don't know why, but a lot of people are afraid of their computers. They think if they press the wrong key or click the wrong button they'll break something or will have to call an expensive repairperson to put things right.

This isn't true.

The important thing to know is that it's difficult to break your computer system. Yes, it's possible to break something if you drop it, but in terms of breaking your system through normal use, it just doesn't happen that often.

It is possible to make mistakes, of course. You can click the wrong button and accidentally delete a file you didn't want to delete or turn off your system and lose a document you forgot to save. You can even take inadequate security precautions and find your system infected by a computer virus. But in terms of doing serious harm just by clicking your mouse, it's unlikely.

So don't be afraid of the thing. Your computer is a tool, just like a hammer or a blender or a camera. After you learn how to use it, it can be a very useful tool. But it's your tool, which means you tell it what to do—not vice versa. Remember that you're in control and that you're not going to break anything, and you'll have a lot of fun—and maybe even get some real work done!

THE ABSOLUTE MINIMUM

Here are the key points to remember from this chapter:

- There are four main types of computer systems available today: desktops, notebooks, tablets, and hybrid models.

- Regardless of type, all personal computers are composed of various hardware components; in a desktop PC, they're separate devices, whereas notebook and tablet PCs combine them all into a single portable unit.

- You interface with your computer hardware via a piece of software called an operating system. The operating system on your new computer is probably some version of Microsoft Windows—Windows 10, Windows 8/8.1, Windows 7, Windows Vista, or Windows XP, depending on when you purchased the computer.

- You use specific software programs or apps to perform specific tasks, such as writing letters and editing digital photos.

- The brains and engine of your system is the system unit, which contains the microprocessor, memory, disk drives, and all the connections for your other system components.

- To make your system run faster, get a faster microprocessor or more memory.

- Data is temporarily stored in your system's memory; you store data permanently on some type of disk drive—either a hard disk or solid-state drive.

2

SETTING UP AND USING A NOTEBOOK COMPUTER

Chapter 1, "How Personal Computers Work," gives you the essential background information you need to understand how your computer system works. With that information in hand, it's now time to connect all the various pieces and parts of your computer system—and get your PC up and running!

As you might expect, setting up a notebook PC is considerably easier than setting up a traditional desktop system, which is one reason why they're so popular. Everything is built into the unit's case, so there's much, much less to connect!

Understanding Notebook PCs

Although desktop systems used to dominate the market, the most popular type of computer today is the notebook PC. A notebook PC does everything a larger desktop PC does, but in a more compact package.

A typical notebook PC combines all the various elements found in a desktop PC system into a single case and then adds a battery so that you can use it on the go. Many users find that portability convenient, even if it's just for using the computer in different rooms of the house.

As you can see in Figure 2.1, a notebook PC looks like a smallish keyboard with a flip-up LCD screen attached. That's what you see, anyway; beneath the keyboard is a full-featured computer, complete with motherboard, CPU, memory chips, video and audio processing circuits, hard drive, and battery (and possibly a CD/DVD drive, depending on the notebook).

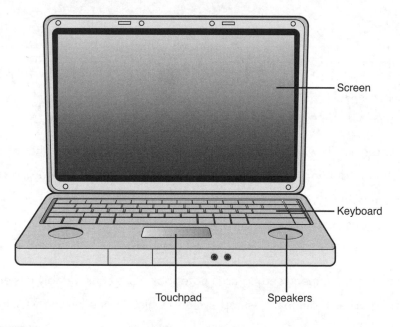

FIGURE 2.1

The important parts of a notebook PC.

When the screen is folded down, the keyboard is hidden and the PC is easy to carry from place to place; when the screen is flipped up, the keyboard is exposed. On the keyboard is some sort of built-in pointing device, like a touchpad, which is used in place of a standalone mouse.

NOTE On some hybrid PCs, the screen may flip or fold in a way to hide the keyboard and make the unit look like and function as a tablet. (It may be the keyboard doing the flipping, on some models.) In some instances, the screen detaches from the keyboard for tablet use. Hybrid PCs have touchscreen displays, which you can operate with your fingers in either notebook or tablet mode.

If you look closely at a notebook, you also see two built-in speakers, typically just above the top edge of the keyboard. Most notebooks also have an earphone jack, which you can use to connect a set of headphones or earphones. (When you connect a set of headphones or earphones, the built-in speakers are automatically muted.)

Somewhere on the notebook—either on the side or along the back edge—should be a row of connecting ports, like what's shown in Figure 2.2. Most notebooks have two or more USB connectors, an Ethernet connector (for connecting to a wired network), a VGA or DVI video connector (for connecting to an external display monitor), and perhaps an HDMI connector (for connecting to a living room TV).

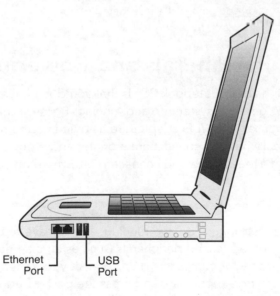

Ethernet
Port

USB
Port

FIGURE 2.2

Connecting ports on a notebook PC.

In addition, many traditional notebooks (but not ultrabooks or hybrids) have a built-in CD/DVD drive, typically on the side of the case. Some notebooks up the ante and include Blu-ray capability as well. Press the little button to open the drive and insert a disc; push the drive back in to begin playing the CD or DVD.

Inside the notebook case are the guts of the computer—everything you have in a desktop PC's system unit but more compact. In fact, most notebooks have *more* inside than a typical desktop does; in particular, most notebook PCs have a built-in Wi-Fi adapter so that the notebook can connect to a wireless home network or public Wi-Fi hotspot.

In addition, virtually all notebook PCs come with some sort of built-in battery. That's because a portable PC is truly portable; in addition to running on normal AC power, a notebook PC can operate unplugged, using battery power. Depending on the PC (and the battery), you might be able to operate a laptop for 3 or 4 hours or more before switching batteries or plugging the unit into a wall outlet. That makes a notebook PC great for use on airplanes, in coffee shops, or anywhere plugging in a power cord is inconvenient.

 TIP   When you unpack your new notebook PC, be sure you keep all the manuals, discs, cables, and so forth. Put the ones you don't use in a safe place in case you need to reinstall any software or equipment at a later date.

Connecting Peripherals and Powering On

One nice thing about notebook PCs is that you don't have nearly as many pieces to connect to get your system up and running. Because the monitor, speakers, keyboard, mouse, and Wi-Fi adapter are all built into the notebook unit, the only things you really have to connect are a printer and a power cable. (And not even a printer, if you already have one connected elsewhere on your home network.)

Getting Connected

To get your notebook PC up and running, all you have to do is connect your printer or any other desired peripherals (such as an external mouse or keyboard) to a USB port on your computer. Then connect your notebook's power cable to a power strip or surge suppressor and press the power button. (You can even skip connecting to a power strip if your notebook runs on internal batteries.)

Powering On for the First Time

The first time you turn on a notebook or tablet computer is different from what you'll experience in later use. There are some basic configuration operations you need to perform.

 NOTE For full installation, activation, and registration, your PC needs to connect to the Internet—typically via the unit's built-in Wi-Fi connection.

This first-time startup operation differs from manufacturer to manufacturer, but it typically includes walking through Windows' configuration process. You may be asked a series of questions about your location, the current time and date, and other essential information. You'll probably also be asked to create a username and password, which you'll use to log into your computer on subsequent occasions.

It's also possible that the computer manufacturer might supplement these configuration operations with setup procedures of its own. Just make sure you follow the onscreen instructions as best you can. After you have everything configured, Windows finally starts, and then you can begin using your system.

THE ABSOLUTE MINIMUM

Here are the key points to remember when connecting and configuring your new computer:

- Notebook PCs contain all the components of a desktop PC, but in a smaller, more portable case—complete with battery.

- You don't have to connect anything to your notebook to get it up and running—save for the power cord, at least until the internal battery is charged up.

- Turning on a notebook is as simple as pressing the power button.

- For full registration and activation, your notebook PC needs to be connected to the Internet.

3

SETTING UP AND USING A DESKTOP COMPUTER

How you set up your computer depends on what type of computer you have. We examined how to set up a notebook PC in Chapter 2, "Setting Up and Using a Notebook Computer." In this chapter, we address the proper way to connect all the components of a traditional desktop PC.

Understanding the Components of a Desktop Computer System

A desktop PC is composed of several different pieces and parts. You have to properly connect all these components to make your computer system work.

On a traditional desktop PC, the most important piece of hardware is the *system unit*. This is the big, ugly box that houses your disk drives and many other components. Most system units, like the one in Figure 3.1, stand straight up like a kind of tower—and are, in fact, called either *tower* or *mini-tower* PCs, depending on the size.

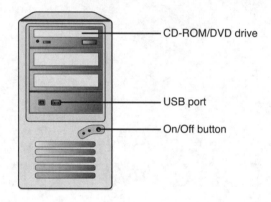

CD-ROM/DVD drive

USB port

On/Off button

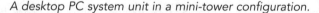

FIGURE 3.1

A desktop PC system unit in a mini-tower configuration.

Know, however, that some desktop systems combine the system unit and the monitor into a single unit. These all-in-one desktops take up less space and, in some instances, provide touch-screen functionality that enables you to use your fingers (instead of a mouse) to navigate the screen.

The system unit is where everything connects; it truly is the central hub for your entire system. For this reason, the back of the system unit typically is covered with all types of connectors. Because each component has its own unique type of connector, you end up with the assortment of jacks (called *ports* in the computer world) that you see in Figure 3.2.

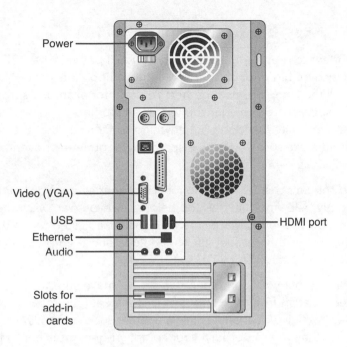

Power

Video (VGA)

USB

Ethernet

Audio

Slots for
add-in
cards

HDMI port

FIGURE 3.2

The back of a typical desktop PC system unit—just look at all those different connectors!

As you've probably noticed, some PCs put some of these connectors on the front of the case, in addition to the back. This makes it easier to connect portable devices, such as an iPod music player or a digital video camcorder, without having to muck about behind your PC.

The connections are on the outside, but all the good stuff in your system unit is inside the case. With most system units, you can remove the case to peek and poke around inside.

To remove your system unit's case, make sure the unit is unplugged, and then look for some big screws or thumbscrews on either the side or the back of the case. (Even better—read your PC's instruction manual for instructions specific to your unit.) With the screws loosened or removed, you should then be able to either slide off the entire case or pop open the top or back.

 CAUTION   Always turn off and unplug your computer before attempting to remove the system unit's case—and be careful about touching anything inside. If you have any built-up static electricity, you can seriously damage the sensitive chips and electronic components with an innocent touch.

Before You Get Started

It's important to prepare the space where you'll put your new PC. Obviously, the space has to be big enough to hold all the components—though you don't have to keep all the components together. You can, for example, spread out your left and right speakers, place your subwoofer on the floor, and separate the printer from the main unit. Just don't put anything so far away that the cables don't reach. (And make sure you have a spare power outlet—or even better, a multiple outlet power strip—nearby.)

You also should consider the ergonomics of your setup. You want your keyboard at or slightly below normal desktop height, and you want your monitor at or slightly below eye level. Make sure your chair is adjusted for a straight and firm sitting position with your feet flat on the floor, and then place all the pieces of your system in relation to that.

Wherever you put your computer, you should make sure that it's in a well-ventilated location free of excess dust and smoke. (The moving parts in your computer don't like dust and dirt or any other such contaminants that can muck up the way they work.) Because your computer generates heat when it operates, you must leave enough room around the system unit for the heat to dissipate. *Never* place your computer (especially a desktop PC's system unit) in a confined, poorly ventilated space; your PC can overheat and shut down if it isn't sufficiently ventilated.

For extra protection to your computer, connect the PC's power cable to a surge suppressor rather than directly into an electrical outlet. A *surge suppressor*—which looks like a power strip but has an On/Off switch and a circuit breaker button—protects your PC from power-line surges that could damage its delicate internal parts. When a power surge temporarily spikes your line voltage (causing the voltage to momentarily increase above normal levels), a surge suppressor helps to keep the level of the electric current as steady as possible. Most surge suppressors also include circuit breakers to shut down power to your system if a severe power spike occurs.

TIP   When you unpack your PC, be sure you keep all the manuals, discs, cables, and so forth. Put the ones you don't use in a safe place in case you need to reinstall any software or equipment at a later date.

CAUTION   Before you connect *anything* to your computer, make sure that the peripheral is turned off.

Connecting a Traditional Desktop PC

Now it's time to get connected—which can be a bit of a chore for a traditional desktop computer system. (It's a lot easier for an all-in-one model, as you'll see in a moment.)

Connect in Order

Start by positioning your system unit so that you easily can access all the connections on the back. Then you need to carefully run the cables from each of the other components so that they hang loose at the rear of the system unit. Now you're ready to get connected.

It's important that you connect the cables in a particular order. To make sure that the most critical devices are connected first, follow these steps:

1. Connect your mouse to an open USB port on your computer.

2. Connect your keyboard to an open USB port on your computer.

 NOTE   Some older mice and keyboards connect to separate mouse and keyboard connections on the back of your PC. Most newer mice and keyboards, however, connect via USB.

3. Connect your video monitor to the video connector on the back of your PC. Most monitors connect via a standard VGA connector; although, some LCD monitors can connect via a DVI or HDMI connector, if one of those is present.

4. Connect the phono jack from your speaker system to the "audio out" or "sound out" connector on the back of your PC. Run the necessary cables between your right and left speakers and your subwoofer, as directed by the manufacturer. (If your speaker system connects via USB, which many newer ones do, just connect the USB cable from the main speaker to an open USB port on your computer.)

5. If you're connecting your computer to a wired router for network and Internet access, connect an Ethernet cable between the router and the Ethernet connector on the back of your computer. (If you're connecting to a wireless router and network, you can skip this step.)

6. If you have a printer, connect it to an open USB port on your computer.

 NOTE   Some older printers connect to a parallel port connector, sometimes labeled "printer" or "LPT1." Most newer printers, however, connect via USB.

7. Connect any other external devices to open USB ports on your PC.

8. Plug the power cable of your video monitor into a power outlet.

9. If your system includes powered speakers, plug them into a power outlet.

10. Plug any other powered external components, such as your printer, into a power outlet.

11. Connect the main power cable to the power connector on the back of your PC.

12. Plug your PC's power cable into a power outlet.

 CAUTION   Make sure that every cable is *firmly* connected—both to the system unit and to the specific piece of hardware. Loose cables can cause all sorts of weird problems, so be sure they're plugged in really well.

Connect by Color

Most PC manufacturers color-code the cables and connectors to make the connection even easier—just plug the blue cable into the blue connector, and so on. If you're not sure what color cable goes to what device, take a look at the standard cable color coding in Table 3.1.

TABLE 3.1   Connector Color Codes

Connector	Color
VGA (analog) monitor	Blue
Digital monitor (DVI)	White
Video out	Yellow
Mouse	Green
Keyboard	Purple
Serial	Teal or turquoise
Parallel (printer)	Burgundy
USB	Black
FireWire (IEEE 1394)	Gray
Audio line out (right)	Red
Audio line out (left)	White
Audio line out (headphones)	Lime

Connector	Color
Speaker out/subwoofer	Orange
Right-to-left speaker	Brown
Audio line in	Light blue
Microphone	Pink
Gameport/MIDI	Gold
HDMI	Black

Connecting an All-in-One Desktop

Connecting an all-in-one desktop is somewhat easier than connecting one with a separate system unit simply because you have fewer components to deal with. You don't have to worry about connecting the monitor to the system unit because they're all one unit. Same thing typically applies with speakers, which are often built into the monitor/system unit.

All you need to worry about connecting, then, are the keyboard and mouse, as well as any peripherals you might have. Follow these steps:

1. Connect your mouse to an open USB port on your computer.

2. Connect your keyboard to an open USB port on your computer.

3. If you're connecting your computer to a wired router for network and Internet access, connect an Ethernet cable between the router and the Ethernet connector on the back of your computer. (If you're connecting to a wireless router and network, you can skip this step.)

4. If you have a printer, connect it to an open USB port on your computer.

5. Connect any other external devices to open USB ports on your PC.

6. Plug any powered external components, such as your printer, into a power outlet.

7. Connect the main power cable to the power connector on the back of your PC.

8. Plug your PC's power cable into a power outlet.

Pretty simple—which is one of the advantages of all-in-one units.

Turning It On and Setting It Up

Now that you have everything connected, sit back and rest for a minute. Next up is the big step—turning it all on.

Getting the Right Order

It's important that you turn on things in the proper order. For a traditional desktop PC, follow these steps:

1. Turn on your video monitor.

2. Turn on your speaker system—but make sure the speaker volume knob is turned down (toward the left).

3. Turn on any other system components that are connected to your system unit—such as your printer, scanner, and so on. (If your PC is connected to an Ethernet network, make sure that the network router is turned on.)

4. Turn on your system unit.

Note that your system unit is the *last* thing you turn on. That's because when it powers on, it has to sense the other components of your system—which it can do only if the other components are plugged in and turned on.

For an all-in-one desktop, there's less to worry about. Just turn on any peripherals connected to the PC, such as your printer, and then press your PC's power button. It's a snap.

Powering On for the First Time

The first time you turn on your PC is a unique experience. A brand-new, out-of-the-box system has to perform some basic configuration operations, which include asking you to input some key information.

 NOTE   For full installation, activation, and registration, your PC needs to be connected to the Internet—typically via a cable or DSL modem connected either to your PC or to a network hub or router.

This first-time startup operation differs from manufacturer to manufacturer, but it typically includes walking through Windows' configuration process. You may be asked a series of questions about your location, the current time and date, and other essential information. You'll probably also be asked to create a username and password, which you'll use to log into your computer on subsequent occasions.

Many computer manufacturers supplement these configuration operations with setup procedures of their own. It's impossible to describe all the different options that might be presented by all the different manufacturers, so watch the screen carefully and follow all the onscreen instructions.

After you have everything configured, Windows finally starts, and then *you* can start using your system.

 NOTE   Some installation procedures require your computer to be restarted. In most cases, this happens automatically; then the installation process resumes where it left off.

THE ABSOLUTE MINIMUM

Here are the key points to remember when connecting and configuring your new computer:

- Most peripherals connect to any USB port on your computer.

- Connecting an all-in-one unit is easier than connecting one with a separate system unit and monitor.

- Make sure your cables are firmly connected; loose cables are the cause of many computer problems.

- Connect all the cables to your system unit before you turn on the power.

- Remember to turn on your printer and monitor before you turn on the system unit.

- For full registration and activation, your computer needs to be connected to the Internet.

4

GETTING TO KNOW WINDOWS 10—FOR NEW COMPUTER USERS

As you learned in Chapter 1, "How Personal Computers Work," the software and operating system make your hardware work. The operating system for most personal computers is Microsoft Windows, and you need to know how to use Windows to use your PC. Windows pretty much runs your computer for you; if you don't know your way around Windows, you can't do much of anything on your new PC.

Introducing Microsoft Windows

Microsoft Windows is a type of software called an *operating system*. An operating system does what its name implies—*operates* your computer *system*, working in the background every time you turn on your PC.

Equally important, Windows is what you see when you first turn on your computer, after everything turns on and boots up. Windows is your gateway to every program and app you run on your computer and to all the documents and files you view and edit.

To use your new computer, you need to learn the ins and outs of operating Windows. Fortunately, it's easy to learn.

 NOTE   Microsoft sells several different versions of Windows 10. It's likely that you're using the basic version, designed for home use, called simply Windows 10. There's also a Windows Pro version, designed for professional and business users, with more sophisticated security and computer management features. If you want to upgrade from the basic version to Windows Pro (and there's little reason you should), it will cost you $99. (Pro sells for $199 on its own.)

Starting and Logging In to Windows

Starting your computer and logging in to Windows is a simple affair that starts when you push the power button on your PC.

Each time you turn on your computer, you see a series of short, perhaps indecipherable text messages flash across your screen. These messages are there to let you know what's going on as your computer *boots up*.

 NOTE   Technical types call the procedure of starting up a computer *booting* or *booting up* the system. Restarting a system (turning it off and then back on) is called *rebooting*.

After a few seconds (during which your system unit beeps and whirrs a little bit), the Windows Lock screen appears. As you can see in Figure 4.1, the Lock screen provides some basic information—today's date and the current time, Internet connection status, and power status—against a pretty photographic background while Windows waits for you to log on.

FIGURE 4.1

The first thing you see in Windows 10—the Lock screen.

To log on to your Windows account, all you have to do is press any key on your keyboard or click the mouse. This displays the login screen, shown in Figure 4.2.

Enter your password and then press the Enter key. After you're past the login screen, you're taken directly to the Windows desktop, and your system is ready to use.

FIGURE 4.2

Select your username and enter your password to proceed.

NOTE It's easy to configure Windows 10 for multiple users, each with their own account and settings; we discuss that in Chapter 8, "Personalizing Windows." If you have only a single user on the machine, only one name appears from the Lock screen.

Getting to Know the Windows Desktop

The desktop is your home base in Windows. It's what you see when you start your computer and Windows launches; it's where all your programs and documents reside.

As you can see in Figure 4.3, the Windows 10 desktop includes a number of key elements. Get to know this desktop; you're going to be seeing a lot of it from now on. Note the following elements:

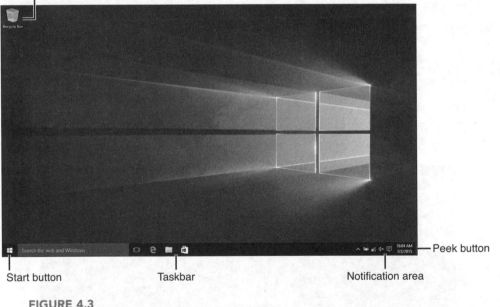

FIGURE 4.3

The Windows 10 desktop.

- **Taskbar**—Displays icons for your favorite applications and documents, as well as for any open window. By default, you see icons for Search, Task View (displays multiple virtual desktops), and File Explorer (the file management tool for Windows). Right-click an icon to see a "jump list" of recent open documents and other operations for that application.

- **Start button**—Click the Start button to display the Start menu. Right-click the Start button to display an Options menu with links to the Control Panel and other important tools and utilities.

- **Notification area**—This far-right section of the taskbar displays icons for a handful of key system functions, power (on notebook PCs), networking/ Internet, and audio (volume). There's also an icon for New Notifications that displays the Notifications panel.

- **Peek button**— Hover over this little rectangle and all open windows go transparent so that you can see what's on the desktop below. Click the Peek button to immediately minimize all open windows.

- **Shortcut icons**—These are links to software programs you can place on your desktop; a "clean" desktop includes just one icon—the one for the Windows Recycle Bin.

- **Recycle Bin**—This is where you dump any files you want to delete.

Learning Basic Operations

To use Windows efficiently on a desktop or notebook PC, you must master a few simple operations with your mouse or touchpad, such as pointing and clicking, dragging and dropping, and right-clicking. When you use your mouse or touchpad in this fashion, you move the onscreen *cursor*—that pointer thing that looks like a little arrow.

Pointing and Clicking

The most common mouse operation is *pointing and clicking*. Simply move your computer's mouse or, on a notebook PC, drag your finger across the touchpad so that the cursor points to the object you want to select, and then click the *left* mouse button once. Pointing and clicking is an effective way to select menu and toolbar items, icons, and the like.

Double-Clicking

In some instances, single-clicking doesn't launch or open an item; it merely selects it. In these instances, you need to *double-click* an item to activate an operation. This involves pointing at something onscreen with the cursor and then clicking the left mouse button twice in rapid succession.

Right-Clicking

Here's one of the secret keys to efficient Windows operation. When you select an item and then click the *right* mouse button, you often see a pop-up menu. This menu, when available, contains commands that directly relate to the selected object. So, for example, if you right-click a file icon, you see commands related to that file—copy, move, delete, and so forth.

Refer to your individual programs to see whether and how they use the right mouse button.

Dragging and Dropping

Dragging is a variation of clicking. To drag an object, point at it with the cursor and then press and hold down the left mouse button. Move the mouse without releasing the mouse button and drag the object to a new location. When you finish moving the object, release the mouse button to drop it onto the new location.

You can use dragging and dropping to move files from one location to another.

Mouse Over

When you position the cursor over an item without clicking your mouse, you *mouse over* that item. (This is sometimes called *hovering*.) Many operations require you to mouse over an item to display additional options or information.

Moving and Resizing Windows

When you have multiple windows open, your desktop can quickly become cluttered. Fortunately, there are ways to deal with this sort of multiple-window desktop clutter.

One approach is to move a window to a new position. You do this by positioning your cursor over a blank area at the top of the window frame and then clicking and holding down the left button on your mouse. As long as this button is depressed, you can use your mouse to drag the window around the screen. When you release the mouse button, the window stays where you put it.

 TIP   The cursor changes shape—to a double-ended arrow—when it's positioned over the edge of a window.

With Windows 10, you can quickly "snap" a window to the left or right side of the desktop. Just drag the window to the left side of the screen to dock it there, and resize it to the left half of the desktop; drag the window to the right side of the screen to dock it on that side. To display a window full-screen, drag it to the top of the desktop.

You also can change the size of most windows. You do this by positioning the cursor over the edge of the window—any edge. If you position the cursor on either side of the window, you can resize the width. If you position the cursor on the top or bottom edge, you can resize the height.

 TIP   You can also "snap" a window full screen by using your mouse to drag the window to the top of the desktop. This automatically maximizes the window.

After the cursor is positioned over the window's edge, press and hold down the left mouse button; then drag the window border to its new size. Release the mouse button to lock in the newly sized window.

Maximizing, Minimizing, and Closing Windows

Another way to manage a window on the Windows desktop is to make it display full screen. You do this by maximizing the window. All you have to do is click the Maximize button in the upper-right corner of the window, as shown in Figure 4.4.

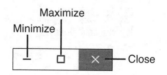

FIGURE 4.4

Use the Minimize, Maximize, and Close buttons to manage your desktop windows.

If the window is already maximized, the Maximize button changes to a Restore Down button. When you click the Restore Down button, the window resumes its previous (pre-maximized) dimensions.

If you would rather hide the window so that it doesn't clutter your desktop, click the Minimize button. This shoves the window off the desktop, onto the taskbar. The program in the window is still running, however—it's just not on the desktop. To restore a minimized window, all you have to do is click the window's icon on the Windows taskbar (at the bottom of the screen).

If what you really want to do is close the window (and close any program running within the window), just click the window's Close button.

CAUTION   If you try to close a window that contains a document you haven't saved, you're prompted to save the changes to the document. Because you probably don't want to lose any of your work, click Yes to save the document, and then close the program.

Scrolling Through a Window

Many windows, whether full screen or otherwise, contain more information than can be displayed onscreen. When you have a long document or web page, only the first part of the document or page displays in the window. To view the rest of the document or page, you have to scroll down through the window using the various parts of the scrollbar (shown in Figure 4.5).

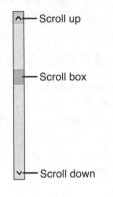

— Scroll up

— Scroll box

— Scroll down

FIGURE 4.5

Use the scrollbar to scroll through long pages.

There are several ways to scroll through a window. To scroll up or down a line at a time, click the up or down arrow on the window's scrollbar. To move to a specific place in a long document, use your mouse to grab the scroll box (between the up and down arrows) and drag it to a new position. You can also click the scrollbar between the scroll box and the end arrow so that you scroll one screen at a time.

If your mouse has a scroll wheel, you can use it to scroll through a long document. Just roll the wheel backward or forward to scroll down or up through a window. Likewise, some notebook touchpads let you drag your finger up or down to scroll through a window. And, if your PC has a touchscreen display, you can simply swipe your finger downward in the document to scroll down or swipe upward to scroll up.

Peeking at the Desktop

Want to quickly see what's beneath all the open windows on the desktop? Have a gadget you want to look at? Then you'll appreciate the *Peek* feature. With Peek you can, well, peek at the desktop beneath all that window clutter.

You activate Peek from the little transparent rectangular button at the far right of the Windows taskbar. Hover the cursor over the Peek button and every open window becomes transparent, as shown in Figure 4.6. This lets you see everything that's on the desktop below.

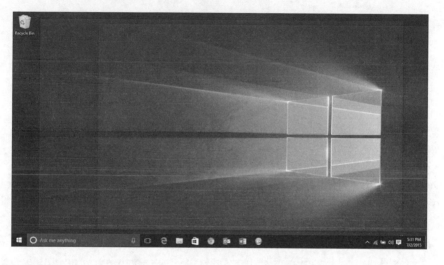

FIGURE 4.6

Windows Peek in action—a great way to view gadgets, shortcut icons, and your Windows desktop wallpaper.

Using Dialog Boxes, Tabs, and Buttons

When Windows or a specific app requires a complex set of inputs, you are often presented with a *dialog box*. A dialog box is similar to a form in which you can input various parameters and make various choices—and then register those inputs and choices when you click OK. (Figure 4.7 shows the Save As dialog box, found in many Windows apps.)

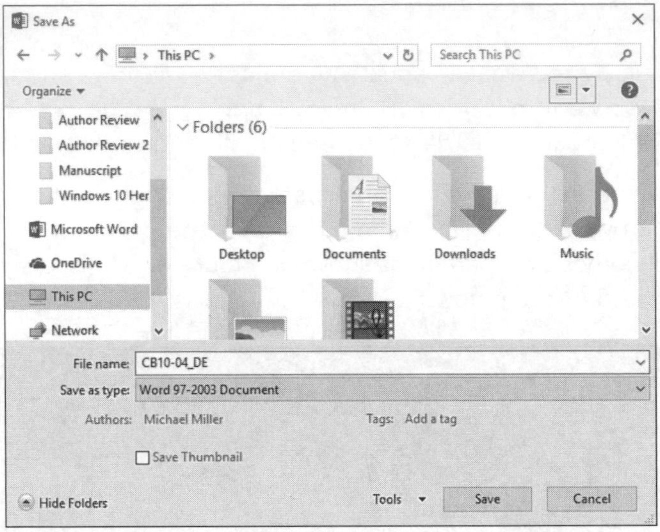

FIGURE 4.7

Use dialog boxes to control various aspects of your Windows applications.

Windows has several types of dialog boxes, each one customized to the task at hand. However, most dialog boxes share a set of common features, which include the following:

- **Buttons**—Most buttons either register your inputs or open an auxiliary dialog box. The most common buttons are OK (to register your inputs and close the dialog box), Cancel (to close the dialog box without registering your inputs), and Apply (to register your inputs without closing the dialog box). Click a button once to activate it.

- **Tabs**—These allow a single dialog box to display multiple "pages" of information. Think of each tab, arranged across the top of the dialog box, as a "thumbtab" to the individual page in the dialog box below it. Click the top of a tab to change to that particular page of information.

- **Text boxes**—These are empty boxes where you type a response. Position your cursor over the empty input box, click your left mouse button, and begin typing.

- **Lists**—These are lists of available choices; lists can either scroll or drop down from what looks like an input box. Select an item from the list with your mouse; you can select multiple items in some lists by holding down the Ctrl key while clicking with your mouse.

- **Check boxes**—These are boxes that let you select (or deselect) various standalone options.

- **Sliders**—These are sliding bars that let you select increments between two extremes, similar to a sliding volume control on an audio system.

Using the Start Menu

All the software programs and utilities on your computer are accessed via Windows' Start menu. You display the Start menu by using your mouse to click the Start button, located in the lower-left corner of your screen.

Navigating the Start Menu

As you can see in Figure 4.8, the Windows 10 Start menu consists of two parts. Your most frequently and recently used programs are listed on the left side; applications you've "pinned" to the Start menu are shown in tiles on the right. To open a specific program or folder, just click the name of or tile for the item.

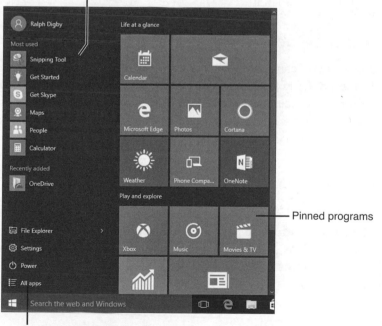

FIGURE 4.8

Access all the programs on your system from the Start menu.

To view the rest of your programs, click All Apps. This changes the left side of the Start menu to display a scrolling list that contains all the applications installed on your PC. (When more programs are contained within a master folder, you see an arrow to the right of the title; click this arrow to expand the menu and display additional choices.)

Launching a Program

Now that you know how to work the Start menu, it's easy to start any particular software program. All you have to do is follow these steps:

1. Click the Start button to display the Start menu.

2. If the program displays on the Start menu, click the program's name or tile.

3. If the program isn't visible on the main Start menu, click All Apps, find the program's name, and then click it.

Another way to find a program to launch is to use the Search box on the Start menu. Just start entering the program's name into the search box, and a list of matching programs appears on the Start menu. When the program you want appears, click it to launch it.

Reopening Recent Documents

In Windows 10 you can quickly access the most recent documents opened with an application directly from the Start menu. Look for a right arrow next to an application on the main Start menu (not the All Apps menu); click this arrow and you see a list of that application's most recent documents. Click a document from this menu, and you open both the application and that document.

Using the Taskbar

That little strip of real estate at the bottom of the Windows desktop is called the *taskbar*. The Windows taskbar lets you open your favorite applications and documents, as well as switch between open windows. You can even add icons for your favorite programs to the taskbar, for quicker and easier launching. Click an icon to launch an app or switch to an open window; taskbar icons exist for both.

Deciphering Taskbar Icons

Because of the multiple functions of the icons on the taskbar, it's difficult to look at an icon on the taskbar and determine whether it represents an open or closed application or document. Difficult, yes, but not impossible. Here's the key.

As you can see in Figure 4.9, an icon for a not-yet-open application or document—essentially a shortcut to that app or doc—appears on the taskbar with no border. An icon for an open window has a white underline, while still appearing translucent. An icon for the currently selected open window also has an underline but is slightly less transparent. And if there is more than one document open for a given application (or more than one tab open in a web browser), the underline on that app's icon button appears "stacked" to represent multiple instances.

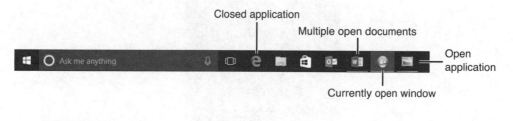

FIGURE 4.9

The Windows taskbar with icons for a (closed) application, open application, open application with multiple documents, and currently selected window.

Opening Applications and Switching Between Windows

Using the taskbar is simplicity itself. Click a shortcut icon to open the associated application or document. Click an open window icon to display that window front and center.

If you click a multiple-window icon, however, something interesting happens: Windows displays thumbnails for each of that application's open windows. (The same thing happens if you mouse over the cursor for any open-window icon, actually.) Move the cursor over a thumbnail, and that window temporarily displays on top of the stack on your desktop, regardless of its actual position. Click a thumbnail to switch to that window, or click the red X on the thumbnail to close the window.

Using Jump Lists

The Windows taskbar becomes even more useful with the addition of Jump Lists— kind of context-sensitive pop-up menus for each icon on the taskbar. To display an icon's Jump List, shown in Figure 4.10, right-click the icon.

FIGURE 4.10

A Windows taskbar Jump List.

What you see in a Jump List depends to some degree on the application associated with the icon. Most Jump Lists contain the following items:

- The most recent documents opened in this application

- A link to open a new instance of this application

- An option to unpin this item from the taskbar (for shortcut icons)

- An option to close the current window (for open-window icons)

Some apps offer more application-appropriate items on their Jump Lists. For example, Windows Media Player has a section for frequent playlists and albums, as well as a Tasks section with the most-recent program operations.

In short, Jump Lists are a lot like traditional right-click pop-up menus, but with more useful options. They make the new taskbar icons more useful than they would have been otherwise.

Managing Taskbar Buttons

Now that you know what the taskbar does, let's look at how to manage it.

First, know that you have total control over the order of icons on the taskbar. Just drag a taskbar icon from one position to another, and there it stays.

To add an application or document shortcut to the taskbar, just navigate to that item using the Start menu or File Explorer, right-click the item's icon, and select Pin to Taskbar. Alternatively, you can drag an icon from any folder to the taskbar. Either approach is quick and easy.

To remove an item from the taskbar, right-click it and select Unpin This Program from the Taskbar.

Switching Between Programs

The taskbar is one way to switch between open programs, but it's not the only way. You can also do either of the following:

- Click any visible part of the application's window, which brings that window to the front.

- Hold down the Alt key and then press the Tab key repeatedly until the application window you want is selected. This lets you cycle through thumbnails of all open windows, as shown in Figure 4.11. When you're at the window you want, release the Alt key.

FIGURE 4.11

Press Alt+Tab to cycle through open apps.

Learning Important Windows Shortcuts

Now that you know how to use your mouse to get around Windows, it's time to learn some shortcuts you can use to speed up important Windows operations. Most of these actions can be initiated with either a mouse or a keyboard, as detailed in Table 4.1.

TABLE 4.1 Essential Windows 10 Operations

Operation	Keyboard	Mouse
Close currently running app or window	Alt+F4	Click the X button in top-right corner of window.
Display context-sensitive options menu	Application (menu) key	Right-click.
Display Notifications panel	Windows+A	Click the Notifications icon on the taskbar.
Display Settings	N/A	Click the Start button; then click Settings.
Display Start menu	Windows key	Click the Start button.
Lock computer	Windows+L	Click the Start button, click your user name, and then click Lock.
Move an item to a new location	N/A	Click and drag, and then release.
Open a program or document	Enter	Click (sometimes double-click).
Open Windows Help	Windows+F1	N/A
Scroll down	Pg Dn or down arrow	Click and drag the scrollbar or click the scroll arrows; use the mouse scroll wheel.
Scroll left	Pg Up or left arrow	Click and drag the scrollbar or click the scroll arrows; use the mouse scroll wheel.
Scroll right	Pg Dn or right arrow	Click and drag the scrollbar or click the scroll arrows; use the mouse scroll wheel.
Scroll up	Pg Up or up arrow	Click and drag the scrollbar or click the scroll arrows; use the mouse scroll wheel.
Search with Cortana	Windows+S	Click within the Search box on the taskbar.
Shut down Windows	Alt+F4	Click the Start button, click Power, and then click Shut Down.
View or switch to other open apps	Alt+Tab	N/A
View or switch to other virtual desktops	Windows+Tab	Click Task View button on taskbar.

TIP When you can't figure out how to perform a particular task, ask Cortana, Windows 10's new virtual assistant. Just type your question in the Ask Me Anything box on the left side of the taskbar, and Cortana displays matching answers.

Shutting Down Windows—and Your Computer

You've probably already noticed that Windows starts automatically every time you turn on your computer. Although you see lines of text flashing onscreen during the initial startup, Windows loads automatically and displays the Windows desktop.

 CAUTION   On a desktop PC, do *not* turn off your computer from your computer's main power button—you could lose data and settings that are temporarily stored in your system's memory. To properly shut down a desktop PC, go through the shutdown operation in Windows.

When you want to turn off your computer, you do it through Windows. In fact, you don't want to turn off your computer any other way—you *always* want to turn off things through the official Windows procedure.

To shut down Windows and turn off your PC, follow these steps:

1. Click the Start button to display the Start menu.

2. Click Power to display the pop-up menu of options, as shown in Figure 4.12.

3. Click Shut Down to shut down your computer. You also have the option of putting your computer into Sleep mode (this mode pauses all operations but still consumes some power) or restarting your PC. (This option shuts down the PC and then powers it back up.)

FIGURE 4.12

Shutting down Windows from the Start menu.

That's it. If you have a desktop PC, you then need to manually turn off your monitor, printer, and other peripherals.

THE ABSOLUTE MINIMUM

This chapter gave you a lot of background about Windows 10—your new PC's operating system. Here are the key points to remember:

- You use Windows to manage your computer system and run apps and programs.

- When you start your computer, you see the Windows Lock screen; click this screen to log in to your account and enter Windows.

- To use Windows 10, you must master basic mouse and keyboard operations.

- Click the Start button to display the Start menu, where all your installed programs are listed.

- The taskbar hosts icons for all open programs, as well as any programs you've "pinned" there for future use.

- To exit Windows and turn off your computer, click the Start button, click the Power Options button, and select Shut Down.

5

GETTING TO KNOW WINDOWS 10—IF YOU'VE USED WINDOWS BEFORE

Windows 10 is the latest version of Windows, the operating system from Microsoft that's been driving personal computers since the late 1980s. It's a considerable improvement over the previous version (Windows 8) and a worthwhile upgrade if you're using any older version of Windows.

A Short History of Windows

If you've recently purchased a new PC, the version of Windows on your PC is probably Windows 10. Microsoft has released different versions of Windows over the years, and Windows 10 (released in July 2015) is just the latest in a 30-year run.

 NOTE If your computer runs an older version of Windows, you should pick up a previous edition of this book covering that operating system. There are editions that cover Windows 8.1, Windows 8, Windows 7, and Windows Vista; you can find these editions at Amazon.com and other online booksellers.

Early Windows

The history of Windows actually goes back further than 30 years. That's because Windows wasn't Microsoft's first operating system. Windows evolved from Microsoft's original DOS operating system, which was released in 1981. The DOS operating system was developed by Bill Gates and Paul Allen to run the then-new IBM Personal Computer, and utilized a stark text-based interface and simple one-word user commands. It wasn't what you would call user-friendly.

 NOTE DOS (stands for *disk operating system*) was the generic name for what were actually two different operating systems. When packaged with IBM's personal computers, DOS was dubbed PC DOS. When sold in a standalone package by Microsoft, DOS was dubbed MS-DOS. Both versions were functionally identical.

Microsoft believed, however, that for personal computers to become mainstream, they had to be easier to use, which argued for a *graphical user interface* (GUI) instead of DOS's command-line interface. With that in mind, development on the inaugural version of Windows started in 1983, with the final product released to market in November, 1985.

Windows was originally going to be called Interface Manager and was nothing more than a graphical shell that sat on top of the existing DOS operating system. While DOS was a keyboard-driven, text-based operating system, Windows supported the click-and-drag operation of a mouse. That said, individual windows could be tiled only onscreen and could not be stacked or overlaid on top of each other.

Windows 1.0 didn't gain a lot of users, but Microsoft kept at it, releasing the next version (Windows 2.0) in 1987. Windows 2.0 added overlapping windows and allowed minimized windows to be moved around the desktop with a mouse. Its big claim to fame, however, was that it came bundled with Microsoft's Word and Excel applications. It still wasn't a big success.

Windows Goes Mainstream

The first commercially successful version of Windows was Windows 3.0, released in 1990. This version of Windows sold more than 10 million copies. Windows 3.0 was the first version of Windows to incorporate true multitasking, thus providing a real alternative to the dominant DOS operating system of the time. In addition, the Windows 3.0 interface was a lot nicer looking, with 3D buttons and such, and users could, for the first time, change the color of the underlying desktop.

Two years later, in 1992, Microsoft released Windows 3.1. This version, more than a simple point upgrade, not only included the requisite bug fixes, but also it was the first version of Windows to display TrueType scalable fonts—which turned Windows into a serious platform for desktop publishing. Also new to Windows 3.1 were screensavers and drag-and-drop operation.

Starting It Up with Windows 95

The next version of Windows would be the biggest so far—and to date, for that matter. Windows 95 was released in 1995, and it was a genuine media event, with live television coverage and customers lined up outside stores waiting for the midnight release of the product. (I know, because I was there.) This was Windows hitting the big time, to the soundtrack of the Rolling Stones' "Start Me Up."

What was the big deal? Windows 95 looked better and worked better, both things for which users had been waiting for years. Windows 95 introduced the taskbar, which held buttons for all open windows. It was also the first version of Windows to use the Start button and Start menu (hence the tie-in to the Rolling Stones' song); desktop shortcuts, right-clicking, and long filenames also debuted in this version.

Three years later, Microsoft introduced Windows 98, an evolutionary change to the previous version. It looked and felt pretty much like Windows 95, even though it did include some useful improvements under the hood. There was also a "Second Edition" of Windows 98 released in 1999, which was more of a bug fix release.

At the turn of the century, Microsoft released a "millennium edition" of Windows, dubbed Windows Me. This version was considered a failure that seemingly broke more things than it fixed. Although Windows Me upgraded the operating system's multimedia and Internet features, added the Windows Movie Maker application, and introduced the System Restore utility—all good things—it was notably bug-ridden and prone to frequent freezes and crashes. This caused many users to skip the upgrade entirely.

Windows XP, Vista, and 7

All those bugs got fixed with the 2001 release of what Microsoft called Windows XP. This was the first version of Windows to bring corporate reliability to the consumer market—and consumer friendliness to the corporate market. From the end user's standpoint, XP was a faster and better-looking version of Windows, and a lot more reliable than the failed Windows Me. It also supported a more modern animated interface, dubbed Luna.

Microsoft stuck with Windows XP for 6 years, not upgrading it until the 2007 release of Windows Vista. Vista added increased security and reliability, improved digital media functionality, and the dazzling Aero 3D user interface. Unfortunately, Vista proved every bit as buggy as the older Windows Me and had a lot of compatibility issues with older computer hardware. It was a bomb, pure and simple—which led Microsoft to replace it with the new and improved Windows 7, released in 2009, just 2 short years after the release of Windows Vista.

What changed in Windows 7? First, it fixed a lot of what people didn't like about Windows Vista. Older hardware and software were more compatible, and there was even a Windows XP Mode that let you run XP-era apps in their native environment—actually a virtual PC running the real honest-to-goodness Windows XP operating system. There were also some subtle interface changes, including a revamping of how the taskbar looked and worked.

Then Came Windows 8

Users loved Windows 7. Even large companies, seemingly wedded to Windows XP, eventually migrated to the better user interface and increased performance of the newer operating system. Everybody was happy.

That wasn't good enough for Microsoft, however. Microsoft was looking at the burgeoning sales of Apple's iPad and feared that traditional notebook and desktop computers would soon be replaced by tablets—a form factor that Microsoft had virtually no presence with. So the brain trust in Seattle put their heads together and came up with a striking reimagining of their core operating system, designed for smaller touchscreen devices.

Windows 8 was released in 2012, and was met with immediate derision. Users took issue with having the new "touch first" interface forced on them, as the vast majority of users were running traditional nontouch notebook and desktop computers, and avoided upgrading to Windows 8.

What exactly was different about Windows 8? First, it didn't boot to the traditional desktop; instead, users saw a new Start screen with clickable tiles for all their installed applications. This Start screen replaced the tried-and-true Start menu, which simply vanished from Windows. Users could no longer click the Start button to see a Start menu full of their installed apps. This was not only confusing to long-term users, but it was also less productive than using the old Start menu.

Many common operations previously done with the mouse or keyboard were translated into touch gestures, which were meaningless for the majority of users who didn't have touchscreen computers. A new class of applications (variously called Metro or Modern or Windows Store apps) was also introduced, displayed solely in full screen mode and designed to operate best on touchscreen devices.

In short, Microsoft abandoned its huge user base and forced them to learn a new way of doing things that they neither wanted nor needed. It's not surprising that Windows 8 was so derisively received, nor that this move almost singlehandedly destroyed the entire personal computer industry. Users not only refused to upgrade their old PCs to Windows 8, but also refused to buy new PCs that were running the despised operating system. Microsoft couldn't have done worse if it tried to.

The company tried to reverse some of the damage with the release of Windows 8.1 in 2013. Windows 8.1 returned the Start button to the taskbar (but tied it to the Start screen; still no Start menu), and let users boot directly to the desktop instead of the Start screen, but the changes were too few to make much of a difference. Microsoft had turned Windows into a joke—and an extremely disliked user experience.

Introducing Windows 10

Lets' face it; Windows 8 was a disaster. Users avoided it like the plague, unless they were forced to buy a new PC with Windows 8 preloaded. Microsoft tried to force a new GUI and operational paradigm on its billions of users, even though users weren't asking for or wanting to change the way they did things on their computers. The result? One of the biggest failures in technology history—a mistake that ranks right up with New Coke and the Edsel.

Fortunately for all those despondent Windows 8 users, that bomb of an operating system has been replaced by Windows 10. Windows 10 undoes pretty much everything that Windows 8 got wrong and is finally a worthy successor to the much-beloved Windows 7.

Windows 10 for Windows 8/8.1 Users

If you were forced to use Windows 8/8.1, you have my sympathy. The good news is, Windows 10 is a lot better. A whole lot better.

What exactly is new in Windows 10? A lot! Here's a short list of changes you'll find:

- The Start button is back, as is the Start menu. Click the Start button and you see a new and (really) improved version of the Start menu, with all your installed programs listed.

- Programs pinned to the Start menu now appear as resizable tiles, some of which display live information without having to be opened.

- Windows boots directly to the desktop. No more full-screen Start screen. (Actually, the Start screen no longer exists in Windows 10; instead, if you run Windows on a tablet, you see a full-screen version of the Start menu.)

- Although you can operate Windows 10 with touch gestures, you don't have to. Everything you need to do you can do with your mouse and keyboard.

- The full-screen Modern apps from Windows 8 have been rewritten to appear in resizable windows on the traditional desktop.

- A new Action Center pane is accessible from the taskbar, which displays important system messages and offers quick access to important system tools.

- There's a new virtual personal assistant, named Cortana, which you can use to search the web or find important information. You can use Cortana with the keyboard or via voice commands.

- A new web browser, called Edge, is faster and more streamlined than the old Internet Explorer.

- The Charms bar from Windows 8 is no more; all configuration options are available from the new Settings tool (or the traditional Control Panel, which is still around).

There are even more new features, including some changes to the interface design, but that gives you a feel of what's new and different. If you still run Windows 8 or Windows 8.1, you need to upgrade to Windows 10.

The good news about upgrading from Windows 8/8.1 is that it's easy and it's free—for the first year of release, anyway. If you have a Windows 8/8.1 PC, open the Windows Store app to download and install Windows 10. You should experience no compatibility issues with hardware or software you ran with Windows 8/8.1.

Windows 10 for Windows 7 Users

It's fair to say that the last great version of Windows was Windows 7. It was so beloved that most Windows 7 users didn't upgrade to Windows 8 or 8.1; they kept running 7 on their old machines and avoided buying new PCs so that they wouldn't have to run the dreaded Windows 8. (Nobody liked Windows 8. Trust me on this one.)

But Windows 7 is starting to get a little long in the tooth, and many of those older Windows 7 PCs are starting to show their age. There's a raft of Windows 7 users who've been holding out on upgrading until something better than Windows 8 came along. That something is Windows 10.

If you're a Windows 7 user, you'll find Windows 10 extremely familiar. I view Windows 10 as the natural upgrade to Windows 7 that Windows 8 should have been but wasn't. Windows 10 sticks with everything that people liked about Windows 7 and makes some natural and quite useful enhancements.

What will Windows 7 users find new in Windows 10? Here's a short list:

- There is no Start screen or full-screen Modern apps to deal with. By moving from Windows 7 directly to Windows 10 you avoid everything that everybody hated about Windows 8.

- The translucent Aero interface is gone, replaced by a more contemporary flat interface design with minimal windows "chrome." (Although the Start menu is still somewhat see-through.)

- There aren't any desktop "gadgets" in Windows 10. Sorry about that.

- The Start menu has been substantially revamped. Pinned apps now appear as live resizable tiles on the Start menu, and the Start menu itself is resizable.

- You now sign into Windows with a Microsoft account. You can sign into multiple PCs (all running Windows 10) with the same account and have your personal options appear on the other PCs.

- There's a newer, faster, more compatible web browser to replace the older, slower Internet Explorer. The new browser is called Edge, and it has a similar (but edgier) "e" shortcut icon as the older Internet Explorer.

- Windows Explorer is renamed to File Explorer, with a new ribbon interface.

- The Task Manager tool is completely overhauled to make it more functional.

- The Windows Defender antivirus/antispyware tool is still included, free of charge.

- Windows adds options to both refresh and reset the operating system in case of severe system problems.

In terms of compatibility, Windows 10 should run just fine on a Windows 7 PC. You may find some compatibility issues with some older software, so check with Microsoft or your software publisher to make sure everything works well together.

You should be able to upgrade from Windows 7 to Windows 10 without losing any of your files, programs, or settings. Any Windows 7 user can upgrade to Windows 10 for free, for the first year of release.

Windows 10 for Windows XP Users

Some people might find it hard to believe, but there are still tens of millions of people and companies still using Windows XP, 14 years after its initial release—and more than a year since Microsoft quit officially supporting it. That loss of support is reason enough to upgrade from XP to Windows 10; you also gain a great deal of functionality by moving to a more modern operating system.

 NOTE   Why are so many installations still using a 14-year-old operating system? In a lot of cases, it's because companies are using purpose-built software that was designed for the Windows XP platform. If this is the main software your company uses, there has been little need to upgrade operating systems—especially if the old software won't run on newer versions of Windows.

How different is Windows 10 from Windows XP? The changes are almost too numerous to note, but include

- Revamped Start menu with live tiles for pinned apps.

- Revamped taskbar to which you can pin shortcuts to your favorite apps. There's also a search button directly on the taskbar, and you can use the search functionality to find apps and files on your computer.

- It's a lot easier to connect your computer to a network, especially with the Homegroup feature.

- The Documents and Settings folder has been replaced by traditional User folders.

- You can more easily switch from one open app to another with the Alt+Tab keyboard shortcut.

- The new and improved Microsoft Edge web browser replaces Internet Explorer.

- Windows 10 runs a lot faster, especially on newer PCs, and crashes less often.

The challenge with upgrading directly from Windows XP to Windows 10 is that you're moving from a 14-year-old operating system to a brand new state-of-the-art one. If you use a computer that's as old as the operating system, it may not run Windows 10; certainly, you're likely to run into some compatibility issues with older peripherals and software programs.

In addition, the upgrade itself won't be easy. You can't just upgrade the operating system; you have to wipe your computer's hard disk completely clean and then install Windows 10 fresh on top of that. (This is called a *clean install.*) You'll lose all your files and programs and settings, so you'll want to back up your files first and then restore them after you install Windows 10. You'll need to reinstall all your software programs from scratch, as well.

In addition, Windows XP users are not eligible for the same free upgrade offered to Windows 7 and 8.1 users. If you want to upgrade to Windows 10, you'll have to pay for it.

For these reasons, it's difficult to recommend that "absolute beginners" upgrade from Windows XP to Windows 10, even with all the benefits that might come from such a move. A better approach is to ditch your older computer (or give it to one of your kids) and buy a new computer with Windows 10 already installed. New computers are a lot less expensive than they were a decade ago, and getting a new PC up and running will take a lot less time and effort than trying to upgrade a Windows XP machine to Windows 10.

The Most Important New Features of Windows 10

Now that you know what's new in this latest version of Windows, let's take an in-depth look at the most important features in Windows 10.

Back to the Desktop (Goodbye, Start Screen)

The biggest mistake that Microsoft made with Windows 8 was trying to apply a single interface paradigm to all possible devices—and then picking the wrong interface. Microsoft assumed that tablets would obliterate desktop and notebook PCs, so it developed a touch-based, full-screen interface that worked fine on those touchscreen devices, but then forced that interface on all traditional PC users. Bad decision.

The biggest change in Windows 10 is the abandonment of that touch-based paradigm—at least if you have a regular notebook or desktop PC. When you boot Windows 10 with a traditional PC, you're booted directly to the desktop, shown in Figure 5.1. There's no Start screen (which is how you had to open apps in Windows 10), no Charms bar you have to swipe in from the right (which is where many system settings were located in Windows 8), no "Modern" or "Metro" apps that took up the entire screen to display a minimal amount of information. You start your PC, you see the same old desktop you've grown to love and expect, and you're off to the races.

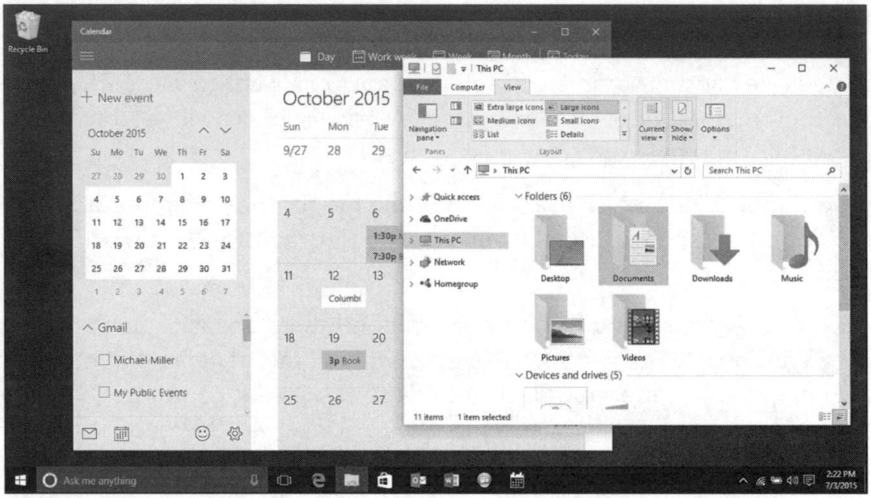

FIGURE 5.1

The Windows 10 desktop, complete with flat design and thinner window frames.

The Windows 10 desktop looks pretty much like the desktop in Windows 7. There's a taskbar at the bottom of the screen, application shortcuts on the desktop itself, even a Start button in the lower-left corner (more on that in a moment). You don't need to touch it to make it work; it's designed for use with your mouse and keyboard, just as you're used to. In short, it's the Windows desktop you want, with no unnecessary interference.

NOTE   If you run Windows 10 on a touchscreen tablet, however, you won't see the desktop—you see a full-screen version of the Start menu, along with much of the touch-based stuff first introduced in Windows 8. And that's as it should be; different interfaces for different types of devices, without negatively impacting traditional desktop users. Learn more about the version of Windows 10 in Chapter 6, "Using Windows 10 on a Touchscreen Device."

By the way, the Windows 10 desktop doesn't look exactly like the Windows 7 desktop. The older operating system's opaque Aero interface is gone, with Windows 10 instead adopting the trendy "flat" design that shows windows floating above the desktop with a slight drop shadow. Individual windows have thinner frames (or no frames at all) so the contents are front and center with a minimum of unnecessary "chrome." And most of the system icons have been redesigned, as well.

At the far-right corner of the notification area of the taskbar you see a new Notifications icon. Click this to display the Action Center, as shown in Figure 5.2, that displays system messages and (if you're using the right email client) new messages in your email inbox. Not necessary, but kind of nice.

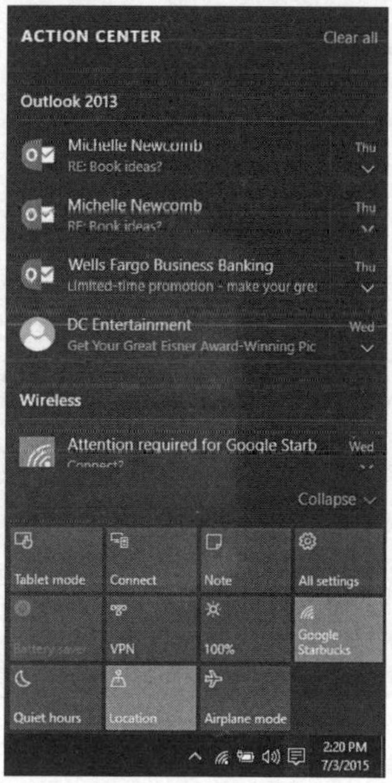

FIGURE 5.2

The Action Center in Windows 10.

The Start Menu Returns—Better Than Ever

Perhaps the most significant change in Windows 10 is that little piece of real estate in the lower-left corner. That's right, the Start button and the Start menu are back!

Perhaps the dumbest thing Microsoft did in Windows 8 was to remove the Start menu, which is how we've all been launching programs since the advent of

Windows 95 two decades ago. In Windows 8, you had to navigate to the Start screen, which took up the entire screen (of course), find your app among the dozens or hundreds displayed there, and then do the tap or click thing. There was no compelling reason for this change, nobody was demanding it, and users quite frankly despised it.

Well, Microsoft heard the complaints, and the Start menu is back in Windows 10. Click the Start button and you see the Start menu—although it looks a little different from what you were used to in Windows 7, as you can see in Figure 5.3.

FIGURE 5.3

The Windows 10 Start menu, complete with live tiles for pinned programs.

Actually, the left side of the new Start menu looks familiar—it's the normal list of favorite and last-used applications, in a slightly different order than before. There's also the requisite All Apps option that, when clicked, displays a scrolling list of all installed programs.

It's the right side of the Start menu that's radically different. Here is where you see any apps you've pinned to the Start menu, but not in the traditional list. Instead, you see a "tile" for each item. These are similar to the tiles on the Windows 8 Start screen, to the extent of being "live"—that is, displaying current information when available. If you pin the Weather app, for example, the Weather tile displays current temperature and weather conditions. The News tile displays current news headlines. And so forth.

These tiles are resizable, and the Start menu can be resized vertically. The tiles create a new level of usability for the Start menu, resulting in a nice addition of Windows 8 functionality into the traditional Windows desktop paradigm.

Modern Apps in Desktop Windows

In Windows 8, Microsoft introduced a new class of applications, originally dubbed Metro (then Modern, and then Windows Store) apps. These apps ran full screen and were designed to be used on touch interfaces.

As a whole, these Modern apps were not successful. In many cases, they presented too little information on too much screen real estate. (Do you really need a Weather app running full screen?) In other cases, the apps were actually pretty good but suffered simply by being associated with the hated Windows 8.

In Windows 10, Microsoft tries to offer the best of both worlds. All the former full-screen Modern apps (now called Universal or just Windows apps) are redesigned to appear in traditional windows on the desktop, as shown in Figure 5.4. You can resize the windows as you like, and display multiple app windows at a time. You get all the functionality of these newer apps but in a desktop-friendly package—just as it should be.

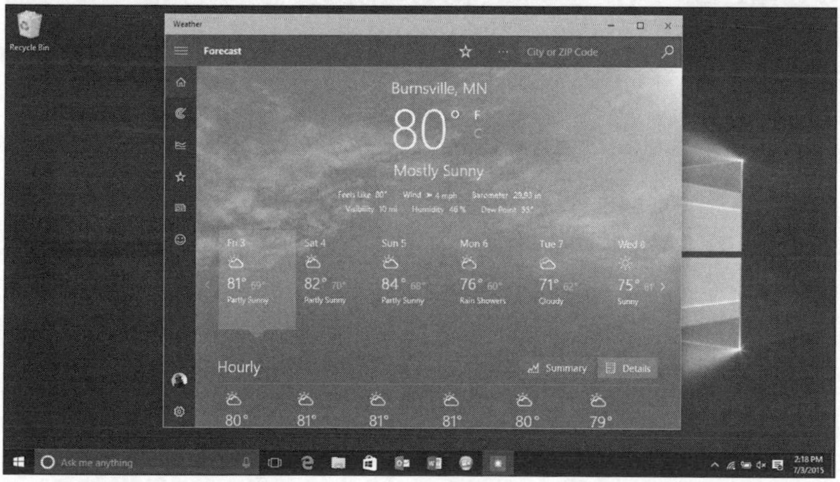

FIGURE 5.4

The Weather app, running in a desktop window.

By the way, in Windows 8 the configuration options for these apps appeared in the swipeable Charms bar. The app-specific Charms bars are gone for these revised Universal apps; instead, all the app options are accessible from a "hamburger" (three bar) button on the app's toolbar. Much more friendly for desktop users.

More New Stuff

Now that Windows 10 takes us back to the desktop, Microsoft has devised a new way to run multiple desktops for better productivity. This new feature is called Task View, and it lets you create multiple desktops, each with its own combination of open windows. Click the new Task View button on the toolbar to switch between desktops, as shown in Figure 5.5.

FIGURE 5.5

Using Task View to switch between two virtual desktops.

Windows 10 also incorporates Cortana, a Siri-like virtual assistant first introduced on Windows Phone devices. You use Cortana to search for content on your PC or on the Web, as well as to set reminders, schedule tasks, and such. You can search with Cortana from your computer keyboard or speak voice commands into your PC's microphone.

In addition, Windows 10 features a new web browser (in addition to the older Internet Explorer), named Edge. This new browser looks and feels more like the more modern Chrome and Firefox browsers and, like those browsers, support browser extensions.

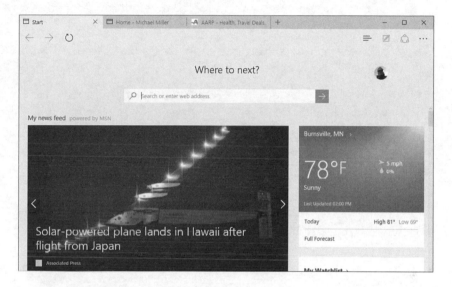

FIGURE 5.6

Windows 10's new Edge web browser.

And there are a lot more changes, big and small, under the hood and hiding in plain sight. This makes Windows 10 a must-have upgrade for both beleaguered Windows 8 users and expectant Windows 7 devotees. It's the upgrade to Windows 7 that Windows 8 should have been—and it's now available on your personal computer.

THE ABSOLUTE MINIMUM

This chapter showed you how Windows 10 differs from older versions of Windows. Here are the key points to remember:

- Windows 10 corrects many of the big issues that users had with the ill-fated Windows 8.

- Windows 10 reintroduces a new and improved Start menu, accessible from the Start button.

- There is no Start screen for notebook and desktop users of Windows 10; you boot directly to and stay on the traditional desktop.

- The Modern apps introduced in Windows 8 now are called Universal apps and run in resizable windows on the traditional desktop.

6

USING WINDOWS 10 ON A TOUCHSCREEN DEVICE

As you learned in Chapter 5, "Getting to Know Windows 10—If You've Used Windows Before," the previous version of Windows, Windows 8, was designed for computers and tablets with touchscreen displays. Most users, however, don't have touchscreen computers, which is why Windows 8 was such a flop.

However, if you do have a computer with a touchscreen display, or if you use a tablet or hybrid PC, you can use Windows 10's touchscreen mode. This version of Windows 10 hides the traditional desktop and instead displays the Start menu and all apps full-screen.

Understanding Windows 10's Tablet Mode

Here's the great thing about Windows 10—it's actually two operating systems in one. It offers the traditional desktop mode for those of us using notebook and desktop computers, and a special tablet mode for those using tablets and other touchscreen devices. In fact, Windows 10's Continuum technology automatically senses what type of device you use and displays either the desktop or the touch-based tablet mode screen accordingly. You don't have to do anything; Windows figures it out for you and provides the optimal interface for your device.

You can, however, manually switch between desktop and tablet modes, just in case you prefer one or the other and that isn't the natural mode for your device. To switch to tablet mode, follow these steps:

1. Click the Notifications icon on the taskbar to display the Action Center.

2. Click Tablet Mode.

To switch back to traditional desktop mode, repeat these steps but deselect the Tablet Mode tile.

Using Tablet Mode

When you use Windows 10 in tablet mode, a few things change. First, all apps display full-screen, not in individual windows. You can still switch from app to app, but you can't display apps in separate windows—although you can display two apps side-by-side. (Also, there's no desktop per se.)

In addition, when you click the Start button, the Start menu displays full-screen, as shown in Figure 6.1. There is no scrolling list of recent apps, as with the desktop Start menu. If you want to display this list, click or tap the Options (three-line) button at the top-left corner of the screen.

FIGURE 6.1

The Start menu in tablet mode.

NOTE Your Start menu probably looks a little different from the one in Figure 6.1, in particular the tiles you see. That's because every person's system is different, depending on the particular programs and apps they have installed on their PC.

As you can see, the tiles on the tablet mode Start menu are big and colorful, ideal for viewing on a tablet or smaller touchscreen computer. Tiles vary in size, with some spanning one-half a column and some spanning two columns; there's no difference between a large tile and a small tile, other than the size.

The taskbar runs across the bottom of the screen; although, it's somewhat simplified over the traditional desktop taskbar. New to the tablet mode taskbar is a back button, which you can click or tap to return to the previously used app or window.

Just above the Start button are two icons, for Power and All Apps. Click or tap the Power icon when you want to power off your computer; click or tap the All Apps icon to display the All Apps list on the left side of the screen.

Scrolling Through the Tiles

There are probably more tiles on your Start menu than will fit on a single screen of your tablet computer display. To view all your Start tiles, scroll down the screen. There are two ways to do this:

- **With your mouse**—Click and drag the scrollbar at the right side of the screen, or click the up and down scroll arrows on the top and bottom of the scrollbar. If your mouse has a scroll wheel, you can also use the scroll wheel to scroll up and down through the tiles.

- **With a touchscreen display**—Swipe the screen with your finger bottom to top to scroll down, or top to bottom to scroll up.

Opening a Tile

Remember that each tile on the Start menu represents a specific app or document. There are three ways to launch an app or open a document from these tiles:

- **With your mouse**—Click the tile, using the left mouse button.

- **With your keyboard**—Use your keyboard's arrow keys to highlight that tile and then press the Enter key.

- **With a touchscreen display**—Tap the tile with your finger.

When you open a program, it opens full-screen. To return to the Start menu, click or tap the Start button on the taskbar. (You can also display the Start menu by pressing the Windows button on your keyboard.)

Finding Additional Apps in the All Apps List

The Start menu is where you find those apps and utilities that you've specifically "pinned" there. When you install a new app, it doesn't automatically appear on the Start menu; you have to manually add the app to it.

If you want to view *all* the apps and utilities installed on your PC, you need to display the All Apps list. To do this, click or tap the All Apps icon at the bottom-left corner of the Start menu. Click or tap an app to launch it from this list.

To add an app to the Start menu, follow these steps:

1. From the All Apps list, right-click the app you want to add.

2. Click Pin to Start.

Using Windows 10 with a Touchscreen Display

If you use Windows on a computer or tablet with a touchscreen display, you can use your fingers instead of a mouse to do what you need to do. To that end, it's important to learn some essential touchscreen operations.

Tapping

The touchscreen equivalent of clicking an item is tapping that item. That is, you tap a tile or button or menu item with the tip of your finger. Just tap and release to open an app or select an option.

Pressing and Holding

As you've learned, right-clicking an item with your mouse often displays additional information or options. The touchscreen equivalent of the right-click is pressing and holding an item. Simply touch an item onscreen with your finger and hold it there until a complete circle appears on the display. You can then lift your finger, and a shortcut menu appears.

Swiping

With a touchscreen display, you can perform many common tasks with a simple swipe of your finger across the screen, typically from one edge or corner into the center of the screen. For example, swiping from the right side of the screen inward to the left displays the Action Center.

Panning

You use panning to scroll down or through a long page or series of screens. Simply touch and drag the page with one or more fingers in the direction you want to pan.

Zooming

You use two fingers to zoom into or out of a given screen—that is, to make a selection larger (zooming in) or smaller (zooming out) onscreen.

To zoom out, use two fingers (or your thumb and first finger) to touch two points on the item, and then move your fingers in toward each other, as if you're pinching the screen. To zoom in, use your fingers to touch two points on the item, and then move your fingers apart from each other, as if you're stretching the screen.

Rotating

You can use your fingers to rotate a picture or other item on the screen in a circular motion, either clockwise or counterclockwise. Simply use two fingers to touch two points on the item and then turn your fingers in the direction you want to rotate it.

Other Important Touch Operations

There's a lot you can do on a touchscreen display—if you know the proper gestures. Peruse the information in Table 6.1, which describes how to perform key operations with your fingers on a touchscreen display.

TABLE 6.1   Essential Touch Operations

Operation	Touchscreen
Close currently running app or window	Touch the top edge of the screen and swipe down about halfway through the screen.
Display Action Center	Swipe in from right side of the screen.
Display context-sensitive options menu	Press and hold item.
Display Start menu	Tap the Start button.
Move an item to a new location	Press and hold, drag to new location, and then release.
Open a program or document	Tap.
View or switch to other open apps	Swipe in from the left edge of the screen.

THE ABSOLUTE MINIMUM

Windows 10's tablet mode is ideal if you have a tablet or hybrid PC. Here are the key points to remember:

- Windows 10 can automatically sense what type of device you have and display the appropriate mode (either desktop or tablet)—although you can manually switch from one mode to another.

- Tablet mode displays the Start menu and all apps maximized full-screen.

- Use a variety of touch gestures to perform basic operations on a touchscreen device.

7

WORKING WITH FILES, FOLDERS, AND ONLINE STORAGE

Managing the data stored on your computer is vital. After you save a file, you might need to copy it to another computer, move it to a new location on your hard drive, rename it, or even delete it. You have to know how to perform all these operations—which means learning how to work with files, folders, and disks in Windows.

Understanding Files and Folders

All the information on your computer is stored in *files*. A file is nothing more than a collection of digital data. The contents of a file can be a document (such as a Word memo or an Excel spreadsheet), a digital photo or music track, or the executable code for a software program.

Every file has its own given name. A defined structure exists for naming files, and you must follow the naming conventions for Windows to understand exactly what file you want when you try to access one. Each filename must consist of two parts, separated by a period—the *name* (to the left of the period) and the *extension* (to the right of the period). A filename can consist of letters, numbers, spaces, and characters and looks something like this: filename.ext.

Windows 10 stores files in *folders*. A folder is like a master file; each folder can contain both files and additional folders. The exact location of a file is called its *path* and contains all the folders leading to the file. For example, a file named filename.doc that exists in the system folder, which is itself contained in the windows folder on your C: drive, has a path that looks like this: C:\windows\system\filename.doc.

Learning how to use files and folders is a necessary skill for all computer users. You might need to copy files from one folder to another or from your hard disk to a floppy disk. You certainly need to delete files every now and then.

 TIP   By default, Windows hides the extensions when it displays filenames. To display extensions in Windows 10, open the View tab in File Explorer and enable the File Name Extensions check box. (You can see this option later in this chapter, in Figure 7.2.)

Using File Explorer

In Windows 10, all the items stored on your computer—including programs, documents, and configuration settings—are accessible from *File Explorer*. This is a desktop application that displays all the disk drives, folders, subfolders, and files on your computer system. You use File Explorer to find, copy, delete, and launch programs and documents.

NOTE   What Microsoft now calls File Explorer used to be called (prior to Windows 8) Windows Explorer. More experienced users may also know File Explorer/Windows Explorer as the My Computer or My Documents folder.

Launching File Explorer

You can launch File Explorer in one of three ways:

- From the taskbar, click the File Explorer icon.

- Click the Start button to display the Start menu, and then click File Explorer.

- Right-click the Start menu to display the Options menu, and then click File Explorer.

Exploring the File Explorer Window

When you open File Explorer, you see a Navigation pane on the left and a contents pane on the right. The Navigation pane is divided into several sections.

The top section, Quick Access, lists your most recently used folders, as well as three folders that are "pinned" to this section: Documents, Music, and Videos. (These are the defaults, but the specific folders listed here can vary.) Next is a OneDrive section, which lists your folders stored on Microsoft's OneDrive Internet-based storage service. Below that is a This PC section, which provides access to all the disk drives and devices connected to your computer. Next is the Network section, which lets you access all your networked computers. Finally, the Homegroup section lets you access other computers in your network homegroup.

Click any icon in the Navigation pane to view the contents of that item. For example, when you click This PC, you see the six main folders, as shown in Figure 7.1: Desktop, Documents, Downloads, Music, Pictures, and Videos—as well as icons for any other devices connected to your computer. Double-click a folder to view its contents.

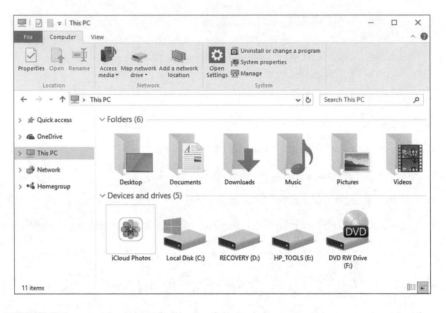

FIGURE 7.1

Navigating through your folders and subfolders with File Explorer.

Working with Ribbons and Tabs

File Explorer displays what is called a *Ribbon* at the top of the window. This Ribbon contains all the operations and commands you need to manage your files and folders, organized into three tabs: File, Computer, and View. The available tabs change depending on what you view in File Explorer; for example, when you view the contents of a folder, you see the File, Home, Share, and View tabs.

If the Ribbon is minimized, you see only the names of the tabs. To view the commands on a given tab, click that tab to expand the tab downward and make visible the tab's commands. You can maximize the entire Ribbon (expand it downward) by clicking the down arrow at the right side of the Ribbon bar.

From time to time, you see additional tabs on the Ribbon, beyond the basic four. That's because Windows displays additional commands relevant to the task at hand. For example, if you open the Recycle Bin, you see a Manage tab that includes commands for managing the Recycle Bin and restoring deleted files (see Figure 7.5, later in this chapter).

Navigating the Folders on Your PC

After you launch File Explorer, you can navigate through all your folders and subfolders in several ways:

 NOTE   A subfolder is a folder that is contained within another folder. Multiple subfolders can be nested in this fashion.

- To view the contents of a disk or folder, double-click the selected item.

- To move back to the disk or folder previously selected, click the Back button (left arrow) on the toolbar beneath the Ribbon.

- To choose from the history of disks and folders previously viewed, click the down arrow in the Address bar at the top of the File Explorer window and select a disk or folder.

- If you've moved back through multiple disks or folders, you can move forward to the next folder by clicking the Forward button (right arrow) on the toolbar.

- Go directly to any disk or folder by entering the path in the Address bar (in the format c:\folder\subfolder) and pressing Enter.

- Move backward through the "bread crumb" path in the Address bar. Click any previous folder location (separated by arrows) to display that particular folder.

 TIP   Click any arrow between locations in the Address bar to view additional paths from that location.

Viewing Files and Folders

There's no set way to view the files and folders stored on your computer. In fact, File Explorer has several options to change the way your files and folders display.

Changing the Way Files Display

You can choose to view the contents of a folder in a variety of ways. To change the file view, select the View tab on the Ribbon bar, as shown in Figure 7.2. From here you can select from eight available views:

- Extra large icons

- Large icons

- Medium icons

- Small icons

- List

- Details

- Tiles

- Content

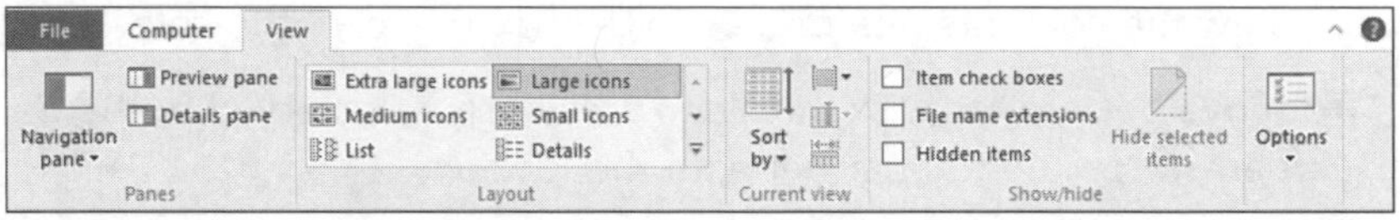

FIGURE 7.2

Use the View tab to change how files display.

> **TIP**   Any of the Icon views are good for working with graphics files or for getting a quick thumbnail glance at a file's contents. The Details view is better if you're looking for files by date or size.

Sorting Files and Folders

When viewing files in File Explorer, you can sort your files and folders in a number of ways. To do this, select the Views tab on the Ribbon bar and then click the Sort By button. You can then choose to sort by a variety of criteria, including Name, Date Modified, Type, Size, Date Created, Folder Path, Authors, Categories, Tags, or Title. You can also choose to sort the items in either ascending or descending order.

If you want to view your files in alphabetical order, choose to sort by Name. If you want to see all similar files grouped together, choose to sort by Type. If you want to sort your files by the date and time you last edited them, choose the Date Modified option. And if you want to sort by a user-applied file tag (assuming you've done this in the file's host program), choose the Tags option.

Grouping Files and Folders

You can also configure File Explorer to group the files in your folder, which can make it easier to identify particular files. For example, if you sort your files by time and date modified, they're grouped by date (Today, Yesterday, Last Week, and so on). If you sort your files by type, they're grouped by file extension, and so on.

To turn on grouping, click the Group By button on the View tab of the Ribbon bar. You can then choose to group by any of the same parameters available for sorting. File Explorer groups your files and folders by the selected criteria.

Searching for Files

As organized as you might be, you might not always find the specific files you want. Fortunately, Windows 10 offers an easy way to locate difficult-to-find files, via the Instant Search function. Instant Search indexes all the files stored on your hard disk (including email messages) by type, title, and contents. So you can search for a file by extension, filename, or keywords within the document.

To use the Instant Search feature, follow these steps:

1. From within File Explorer, locate the search box at the top right of the window.

2. Enter one or more keywords into the search box.

3. Press Enter.

Windows displays a list of items that match your search criteria. Double-click any icon to open that file.

 TIP   You can also search for files from anywhere in Windows 10. Press Win+Q or click the Search button on the taskbar to display the Search pane, enter your query, and press Enter.

Performing Basic File and Folder Operations

In Windows 10, you accomplish most of the file and folder operations you want to do via the Home tab on the Ribbon bar, as shown in Figure 7.3. You use the buttons on this tab to move, copy, and delete items—as well as perform other key operations.

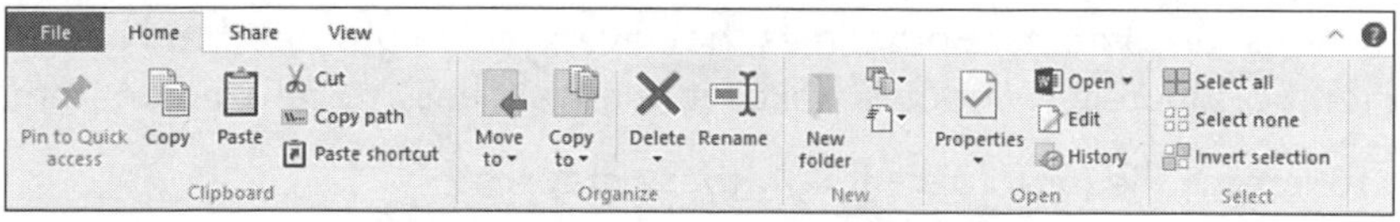

FIGURE 7.3

Use the Home tab to perform essential file and folder operations.

Creating New Folders

The more files you create, the harder it is to organize and find things on your hard disk. When the number of files you have becomes unmanageable, you need to create more folders—and subfolders—to better categorize your files.

To create a new folder, follow these steps:

1. Navigate to the drive or folder where you want to place the new folder.

2. Select the Home tab on the toolbar.

3. Click the New Folder button.

4. A new, empty folder appears within the File Explorer window, with the filename New Folder highlighted.

5. Type a name for your folder (which overwrites the New Folder name), and press Enter.

 CAUTION   Folder and filenames can include up to 255 characters—including many special characters. Some special characters, however, are "illegal," meaning that you *can't* use them in folder or filenames. Illegal characters include the following: \ / : * ? " < > |.

 CAUTION   The one part of the filename you should never change is the extension—the part that comes after the "dot." That's because Windows and other software programs recognize different types of program files and documents by their extension. This is why, by default, Windows hides these file extensions—so you can't change them by mistake.

Renaming Files and Folders

When you create a new file or folder, it helps to give it a name that somehow describes its contents. Sometimes, however, you might need to change a file's name. Fortunately, Windows makes it relatively easy to rename an item.

To rename a file (or folder), follow these steps:

1. Click the file or folder you want to rename.

2. Select the Home tab on the Ribbon bar.

3. Click the Rename button to highlight the filename.

4. Type a new name for your file or folder (which overwrites the current name), and press Enter.

Copying Files

Copying a file lets you re-create that file in a different location, either on your computer's hard drive or on some sort of external media. Here's how to do it:

 NOTE   It's important to remember that copying is different from moving. When you *copy* an item, the item remains in its original location—plus you have the new copy. When you *move* an item, the file is no longer present in the original location—all you have is the item in the new location.

1. Select the item you want to copy.

2. Select the Home tab on the Ribbon bar.

3. Click the Copy To button; this displays a pull-down menu of popular and recently visited locations.

4. To copy directly to one of the listed locations, click that location from the list.

5. To copy to another location, click Choose Location from the pull-down menu to display the Copy Items dialog box. Navigate to the new location for the item, and then click the Copy button.

That's it. You've just copied the file from one location to another.

Moving Files

Moving a file (or folder) is different from copying it. Moving cuts the item from its previous location and places it in a new location. Copying leaves the original item where it was *and* creates a copy of the item elsewhere.

In other words, when you copy something, you end up with two of it. When you move something, you have only the one instance.

To move a file, follow these steps:

1. Select the item you want to move.

2. Select the Home tab on the Ribbon bar.

3. Click the Move To button; this displays a list of popular and recently visited locations.

4. To move an item to one of the listed locations, click that location from the list.

5. To move the item to another location, click Choose Location on the pull-down menu to display the Move Items dialog box. Navigate to the new location for the item, and then click the Move button.

Deleting Files

Too many files eat up too much hard disk space—which is a bad thing because you have only so much disk space. (Music and video files, in particular, can chew up big chunks of your hard drive.) Because you don't want to waste disk space, you should periodically delete the files (and folders) you no longer need.

Deleting a file is as easy as following these simple steps:

1. Select the file or files you want to delete.

2. Select the Home tab on the Ribbon bar.

3. Click the Delete button.

This simple operation sends the file to the Windows Recycle Bin, which is kind of a trash can for deleted files. (It's also a trash can that periodically needs to be dumped—as we discuss momentarily.)

 TIP   You can also delete a file by selecting it and then pressing the Delete key on your computer keyboard.

Working with the Recycle Bin

As just discussed, all recently deleted files are stored in what Windows calls the Recycle Bin. This is a special folder on your hard disk that temporarily stores all deleted items—which is a good thing.

Restoring Deleted Files

Have you ever accidentally deleted the wrong file? If so, you're in luck, thanks to the Recycle Bin. As you now know, Windows stores all the files you delete in the Recycle Bin, at least temporarily. If you've recently deleted a file, it should still be in the Recycle Bin folder.

To "undelete" a file from the Recycle Bin, follow these steps:

1. Double-click the Recycle Bin icon on the desktop (shown in Figure 7.4) to open the Recycle Bin folder.

FIGURE 7.4

The Recycle Bin, where all your deleted files end up.

2. Click the file(s) you want to restore.

3. Select the Manage tab on the Ribbon bar, as shown in Figure 7.5.

4. Click the Restore the Selected Items button.

FIGURE 7.5

Managing deleted files in the Recycle Bin.

The deleted file is copied back to its original location, ready for continued use.

Managing the Recycle Bin

Deleted files do not stay in the Recycle Bin indefinitely. When you delete enough files to exceed the space allocated for these files, the oldest files in the Recycle Bin are automatically and permanently deleted from your hard disk.

If you'd rather dump the Recycle Bin manually (and thus free up some hard disk space), follow these steps:

1. Double-click the Recycle Bin icon on your desktop to open the Recycle Bin folder.

2. Select the Manage tab on the Ribbon bar.

3. Click the Empty the Recycle Bin button.

4. When the confirmation dialog box appears, click Yes to completely erase the files; click No to continue storing the files in the Recycle Bin.

Working with Compressed Folders

Really big files can be difficult to move or copy. They're especially difficult to transfer to other users, whether by email or USB drive.

Fortunately, Windows includes a way to make big files smaller. *Compressed folders* (sometimes called *zip files*) take big files and compress their size, which makes them easier to copy or move. After you transfer the file, you can uncompress the file to its original state.

Compressing a File

Compressing one or more files is a relatively easy task from within any Windows folder. Just follow these steps:

1. Select the file(s) you want to compress.

2. Select the Share tab on the Ribbon bar, shown in Figure 7.6.

3. Click the Zip button.

FIGURE 7.6

Use the Share tab to compress large files to a zip file.

Windows now creates a new folder that contains compressed versions of the file(s) you selected. (This folder is distinguished by a little zipper on the folder icon.) You can now copy, move, or email this folder, which is a lot smaller than the original file(s).

 NOTE The compressed folder is actually a file with a .ZIP extension, so you can use it with other compression/decompression programs, such as WinZip.

Extracting Files from a Compressed Folder

The process of decompressing a file is actually an *extraction* process. That's because you extract the original file(s) from the compressed folder. Follow these steps:

1. Select the compressed folder.

2. Select the Extract tab on the Ribbon bar.

3. Pull down the Extract To list and select a location for the extracted files.

4. Click the Extract All button.

Copying Files to Another Computer

Of course, you're not limited to copying and moving files from one location to another on a single PC. You can also copy files to other PCs via either a network connection or some sort of portable disk drive.

Copying Files over a Network

We talk more about network operations in Chapter 11, "Setting Up a Home Network." For now, it's important to know that if your PC is connected to a network and has file sharing activated, you can copy and move files from one network computer to another just as you can within folders on a single computer.

Copying Files with a Portable Drive

If you're not on a network, you can use a portable drive to transport files from one computer to another. The most popular type of portable drive today is the USB drive (sometimes called a flash drive or thumb drive), such as the one shown in Figure 7.7, which stores computer data in flash memory. You can find USB drives with capacities up to 256GB—more than big enough to hold even your biggest files.

FIGURE 7.7

Use a USB drive to transport files from one computer to another.

To use a USB drive, simply insert the device into an open USB port on your computer. After you insert it, the drive appears as a new drive in the This PC section of the File Explorer navigation pane. Double-click the USB drive icon to view the contents of the drive; you can then copy and paste files from your hard drive to the USB drive and vice versa. When you finish copying files, just remove the USB device. It's that simple.

Copying Files via Email

Another popular way to send files from one computer to another is via email. You can send any file as an email *attachment*; a file is literally attached to an email message. When the message is sent, the recipient can open or save the attached file when reading the message.

To learn how to send files as email attachments, turn to Chapter 15, "Sending and Receiving Email."

Working with Cloud-Based Storage

In addition to the local storage found on your personal computer, Microsoft offers online storage for all your documents and data, via its OneDrive service. When you store your files on OneDrive, you can access them via any computer or mobile device connected to the Internet.

This type of online file storage is called *cloud storage* because the files are stored on the "cloud" of computers on the Internet. The advantage of cloud storage is that you can access files from any computer (work, home, or other) at any location. You're not limited to using a given file on one particular computer.

Cloud storage is also great if you want to share your files with others. You can configure your files so that your friends and family can view them, or so that your work colleagues can edit and collaborate on them. It's all up to you, and all available to any person with a web browser and an Internet connection.

Accessing OneDrive from File Explorer

You can use File Explorer to view and manage the files stored online with OneDrive. Follow these steps:

1. From within File Explorer, click OneDrive in the navigation pane. This displays all your OneDrive files and folders, as shown in Figure 7.8.

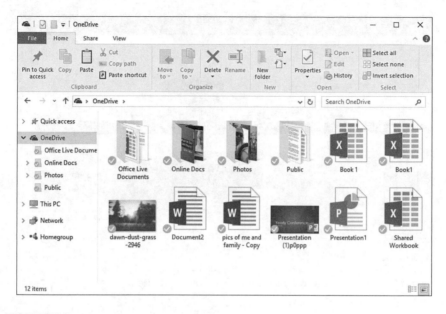

FIGURE 7.8

Viewing OneDrive contents in File Explorer.

2. Double-click to open a folder.

3. Double-click to open a file.

4. To manage your files, click any file, and then click the appropriate option on File Explorer's Home Ribbon.

Using Microsoft OneDrive

You can also view and manage your OneDrive files from the OneDrive website. Follow these steps:

1. From within Microsoft Edge or any web browser, go to onedrive.live.com.

2. As you can see in Figure 7.9, the OneDrive website displays the files you uploaded. If you organized your files into folders, you see those folders on the main page. Click a folder to view its contents.

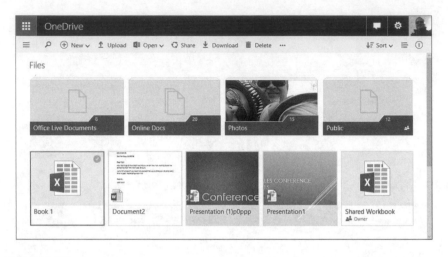

FIGURE 7.9

Viewing online folders and files on the OneDrive website.

3. Click a file to view it, or in the case of an Office document, open it in its online application.

4. To copy, cut, or rename a file, mouse over the file to display the selection circle, and then click the circle to select the file. You can then select the action you want from the toolbar.

5. To download a file from OneDrive to your local hard disk, select the file and then click Download from the toolbar.

6. To upload a file from your computer to OneDrive, click Upload and then select Files; when the Open dialog box appears, select the file to upload and then click Open.

 NOTE Microsoft gives you 15GB of storage in your free OneDrive account, which is more than enough to store most users' documents, digital photos, and the like. If you need more storage, you can purchase an additional 100GB for $1.99/month.

Syncing Files on Your PC to OneDrive

You can also use OneDrive to synchronize files stored on your computer with those stored in the cloud. You do this by utilizing the OneDrive folder in File Explorer.

To synchronize a file in this fashion, it must be stored in a special OneDrive folder. Then, whenever you connect to the Internet, any changes you make to that file are automatically made to the version of that file stored on OneDrive.

All you have to do is use File Explorer to move the file in question to the OneDrive folder. Navigate to the file, and then drag it onto the OneDrive folder in the Navigation pane. It's that easy; OneDrive does all the syncing for you.

Evaluating Other Online Storage Services

Microsoft OneDrive is just one of many cloud storage services you can use to store and share your files online. Other popular services are compared in Table 7.1.

TABLE 7.1   Online Storage Services

Service	URL	Free Storage	Other Plans
Apple iCloud	www.icloud.com	5GB	20GB $0.99/month
			200GB $3.99/month
			500GB $9.99/month
			1TB $19.99/month
Box	www.box.com	10GB	100GB $5/month
			Unlimited $15/month
Dropbox	www.dropbox.com	2GB	1TB $9.99/month
			Unlimited $15/month
Google Drive	www.google.com/drive	15GB	100GB $1.99/month
			1TB $9.99/month
Microsoft OneDrive	onedrive.live.com	15GB	100GB $1.99/month
			200GB $3.99/month
			1TB $6.99/month

All these services work in a similar fashion. Some, such as Google Drive, are focused on collaboration and sharing. Check out the various services before you commit—especially for a paid plan.

THE ABSOLUTE MINIMUM

Here are the key points to remember from this chapter:

- You manage your files and folders from File Explorer.

- Most common file and folder operations are found on the Home tab of the File Explorer Ribbon bar.

- If you accidentally delete a file, you might recover it by opening the Recycle Bin window.

- If you need to share a really big file, consider compressing it into a compressed folder (also known as a zip file).

- To copy a file to another PC, you can copy the file over a network, send the file as an email attachment, or copy the file to a portable USB drive.

- You can also store your files online, using Microsoft's OneDrive or other cloud-based file storage services.

8

PERSONALIZING WINDOWS

One of the nice things about Windows is that your version of Windows doesn't have to look or feel exactly like your neighbor's version. You can easily personalize various aspects of the operating system by tweaking a handful of configuration settings. Make Windows reflect your personality!

Personalizing the Windows Desktop

As with previous versions of Windows dating all the way back to Windows 3, you can personalize the Windows 10 desktop in a number of ways. You can change the color scheme and the desktop background and even "pin" your favorite programs to the taskbar or directly to the desktop.

Changing the Desktop Background

One of the most popular ways to personalize the desktop is to use a favorite picture or color as the desktop background. Follow these steps:

1. Right-click in any open area of the desktop to display the pop-up menu.

2. Click Personalize to display the Personalization window.

3. Click to select the Background tab, as shown in Figure 8.1.

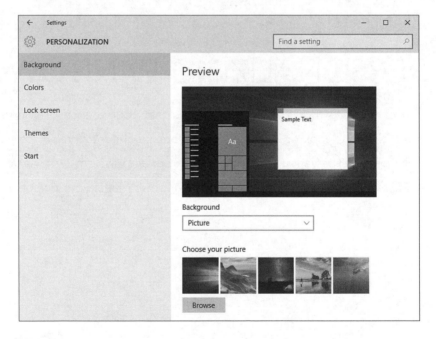

FIGURE 8.1

Choosing a desktop background.

4. Pull down the Background list, and select the type of background image you want: Picture, Solid Color, or Slide Show.

5. If you selected Picture, choose from one of the image options, or click Browse to select another picture stored on your PC. If the image is a different size from your Windows desktop, pull down the Choose a Fit list and select a display option: Fill, Fit, Stretch, Tile, Center, or Span.

6. If you select Solid Color, choose from one of the Background Colors presented.

7. If you select Slide Show, click Browse to choose the albums for your slideshow, and then select how often you want the picture to change and the fit.

Changing the Accent Color

You can select any accent color for your Windows desktop, as well as the background color for the Start menu and taskbar. Follow these steps:

1. Right-click in any open area of the desktop to display the pop-up menu.

2. Click Personalize to display the Personalization window.

3. Click to select the Colors tab, as shown in Figure 8.2.

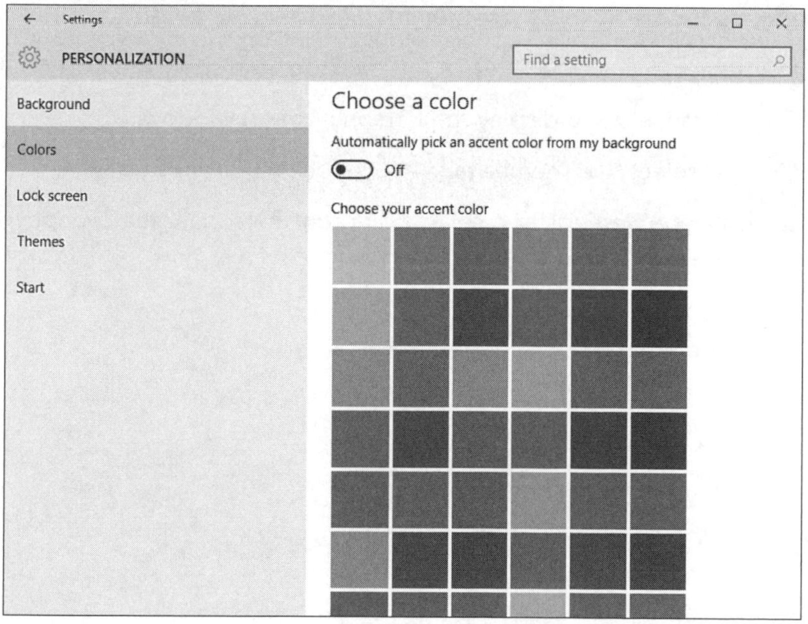

FIGURE 8.2

Choosing an accent color.

4. Click to select an accent color from the choices displayed.

5. To change the window color based on the color of the current background image, click "on" the Automatically Pick an Accent Color from My Background control.

6. By default, the Start menu, taskbar, and Action Center display in black. To have these elements display in color, click "on" the Show Color on Start, Taskbar, and Action Center control.

7. By default, the Start menu, taskbar, and Action center are transparent. To turn off this transparency, click "off" the Make Start, Taskbar, and Action Center Transparent control.

Choosing a Windows Theme

Rather than configuring each desktop element separately, you can choose a predesigned *theme* that changes all the elements together, in a visually pleasing configuration. A theme combines background images, color schemes, system sounds, and a screensaver to present a unified look and feel. Some themes even change the color scheme to match the current background picture.

To select a theme, follow these steps:

1. Right-click in any open area of the desktop to display the pop-up menu.

2. Click Personalize to display the Personalization window.

3. Click to select the Themes tab.

4. Click Theme Settings to display a different Personalization window, as shown in Figure 8.3.

5. Click a theme to begin using it.

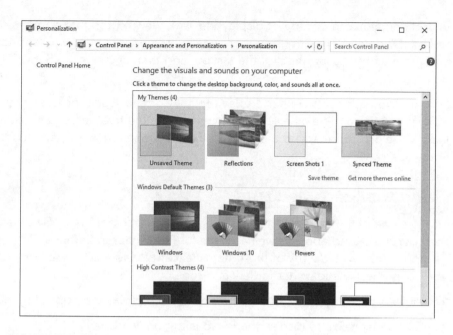

FIGURE 8.3

Choosing a new Windows theme.

Customizing the Taskbar

By default, the taskbar displays at the bottom of the screen. You can move it to either side of the screen (vertically) or the top of the screen by following these steps:

1. Right-click the taskbar to display the pop-up menu.

2. Click Properties to display the Taskbar and Start Menu Properties dialog box with the Taskbar tab selected.

3. Click the Taskbar Location on Screen menu and select the wanted location.

4. Click OK.

 TIP   From this same dialog box, you can opt to auto-hide the taskbar so that it appears only when you mouse over that area of the screen; lock the taskbar so that it can't be changed; use smaller taskbar buttons; and configure the way buttons display on the taskbar.

In addition, you can opt to not display the Task View button that appears on the taskbar by default. (This frees up more space on the taskbar for your shortcuts and other icons.) Just right-click the taskbar and then uncheck the Show Task View Button.

Similarly, you can opt to either display the full Cortana search box, display only a Cortana icon, or hide all evidence of Cortana on the taskbar. Right-click the taskbar, select Cortana, and then choose from Hidden, Show Cortana Icon, or Show Search Box.

Customizing the Start Menu

The left side of the Start menu can display a lot of different items. By default, you see your most-used apps, as well as icons for File Explorer, Settings, Power, and All Apps. You can hide any of these items (except Power and All Apps), or choose to display shortcuts for other folders and tools.

1. Right-click in any open area of the desktop to display the pop-up menu.

2. Click Personalize to display the Personalization window.

3. Click to select the Start tab.

4. Click "off" any option you don't want to see.

5. If you want the Start screen to always display full-screen (tablet mode), click "on" the Use Start Full Screen control.

6. To choose which folders appear on the Start menu, click Choose Which Folders Appear on Start.

7. When the next page appears, click "on" those items you want to see and click "off" those items you want to hide.

Personalizing the Lock Screen

You can also personalize the Lock screen that you see when you first start or begin to log in to Windows. You can change the background picture of the Lock screen, turn the Lock screen into a photo slide show, and add informational apps to the screen.

Changing the Lock Screen Background

To change the background picture you see on the Lock screen, follow these steps:

1. Right-click in any open area of the desktop to display the pop-up menu.

2. Click Personalize to display the Personalization window.

3. Click to select the Lock Screen tab, as shown in Figure 8.4.

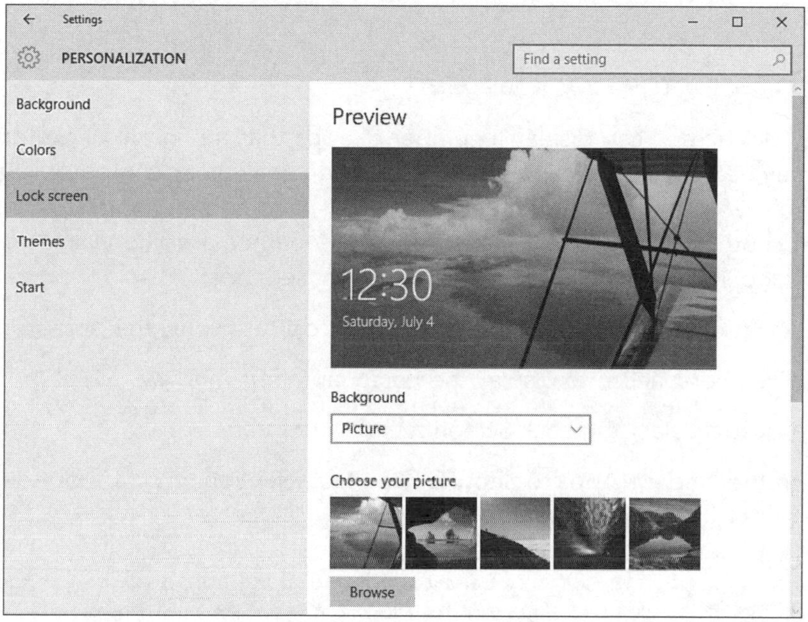

FIGURE 8.4

Personalizing the Lock screen.

4. Make sure Picture is selected in the Background list.

5. Click the thumbnail for the picture you want to use, or click Browse to select a different picture stored on your computer.

Displaying a Slide Show on the Lock Screen

Windows 10 lets you turn your computer into a kind of digital picture frame by displaying a slide show of your photos on the Lock screen while your PC isn't used. Follow these steps:

1. Right-click in any open area of the desktop to display the pop-up menu.

2. Click Personalize to display the Personalization window.

3. Click to select the Lock Screen tab.

4. Pull down the Background list and select Slideshow.

5. Click Add a Folder to select the picture folder you want to display in your slide show. (Otherwise, Windows always chooses pictures from your Pictures folder.)

6. Click Advanced Slideshow Settings to display additional options.

Adding Apps to the Lock Screen

The Lock screen can display a number of apps that run in the background and display useful or interesting information, even while your computer is locked. By default, you see the date/time, power status, and connection status, but it's easy to add other apps and information (such as weather conditions and unread email messages) to the Lock screen. Just follow these steps:

1. Right-click in any open area of the desktop to display the pop-up menu.

2. Click Personalize to display the Personalization window.

3. Click to select the Lock Screen tab.

4. In the Choose Apps to Show Quick Status section, click a + button and then select the app you want to add.

 TIP   You can also opt for one of the apps to display detailed live information. For example, you might want the Lock screen to display current weather conditions from the Weather app or upcoming appointments from the Calendar app. To select which app displays detailed information, click or tap the app button in the Choose an App to Display Detailed Status section.

Changing Your Account Picture

When you first configured Windows, you may have picked a default image to use as your profile picture—or not. You can, at any time, select a new or different profile picture that's more to your liking. Follow these steps:

1. Click the Start button to display the Start menu.

2. Click your name or picture at the top of the Start menu, and then click Change Account Settings.

3. The Settings window opens with the Your Account tab selected, as shown in Figure 8.5. Scroll to the Your Picture section and an existing picture.

Or...

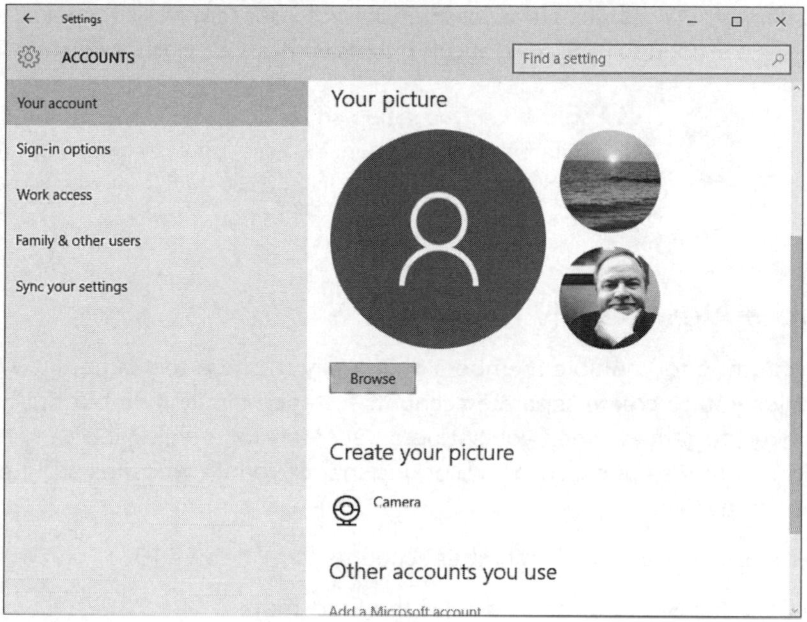

FIGURE 8.5

Changing your account picture.

4. Click the Browse button to display the Open dialog box, and then navigate to and select the picture you want.

 TIP   If your computer has a webcam, you can take a picture with your webcam to use for your account picture. From the Your Account tab, scroll to the Create Your Picture section, click the Camera button, and follow the onscreen directions from there.

Setting Up Additional User Accounts

Chances are you're not the only person using your computer; it's likely that you'll be sharing your PC with your spouse or kids, at least to some degree. Fortunately, you can configure Windows so that different people using your computer sign on with their own custom settings—and access to their own personal files.

The way to do this is to assign each user in your household her own password-protected *user account*. Anyone trying to access another user's account and files without the password is denied access.

You can set up new accounts for members of your family, with special safety options for younger children, and for users who aren't part of your family.

 NOTE When you set up an account, you can choose from three different ways to log in. You can log in to an account with a traditional password, with a PIN code, or with a picture password that you sketch onscreen with your finger or mouse.

Setting Up a New Family Member

It's common for multiple members of a family to share the same PC. Windows 10 enables you to create separate accounts for each family member but have them all linked together. When you set up an account for a child, you can also configure various safety settings, such as blocking inappropriate websites and tracking his online activities.

Here's how to add family member accounts to Windows 10:

1. Click the Start button to display the Start menu.

2. Click select Settings to display the Settings window.

3. Click Accounts to display the Accounts page.

4. Click the Family & Other Users tab.

5. Click Add a Family Member to display the Add as Child or Adult? window.

6. Select either Add a Child or Add an Adult.

7. Enter that person's email address.

8. Click Next.

9. When asked to confirm this new user, click Confirm. The person now receives an invitation to join your account.

Or…

10. If this person doesn't have an email address, click The Person I Want to Add Doesn't Have an Email Address.

11. This displays the Let's Create an Account page, as shown in Figure 8.6. Enter the person's name into the First Name and Last Name boxes.

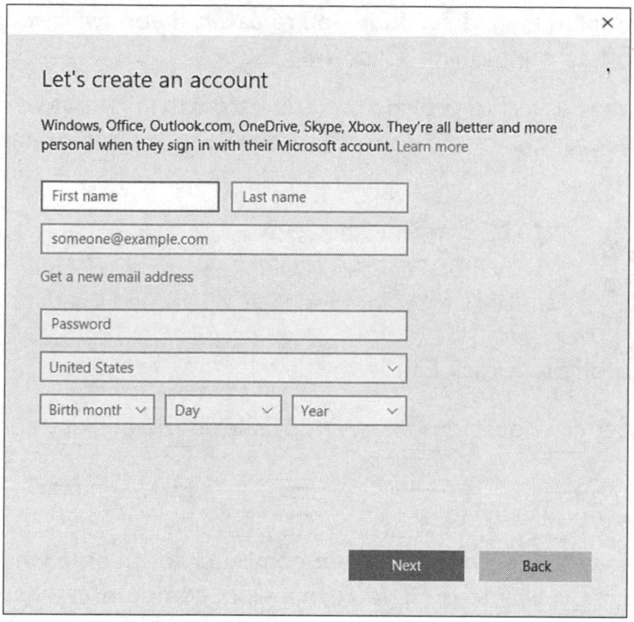

FIGURE 8.6

Creating a new user account.

12. Click Get a New Email Address.

13. Enter the desired email username into the New Email box. (You may have to try several names to get one that isn't already taken.)

14. Enter the desired password into the Password box.

15. Accept or change the country selection (United States by default).

16. Enter this person's birthdate.

17. Click Next.

18. On the next screen, enter a phone number you can use if you need to recover this account's password.

19. Click Next.

20. On the next screen, *uncheck* both options. (Unless you want them to receive promotional offers from Microsoft, which you probably don't.)

21. Click Next.

22. If you created a child account, you're asked if you want your child to use her Microsoft account online. Click Yes.

23. You're now asked to provide a credit card to verify that you're an adult. (This also charges your card $0.50.) Enter the requested information, and then click Confirm.

 NOTE   The $0.50 charge is required by the Children's Online Privacy Protection Act (COPPA). Microsoft donates this fee to The National Center for Missing and Exploited Children.

24. When prompted, click Finish.

This new user can now sign in to Windows from the Lock screen.

Setting Up Other Users

You can also set up accounts on your computer for people who aren't in your family. This is the way to go if you use a work computer or share your computer with friends or other people in your house.

Follow these steps:

1. Click the Start button to display the Start menu.

2. Click select Settings to display the Settings window.

3. Click Accounts to display the Accounts page.

4. Click the Family & Other Users tab.

5. Scroll to the Other Users section, and click Add Someone Else to This PC.

6. This displays the How Will This Person Sign In? window. If the person has a Microsoft email address, enter that address and click Next.

Or...

7. If the person doesn't have a Microsoft account, click The Person I Want to Add Doesn't Have an Email Address.

8. Follow steps 11 through 24 from the previous section to complete the process.

Switching Users

If other people use your computer, they might want to log in with their own accounts. To switch users on a Windows 10 computer, follow these steps:

1. Click the Start button to display the Start menu.

2. Click your name or picture at the top of the Start menu. All users for this PC now display, as shown in Figure 8.7.

FIGURE 8.7

Switching users from the Start menu.

3. Click the desired user's name.

4. Enter the new user's password and then press Enter.

Logging Out

When you switch users, both accounts remain active; the original user account is just suspended in the background. If you'd rather log out completely from a given account and return to the Windows Lock screen, follow these steps:

1. Click the Start button to display the Start menu.

2. Click your name or picture at the top of the Start menu.

3. Click Sign Out.

Logging In with Multiple Users

In Chapter 4, "Getting to Know Windows 10—For New Computer Users," you learned how to log in to Windows when your computer first starts up. If you have more than one user assigned to Windows 10, however, the login process is slightly different. Follow these steps:

1. From the Windows Lock screen, press any key on your keyboard or click anywhere the screen.

2 By default, the login screen displays the main user of this computer, with other users displayed in the lower-left corner. Click the username of the user who wants to sign in.

3. That user's personal login screen displays. Enter the password, and then press the Enter key.

Configuring Other Windows Settings

There are many other Windows system settings that you can configure. In most cases, the default settings work fine, and you don't need to change a thing. However, you *can* change these settings, if you want to or need to.

Configuring Settings with the Settings Tool

You configure the most common Windows 10 settings from the Settings tool. This tool offers a series of options that present different types of settings.

Here's how it works:

1. Click the Start button to display the Start menu.

2. Select Settings to display the Settings window, as shown in Figure 8.8.

3. Click the appropriate option to configure related settings.

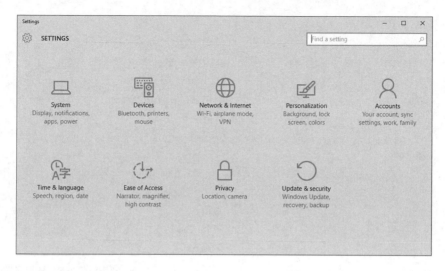

FIGURE 8.8

Configuring Windows from the PC Settings window.

NOTE   You can also open the Settings tool by clicking the Notifications icon on the taskbar to open the Action Center and then clicking All Settings.

Table 8.1 details the settings in the Settings tool.

TABLE 8.1   Windows Settings

Option	Settings
System	Display
	Notifications & Actions
	Apps & Features
	Multitasking
	Tablet Mode
	Battery Saver
	Power & Sleep
	Storage
	Offline Maps
	Default Apps
	About

TABLE 8.1 (continued)

Option	Settings
Devices	Printers & Scanners
	Connected Devices
	Mouse & Touchpad
	Typing
	AutoPlay
Network & Internet	Wi-Fi
	Airplane Mode
	Data Usage
	VPN
	Dial-Up
	Proxy
	Ethernet (if PC is connected to Ethernet connection)
Personalization	Background
	Colors
	Lock Screen
	Themes
	Start
Accounts	Your Account
	Sign-In Options
	Work Access
	Family & Other Users
	Sync Your Settings
Time & Language	Date & Time
	Region & Language
	Speech
Ease of Access	Narrator
	Magnifier
	High Contrast
	Closed Captions
	Keyboard
	Mouse
	Other Options

Option	Settings
Privacy	General
	Location
	Camera
	Microphone
	Speech, Inking, and Typing
	Account Info
	Contacts
	Calendar
	Messaging
	Radios
	Other Devices
	Feedback & Diagnostics
	Background Apps
Update & Security	Windows Update
	Windows Defender
	Backup
	Recovery
	Activation
	For Developers

Configuring Settings from the Traditional Control Panel

If you've used older versions of Windows, you're probably familiar with the Control Panel. This tool offers many of the same configuration settings as the new Settings tool, and a few more, to boot.

To access the Control Panel follow these steps:

1. Right-click the Start button to display the Quick Access menu.

2. Click Control Panel to open the Control Panel, shown in Figure 8.9.

3. Click the link for the type of setting you want to configure.

FIGURE 8.9

Configuring Windows from the Control Panel.

THE ABSOLUTE MINIMUM

This chapter showed you pretty much everything you need to know to customize Windows 10 for your own personal usage. Here are the key points to remember:

- You can personalize the Windows 10 desktop by choosing new background images, color schemes, and even complete system themes.

- You can customize the Lock screen with a selected image or display a photo slide show instead.

- If you have multiple people using your computer, you can create separate user accounts for each person.

- You can configure additional Windows settings from the Settings tool or from the traditional Control Panel.

9

CONNECTING OTHER DEVICES TO YOUR PC— AND YOUR PC TO OTHER DEVICES

If you just purchased a brand-new, right-out-of-the-box personal computer, it probably came equipped with all the components you could ever want—or so you think. At some point in the future, however, you might want to expand your system by adding a printer, a scanner, an external hard drive, better speakers, a different mouse or keyboard, or something equally new and exciting.

Adding new hardware to your system is relatively easy if you know what you're doing. That's where this chapter comes in.

Getting to Know the Most Popular Peripherals

When adding stuff to your PC, what are the most popular peripherals? Here's a list of hardware you can add to or upgrade on your system:

- **Hard drive**—Adds more storage capacity to your system or performs periodic backups from your main hard disk. The easiest type of hard drive to add is an external unit, which typically connects via USB and costs under $100. If you have a traditional desktop PC, you might also be able to add a second internal drive inside your system unit, but that's a lot more work.

 NOTE Learn more about adding a hard drive to your system in Chapter 10, "Adding Storage and Backup."

- **Solid-state drive**—On many systems, a replacement for the traditional hard drive. A solid-state drive has less storage space than a hard drive but is much faster for accessing that data. Some systems use a solid-state drive to store the Windows operating system (which makes everything run faster) and a separate hard drive to store files and other data.

- **Memory card reader**—Enables you to read data from devices (such as digital cameras) that use various types of flash memory cards.

- **USB memory device**—Provides gigabytes of removable storage; you can transport the USB memory device from one computer to another, connecting to each PC's USB port.

- **Monitor**—Replaces or supplements the built-in display on a notebook computer or replaces the existing monitor on a desktop system (typically with a larger screen).

- **Video card**—On traditional desktop PCs, upgrades your system's video playback and graphics, typically for video editing or playing visually demanding PC games.

- **Sound card**—On traditional desktop PCs, improves the audio capabilities of your systems; this is particularly important if you play state-of-the-art PC games, watch surround-sound DVD movies, or mix and record your own digital audio.

- **Speakers**—Upgrades the quality of your computer's sound system. (Surround-sound speaker systems with subwoofers are particularly popular, especially with PC gamers.)

- **Keyboard**—Supplements a notebook's built-in keyboard with a larger, more fully featured model, or upgrades the capabilities of a desktop's included keyboard.

- **Mouse**—Provides a more traditional input in place of a notebook PC's touchpad, or upgrades the capabilities of a desktop system's mouse. (For example, many users like to upgrade from wired to wireless mice.)

- **Gamepad or other game controller**—Enables you to get better action with your favorite games.

- **CD/DVD drive (burner)**—Adds recordable/rewritable capabilities to a netbook or ultrabook that doesn't have a built-in CD/DVD drive. (Some CD/DVD drives also have Blu-ray capability.)

- **Printer**—Improves the quality of your printouts, adds color to your printouts, or adds photo-quality printing to your system.

- **Scanner**—Enables you to scan photographs and documents into a digital format to store on your computer's hard drive.

- **Webcam**—Enables you to send real-time video to friends and family.

- **Wireless router**—Enables you to create a wireless network in your home—and share your broadband Internet connection among multiple computers.

- **Wireless network adapter**—Enables you to connect a desktop computer to any wireless network.

Adding New Hardware to Your System

Everything that's hooked to your PC is connected via some type of *port*. A port is simply an interface between your PC and another device—either internally (inside your PC's system unit) or externally (via a connector on the back of the system unit).

Given the choice, the easiest way to add a new device to your system is to connect it externally. In fact, if you have an all-in-one desktop, notebook, or tablet computer, it's the *only* way to add new hardware; you can't get inside the case to add anything else. And even if you have a traditional desktop PC with a separate system unit, it's still a whole lot easier to add a new device via an external USB port than it is to open the case and add it that way.

 NOTE No matter how you connect a new device, make sure to read the installation instructions for the new hardware and follow the manufacturer's instructions and advice.

The most common external connector today is the USB port, like the one shown in Figure 9.1. USB is a great concept (and truly "universal") in that virtually every type of new peripheral comes in a USB version. Want to add a second hard disk? Don't open the PC case; connect an external drive via USB. Want to add a new printer? Connect a USB printer. Want to connect to a home network? Don't bother with Ethernet cards; get a USB-compatible wireless adapter.

FIGURE 9.1

A USB port on a notebook PC. (Photograph courtesy Aidan C. Siegel via the Creative Commons Attribution-Share Alike 3.0 Unported license.)

There are a few other types of ports that you might occasionally run into or need to use. For example, if you want to connect your PC to your TV (which we discuss later in this chapter), you'll probably connect a cable to your PC's HDMI port. (HDMI is a special kind of connection for transmitting high-definition audio/video.) And some high-speed devices (such as really big and expensive hard drives) might connect via FireWire, which is kind of a faster version of USB. But for most purposes, USB is all you need to know about and use.

 NOTE There are a few variations on the USB tech standard. The older USB 2.0 connections, still common on computers today, have been superseded by the newer and faster USB 3.0 standard. USB 3.0 cables and connectors are slightly different from 2.0 versions but designed to work with older ports. Whenever possible, use USB 3.0 cables and ports for faster performance. (Most new PCs come with a combination of USB 2.0 and 3.0 ports.)

USB is popular because it's so easy to use. When you connect a USB device, not only do you not have to open your PC's case, but you don't even have to turn off your system when you add the new device. That's because USB devices are *hot swappable*. That means you can just plug the new device into the port, and Windows automatically recognizes it in real time.

 TIP If you connect too many USB devices, you might run out of USB connectors on your PC. If that happens to you, buy an add-on USB hub for $25 or so, which enables you to plug multiple USB peripherals into a single USB port.

To connect a new USB device, follow these steps:

1. Find a free USB port on your system unit and connect the new peripheral.

2. Windows should automatically recognize the new peripheral and install the proper device driver automatically.

That's it! The only variation on this procedure is if the peripheral's manufacturer recommends using its own installation program, typically provided on an installation CD. If this is the case, follow the manufacturer's instructions to perform the installation and setup.

 NOTE A *device driver* is a small software program that enables your PC to communicate with and control a specific device. Windows includes built-in device drivers for many popular peripherals. If Windows doesn't include a particular driver, you typically can find the driver on the peripheral's installation disk or on the peripheral manufacturer's website.

Connecting and Using a Printer

Your computer monitor displays images in real time, but they're fleeting. To conveniently create permanent visual records of your work, you need to add a printer to your system. Printers create hard copy output from your software programs—or just make prints of your favorite pictures.

Understanding Different Types of Printers

You can choose from various types of printers for your system, depending on your exact printing needs. The two main types of printers today are inkjet and laser, and both are suitable for home use.

The most popular type of printer for home use is the *inkjet* printer, like the one shown in Figure 9.2. An inkjet printer works by shooting jets of ink to the paper's surface to create the printed image.

FIGURE 9.2

A typical color inkjet printer. (Photo courtesy HP.)

To work, an inkjet printer needs to be filled with one or more replaceable ink cartridges. The typical inkjet printer has two cartridges—one that contains red, yellow, and blue ink (for color printing) and another with just black ink. You'll likely use up the black ink cartridge first because you'll probably print more single-color text documents than full-color pictures. Your printer should display a message on its front panel when a cartridge is running low; replacement ink cartridges are available at most home office stores.

Inkjet printers are typically lower priced than the other major type of printer, the laser printer. That's because inkjet models are not quite as heavy duty as laser printers, which are more suited for larger print jobs. An inkjet printer is fine for typical home use, but it might not hold up as well in a busy office environment.

Laser printers work a little differently than inkjet models. Instead of shooting liquid ink at the paper, a laser printer works much like a traditional copying machine, applying powdered ink (toner) to paper by using a small laser.

As such, laser printers (like the one in Figure 9.3) typically print a little faster than similar inkjets, and they produce slightly sharper results. This makes laser printers better suited for heavy-duty use, such as what you might get in an office environment.

FIGURE 9.3

A typical laser printer. (Photo courtesy HP.)

Of course, everything comes at a cost, and laser printers tend to be a little bigger and more expensive than comparable inkjet models. In addition, where most inkjets offer full-color printing, not all laser printers do; you can find both black-and-white and color laser printers for home and office use.

 NOTE Especially when considering a laser printer, you'll have your choice of either black-and-white or color printers. (Almost all consumer inkjet printers today are full color.) Black-and-white printers are faster than color printers and better if you're printing memos, letters, and other single-color documents. Color printers, however, are great if you have kids, and they're essential if you want to print pictures taken with a digital camera. As such, most home users tend to choose color printers—they're just more versatile.

You also have the option of purchasing a "multifunction" printer. This combines a traditional desktop printer with a scanner, a fax machine, and a copier—all-in-one multifunction unit. As you can see in Figure 9.4, multifunction printers are slightly larger than single-function printers. You can find multifunction printers of both the inkjet and laser varieties; these printers can be either black and white or color.

FIGURE 9.4

A multifunction color laser printer. (Photo courtesy Brother.)

If you need all these functions, by all means consider such a multifunction printer. Know, however, that you'll pay extra to get all this functionality; single-function printers are more affordable than multifunction units.

Connecting a Printer to Your Computer

Most printers connect directly to your computer, typically via USB. Some printers, however, can connect to your home network, typically via Wi-Fi, without being connected to a single PC.

In most instances, connecting a USB printer to your computer is a simple process:

1. Connect one end of a USB cable to the USB port on your printer.

2. Connect the other end of the USB cable to a USB port on your computer.

3. Connect the printer to a power outlet.

4. Turn on the printer.

Windows should automatically recognize the new printer and install the proper device driver automatically. Follow the onscreen instructions to finish the installation.

 NOTE Your printer might offer additional functionality, such as scanning, which is common in multifunction units. If so, you might need to install the printer and any necessary software from the accompanying installation CD or DVD. As always, follow the manufacturer's instructions for best results.

Connecting a Printer to Your Network

If you share a printer between multiple computers on your home network, you might want to go with a network printer—one that connects to your wireless network but doesn't physically connect to any single computer. The primary benefit of a network printer is that you can place it anywhere in your home; because it's not tethered to a given PC, it doesn't have to sit next to any computer. In fact, most network printers can connect to your network wirelessly or via Ethernet.

In general, the setup goes something like this:

1. Turn on your printer.

2. Connect the printer to your wireless router, either via Wi-Fi or Ethernet. In most instances, the printer automatically detects and connects to your network.

3. If your wireless network has a security password (and it should), enter that password on your printer's keypad.

Follow any additional instructions in your printer's installation manual. When the printer is properly configured, it should appear as a printing option for all computers connected to your network.

Printing to Your System's Printer

Printing from a given program is typically as easy as clicking or tapping the Print button. In some instances, the print function might be contained within a pull-down File or Print menu.

In any case, one-click printing is the norm. That is, you click the Print button, and printing ensues. In most programs, however, you can fine-tune your printing options by selecting the File menu and clicking Print. This typically displays a Print Options dialog box or page, like the one shown in Figure 9.5. From here you can select which printer to print to, which pages to print, how many copies to print, whether to print in portrait (vertical paper) or landscape (horizontal paper) modes, and so forth.

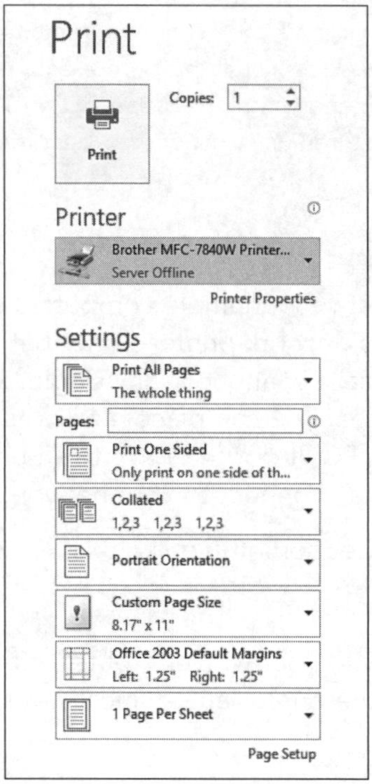

FIGURE 9.5

The print options page in Microsoft Word.

Know, however, that print functionality does differ from program to program. Make sure you consult a given app's help files if you need assistance in configuring various print options.

Connecting Portable Devices to Your PC

These days, a lot of the devices you connect to your PC actually aren't computer peripherals. Instead, they are gadgets that you use on their own but plug into your PC to share files.

What kinds of portable devices are we talking about? Here's a short list:

- Smartphones, including iPhones, Android phones, and Windows phones
- Tablets, such as the Apple iPad or Kindle Fire
- Portable music players, such as Apple's popular iPod
- Digital cameras
- Digital camcorders
- USB memory devices

All these devices connect to a USB port on your PC, which makes for an easy hookup. As mentioned earlier, USB ports are hot swappable, which means that all you have to do is connect the device to the proper port—no major configuration necessary. In some cases, the first time you connect your device to your PC, you need to run some sort of installation utility to install the device's software on your PC's hard drive. Each subsequent time you connect the device, your PC should recognize it automatically and launch the appropriate software program.

After your portable device is connected to your PC, what you do next is up to you. Most of the time, you'll transfer files either from your PC to the portable device, or vice versa. Use the device's software program to perform these operations, or use File Explorer to copy files back and forth.

For example, you can use a USB memory device as a removable and portable memory storage system. One of these USB drives is smaller than a pack of chewing gum and can hold several gigabytes' worth of data in electronic flash memory. Plug a USB memory device into your PC's USB port, and your PC recognizes it just as if it were another disk drive. You can then copy files from your PC to the USB drive to take your work (or your digital music or photo files) with you.

For more detailed information, see the instructions that came with your portable device.

Connecting Your PC to Your Living Room TV

As you'll no doubt soon discover, there are a lot of good movies and TV shows on the Internet that you can watch on your PC—often for free. Although you can watch this programming on your computer screen, that might be a little small for those of us more familiar with the large screen experience.

 NOTE Learn more about finding movies and TV shows on the Internet in Chapter 23, "Watching Movies, TV Shows, and Other Videos."

Fortunately, there might be a way to connect your computer to your living room TV and watch your Internet-based programming in full big-screen glory. It's all a matter of which ports you have on the back (or side) of your PC and whether you have similar connectors on your flat-screen television.

The most common way to connect a computer to a flat-screen TV is via HDMI. You might already be familiar with HDMI, which is used to connect many Blu-ray players, cable boxes, and the like to high-definition television sets. (Figure 9.6 shows an HDMI port on a typical notebook PC.) HDMI is nice because it feeds both video and audio via a single cable, in full 1080p high definition.

FIGURE 9.6

An HDMI port on a notebook PC.

If your computer has an HDMI connector, it's easy to connect an HDMI cable between your PC and an HDMI input on your TV. Connect that single cable, and the picture and sound (in full 5.1-channel surround!) from whatever you're watching on your computer is fed to your flat-screen TV.

If your PC doesn't have an HDMI port, you might still be able to connect it to your TV. Here's what to look for:

- Some TVs have a standard VGA connector (typically labeled "PC") that can connect (via a standard VGA cable) to the VGA or monitor output found on almost all PCs.

- If your computer has a DVI output, you can connect a DVI-to-HDMI adapter to this port and then use an HDMI cable to connect to your TV. Because DVI is video only, you also need to run an audio cable from your PC's audio output to your TV's audio inputs.

 NOTE *DVI* (short for *digital video interface*) is a digital connection for transmitting video signals and is often used to connect computers to LCD monitors. Both DVI and HDMI are digital formats, which is why you can convert DVI to HDMI.

After you connect your computer to your TV, you can see and hear everything your PC is doing through your TV. Just connect to the movie or TV website of choice, switch your TV to the appropriate video input, and get out the popcorn!

 TIP Windows 10 includes support for Miracast technology, which enables you to beam your PC's screen contents wirelessly to a Miracast-compatible TV or streaming media box. With Miracast, you can queue up your TV or movie programming on your computer and then watch it on your big-screen TV. As of this writing, however, there aren't a lot of TVs with Miracast built in; that may change over time.

THE ABSOLUTE MINIMUM

Here's what you need to know if you're adding new equipment to your computer system:

- The easiest way to connect a new peripheral is via an external USB connection.

- In most cases, Windows automatically recognizes your new hardware and installs all the necessary drivers.

- There are two types of consumer printers in use today: inkjet and laser.

- A printer can connect directly to a PC via USB or (in some models) wirelessly to your home network.

- Connecting a portable device, such as a portable music player or digital camera, is also done via an external USB port.

- You can connect your PC to your TV, typically via HDMI, to watch web-based programming on the bigger display.

10

ADDING STORAGE AND BACKUP

Most desktop and traditional notebook computers these days come with a fairly large amount of internal hard disk storage, anywhere from 500GB (for a basic notebook) up to 6TB (that's 6 *terabytes*—one of which is equivalent to 1000 gigabytes) or more. That's plenty of storage for most people, even if you download a lot of music and videos or store a ton of digital photos.

Some smaller notebook PCs don't have that much internal storage, however, because they don't have hard drives. These lightweight computers use solid-state flash storage that typically provides anywhere from 32GB to 256GB storage capacity—enough for basic tasks but certainly not for storing a lot of large documents, photos, or videos.

What do you do, then, if you need more storage space for your valuable files? The solution is to add more capacity with an external hard drive. (And you can use that same external drive to back up your data.)

Understanding External Storage

Most traditional computers use internal hard drives to store digital data: software applications, documents, photos, music, and so forth. This same hard disk technology is available in external drives that connect to your computer via USB.

When it has been connected, an external hard disk appears as another drive in the Computer section of File Explorer. You can access it just like your internal hard drive, and you can use it to store files or software programs.

You can find external hard drives in a variety of capacities, starting at 500GB or so and going all the way up to 12TB or more. Most manufacturers offer traditional desktop hard drives, like the one in Figure 10.1, as well as smaller portable drives. As you might suspect, the portable drives are designed to work better with portable notebook PCs.

FIGURE 10.1

A typical desktop external hard drive. (Photo courtesy Western Digital.)

Connecting an External Hard Drive

In most instances, connecting an external hard drive is a simple two-step process:

1. Connect the external hard drive to a power source. (Not necessary if you're connecting a portable drive, which typically gets its power from the computer via USB.)

2. Use a USB cable to connect the external hard drive to a USB port on your computer.

Some desktop hard drives have power switches. If yours does, you need to turn it on, as well.

When the hard drive is powered up and connected to your computer, it should appear in the This PC section of File Explorer as a new drive. It should take the next available letter; for example, if your internal hard drive is drive C: and your CD/DVD drive is drive D:, then the new external drive should be labeled as drive E:.

Backing Up Your Important Files

Protecting your valuable data—including all your music and personal photos—is something you need to do. After all, what would you do if your computer crashed or your hard disk died? Do you really want to lose all your valuable documents and files?

Of course, you don't—which is why you need to back up your key files on a regular basis.

Backing Up to an External Hard Drive

The easiest way to back up your files is with an external hard drive. Get a big enough external drive (about the same size as your main hard disk), and you can copy your entire hard disk to the external drive. Then, if your system ever crashes, you can restore your backed up files from the external drive to your computer's system unit.

Most external hard drives come with some sort of backup software installed, or you can use a third-party backup program. The backup process can be automated, so that it occurs once a day or once a week and backs up only those new or changed files since your last backup.

Whichever program you use, you should back up your data at least weekly—if not daily. That way you won't lose much fresh data if the worst happens.

TIP Given the affordability of external hard drives and how easy most backup programs make the process, there's no excuse not to back up your data on a regular basis. It's cheap protection in case something bad happens to your computer.

Using Windows' File History Utility

In Windows 10, you can back up all your important files with the File History utility. By default, File History saves copies of files every hour, and it keeps all saved versions forever.

To activate File History on your computer, follow these steps:

1. Click the Start button to display the Start menu, and then select Settings.

2. In the Settings window, click Update & Security.

3. From the Update & Security page, click to select the Backup tab, as shown in Figure 10.2.

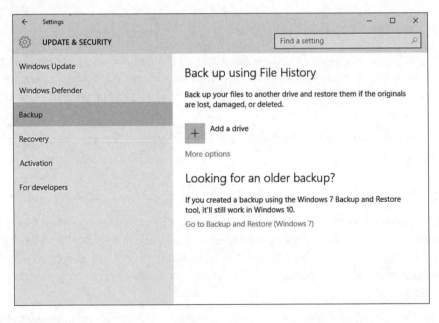

FIGURE 10.2

Backing up important files with File History.

4. Click + Add a Drive.

5. Select the drive you want to back up to.

6. Click "on" the Automatically Back Up My Files control.

To restore any or all files you've backed up, right-click the Start button and open the Control Panel. Click System and Security, and then click File History. This opens the File History panel; in the left column, click Restore Personal Files. This opens a new File History window. You can now navigate to and select those files or folders you want to restore; click the Restore button to restore these files to their original locations.

 TIP   You can also use File History to restore a given file to an earlier state. This is useful if you're editing a document, for example, and want to use an earlier version of the document before more recent editing.

Backing Up Online

The newest way to back up your data is to do it over the Internet, using an online backup service. This type of service copies your important files from your computer to the service's own servers, over the Internet. This way, if your local data is lost or damaged, you can then restore the files from the online backup service's servers.

The benefit of using an online backup service is that the backup copy of your library is stored offsite, so you're protected in case of any local physical catastrophe, such as fire or flood. Most online backup services also work in the background, so they're constantly backing up new and changed files in real time.

The downside of an online backup service comes if you need to restore your files. It takes a long time to transfer a lot of big files to your computer over an Internet connection. Plus, you have to pay for the backup service—on an ongoing basis. Most online backup services run $50 or more per year, per computer.

If online backup appeals to you, check out these popular online backup services designed for home users:

- Carbonite (www.carbonite.com)
- IDrive (www.idrive.com)
- Mozy (www.mozy.com)
- Norton Online Backup (us.norton.com/online-backup/)
- SOS Online Backup (www.sosonlinebackup.com)

NOTE   You can also use cloud storage services, such as Microsoft OneDrive or Google Drive, to store backup copies of your files. Unfortunately, these services don't offer the same type of automatic backup functionality as the full-featured backup services, which means you need to manually copy your files to these services, which isn't nearly as convenient. Learn more about these services in Chapter 7, "Working with Files, Folders, and Online Storage."

THE ABSOLUTE MINIMUM

Here are the key points to remember when connecting and configuring your new computer:

- External hard drives let you add extra storage capacity to your system—up to 12TB extra.

- You can find both desktop-type external drives and smaller, portable drives for use with notebook PCs.

- Connecting an external drive is typically as easy as connecting it to one of your PC's USB ports.

- An external drive shows up in File Explorer as just another drive on your system.

- You can also use an external hard drive to back up valuable data from your main hard drive.

- Windows 10 includes a File History utility that automates the backup process for files on your computer.

- Also available are online backup services, which back up your data over the Internet.

11

SETTING UP A HOME NETWORK

When you need to connect two or more computers, you need to create a computer *network*.

Why would you want to connect two computers? Maybe you want to transfer files or digital photos from one computer to another. Maybe you want to share an expensive piece of hardware (such as a printer) instead of buying one for each PC. Or most likely, you want to connect all your computers to the same Internet connection. Whatever your reasons, it's easy to set up and configure a simple home network. Read on to learn how!

How Networks Work

To physically connect your network, you have two ways to go—wired or wireless. A wireless network is more convenient (no wires!), but a wired network is faster and more secure. Which you choose depends on how you use the computers you network.

If you use your network primarily to share an Internet connection or a printer or to transfer the occasional word processing file, wireless should work just fine; most homes today have wireless networks installed. However, if you plan on using your network for multiplayer gaming or deal with highly sensitive files that you cannot afford to have hacked, you should to stick to a more secure (and faster) wired network.

Wired Networks

A *wired network* is the kind that requires you to run a bunch of cables from each PC to a central hub or router. In a wired network, all your PCs connect through a central *network router* via Ethernet cables. (Most new PCs come with built-in Ethernet capability, so you don't have to purchase anything additional to connect to the network—other than the cables and router, that is.) Although this type of network is fast and easy enough to set up, you still have to deal with all those cables—which can be a hassle if your computers are in different areas of your house.

The speed you get from a wired network depends on the type of Ethernet technology used by each piece of equipment. The oldest Ethernet technology transfers data at just 10Mbps; Fast Ethernet transfers data at 100Mbps; and the newer Gigabit Ethernet transfers data at 1 *gigabit* per second. (That's 1,000Mbps.) Either Fast Ethernet or Gigabit Ethernet is fine for transferring really big files between computers or for playing real-time PC games.

 NOTE   How quickly data is transferred across a network is measured in megabits per second, or Mbps. The bigger the Mbps number, the faster the network—and faster is always better than slower.

Wireless Networks

The popular alternative to a wired network is a *wireless network*. Wireless networks use radio frequency (RF) signals to connect one computer to another. The advantage of wireless, of course, is that you don't have to run cables. This is a big plus if you have a large house with computers on either end or on different floors.

Most home networks today are wireless, using Wi-Fi technology. The original Wi-Fi standard, known as 802.11b, transferred data at 11Mbps—slower than Fast Ethernet, but fast enough for most practical purposes. Next up was 802.11g, which transferred data at 54Mbps—more than fast enough for most home-networking needs.

 NOTE   Wi-Fi is short for *wireless fidelity*.

Even faster is the 802.11n standard, which delivers a blazing 600Mbps data transmission with a substantially longer range than older equipment. Current 802.11b and g equipment has a range of approximately 100 feet between transmitter and receiver; 802.11n gives you a 160-foot range, with less interference from other wireless household devices.

 NOTE   The 600Mbps rate for 802.11n networks is the theoretical maximum. In practice, expect rates between 200Mbps and 300Mbps.

Then there's the latest version of Wi-Fi, dubbed 802.11ac. Equipment running 802.11ac Wi-Fi is roughly twice **as fast as** 802.11n equipment, with a theoretical maximum speed of 1.3GBps. (That's *gigabytes* per second.) Naturally, 802.11ac routers will be a little more expensive than older models—but better suited for streaming high-definition video, if you do that.

A wireless network is a necessity if you have other non-PC devices in your home that need to connect to the Internet. So if you want to surf the Internet from your smartphone or iPad, play online games with your Xbox or PlayStation, or watch streaming video on your Roku media player box, you need a wireless network.

Of course, you can combine wired and wireless technologies into a single network because most wireless routers also have Ethernet connections. If you want, some PCs in your house can connect directly to a wireless router via Ethernet, whereas others can connect via wireless Wi-Fi signals. This type of mixed network is quite common.

Connecting and Configuring

Whether you're going wired or wireless, the setup is surprisingly easy. You have to assemble the appropriate cables, along with a network router, and then install and connect it all. After everything is hooked up properly, you then have to configure all the PCs on your network. The configuration can be made from within Windows or via the configuration utility provided with your network router or wireless adapter. You run this utility on each computer you connect to your network and then configure the network within Windows.

Setting Up a Wireless Network in Your Home

Connecting multiple computers in a home network is fairly simple. Just make sure that you do the proper planning beforehand and buy the appropriate hardware and cables; everything else is a matter of connecting and configuration.

 NOTE For the purposes of this chapter, the assumption is that you're setting up a wireless network, as that's what most people today use. Connecting a wired network is equally easy; the big difference is that you have to connect Ethernet cables between your router and each computer instead of making a wireless connection.

How It Works

A wireless network revolves around a device called a *wireless router.* This device functions like the hub of a wheel and serves as the central point in your network; each computer on your network connects through the wireless router.

 NOTE Most wireless routers can make both wireless and wired connections. A typical wireless router includes four or more Ethernet ports in addition to wireless capabilities.

Every computer in a wireless network connects to the router wirelessly—assuming, that is, that each computer contains wireless functionality. Almost all notebook PCs (as well as tablets and smartphones) have built-in wireless connectivity, but many desktop PCs don't. (Although some do, of course.) You can add wireless functionality to a desktop PC via a wireless adapter, which is a small device that connects to your PC via USB.

When complete, your network should look something like the one in Figure 11.1.

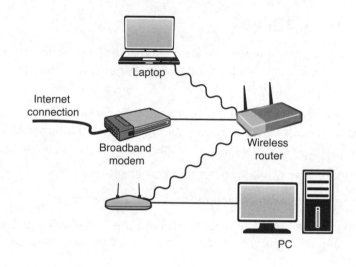

FIGURE 11.1

A typical wireless network.

What You Need

Here's the specific hardware you need to set up your network:

- Wireless router (one for the entire network)

- Broadband modem (typically supplied by your Internet service provider, or ISP; either cable modem or DSL modem, depending on your service)

 NOTE Some ISPs supply boxes (sometimes called Internet gateways) that combine a broadband modem with a wireless router. If you have one of these devices, you don't need a separate wireless router; it's all built into the modem.

- Wireless network adapters (one for each desktop PC; these are already built into notebook and tablet PCs, and they are sometimes built into desktops)

If you're connecting only notebook PCs to your network, you don't need wireless adapters (they're built into all portable computers)—you need only the wireless router and broadband modem. In addition, some desktop PCs have built-in wireless connectivity; if your desktops are so enabled, you don't need wireless adapters for them, either.

Making the Connections

Naturally, you should follow the instructions that come with your networking hardware to properly set up your network. In general, however, here are the steps to take:

1. Run an Ethernet cable from your broadband modem to your wireless router and connect it to the port on your router labeled Internet or WAN. (If your router doesn't have a dedicated Internet port, you can connect it to any port.)

2. Connect your wireless router to a power source.

3. Power on your broadband modem and wireless router.

4. Connect the first PC in your network to the router, as discussed in the "Connecting Your Computer to Your New Network" section, later in this chapter.

5. Follow the instructions provided by the router's manufacturer to create and configure a new wireless network. Make sure you configure your network to use wireless security, which requires a password (sometimes called a *network key*) before a device can connect to the network.

6. Configure the first PC for your new network.

7. Connect and configure all your remaining PCs for your new network.

 TIP   When you first connect a new router to your network, you should configure the router using the software that came with the device. Follow the manufacturer's directions to configure the network and wireless security.

After you connect all the computers on your network, you can proceed to configure any devices (such as printers) you want to share over the network. For example, if you want to share a single printer over the network, you can connect it to one of the network PCs and then share it through that PC. (You can also install network printers that connect directly to your wireless router, not to any specific PC.)

Connecting Your Computer to Your New Network

After your network hardware is all set up, you have to configure Windows to recognize and work with your new network. With Windows 10, this is a relatively painless and practically transparent step.

Connecting via Ethernet

If you connect to your network via Ethernet, you don't have to do a thing. After you connect an Ethernet cable between your PC and your router, Windows 10 recognizes your new network and starts using it automatically.

Connecting Wirelessly

If you connect via a wireless connection, the configuration is only slightly more involved. All you have to do is select which wireless network to connect to. Follow these steps:

1. In the notification area of the taskbar, click the Connections icon. This icon is typically labeled Not Connected—Connections Are Available if no network is currently connected.

2. This displays the Connections panel, as shown in Figure 11.2, which lists all nearby wireless networks. Locate your home network in this list and then click it. The panel for this network expands.

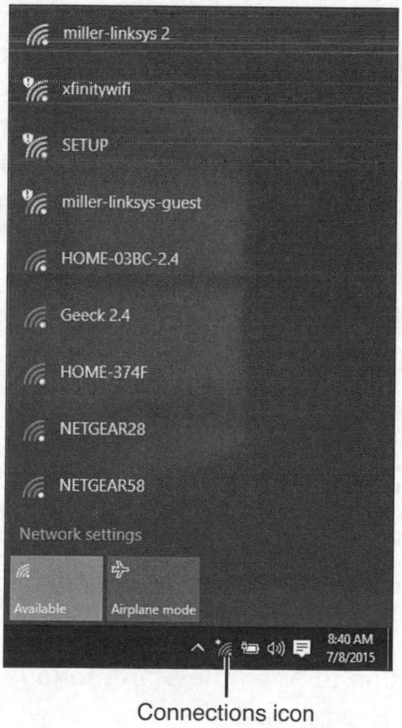

Connections icon

FIGURE 11.2

Select your wireless network from the list.

3. Check the Connect Automatically box to connect automatically to this network in the future.

4. Click Connect.

5. When prompted, enter the password (called the *network security key*) for your network. You should have created this password when you first set up your wireless router. Click Next to continue.

6. When the next screen appears, click Yes to connect with other PCs and devices on your home network. (This lets you share pictures, music, and other files with other computers connected to your home network.) You're now connected to your wireless router and should have access to the Internet.

 NOTE If the wireless router on your network supports "one-button wireless setup" (based on the Wi-Fi Protected Setup technology), you might be prompted to press the Connect button on the router to connect. This is much faster than going through the entire process outlined here.

Connecting Computers in a Homegroup

The easiest way to connect multiple computers to your home network is to create what Microsoft calls a *homegroup*. A homegroup is kind of a simplified network that enables you to automatically share files and printers between connected computers.

 NOTE Only PCs running Windows 7, 8, 8.1, or 10 can be part of a homegroup. PCs running older versions of Windows do not have the homegroup feature and must use the normal networking functions instead.

Creating a New Homegroup

When you connect your first computer to your wireless network, you need to create a new homegroup. Follow these steps:

1. Click the Start button to open the Start menu, and then select Settings to display the Settings window.

2. Click Network & Internet.

3. Click to select the Wi-Fi tab.

4. Scroll down the page to the Related Settings section, and then click HomeGroup to open the HomeGroup panel.

5. Click Create a Homegroup to display the Create a Homegroup panel.

6. Click Next to display the Share with Other Homegroup Members panel, as shown in Figure 11.3.

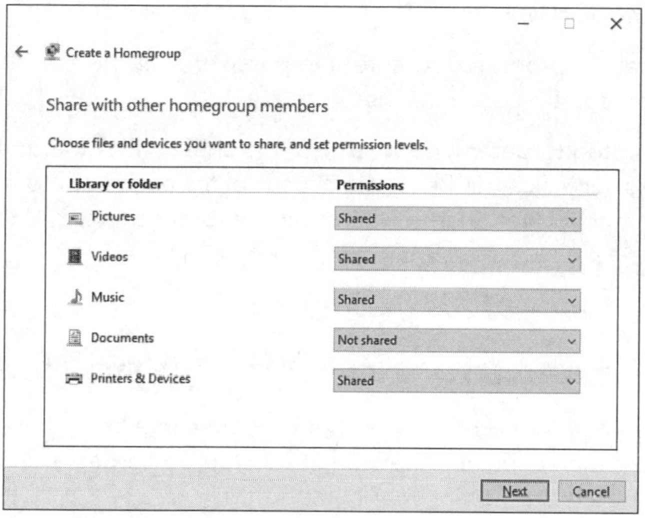

FIGURE 11.3

Setting up a homegroup on your network.

7. You now see all the items you can share with other members of your homegroup—Pictures, Videos, Music, Documents, and Printers & Devices. Click the Permissions control for each item to determine whether it is Shared or Not Shared with other computer users, and then click Next.

8. Windows displays the password for this homegroup in the Password section. Write it down; you need to provide this to users of other computers on your network who want to join your homegroup.

9. Click Finish.

Connect to an Existing Homegroup

Each additional computer you connect to your network needs to join your existing homegroup. To connect a computer to an existing homegroup, follow these steps:

1. Click the Start button to open the Start menu, and then select Settings to display the Settings window.

2. Click Network & Internet.

3. Click to select the Wi-Fi tab.

4. Scroll down the page to the Related Settings section, and then click HomeGroup to open the HomeGroup panel.

5. Windows now searches for and finds the existing homegroup on your network. Click the Join Now button.

6. You may be prompted to enter the password for this homegroup. If so, enter the homegroup password then click Next.

7. If prompted to determine what items to share with other members of the homegroup, click the Permissions control for each item to determine whether it is Shared or Not Shared with other computer users, and then click Next.

8. Click the Finish button.

Accessing Computers on Your Network

After you have your home network set up, you can access shared content stored on other computers on your network. How you do so depends on whether the other computers are part of your homegroup.

Accessing Homegroup Computers

You access the content of other computers connected to your homegroup via File Explorer. Follow these steps:

1. Click the File Explorer icon on the taskbar.

2. When File Explorer opens, go to the Homegroup section of the Navigation pane. This section lists all the users in your homegroup.

3. Click the name of the user whose files you want to access. Any given user might have accounts on multiple computers.

4. Windows displays the folders shared by that user, as shown in Figure 11.4. Double-click a folder to access that particular content.

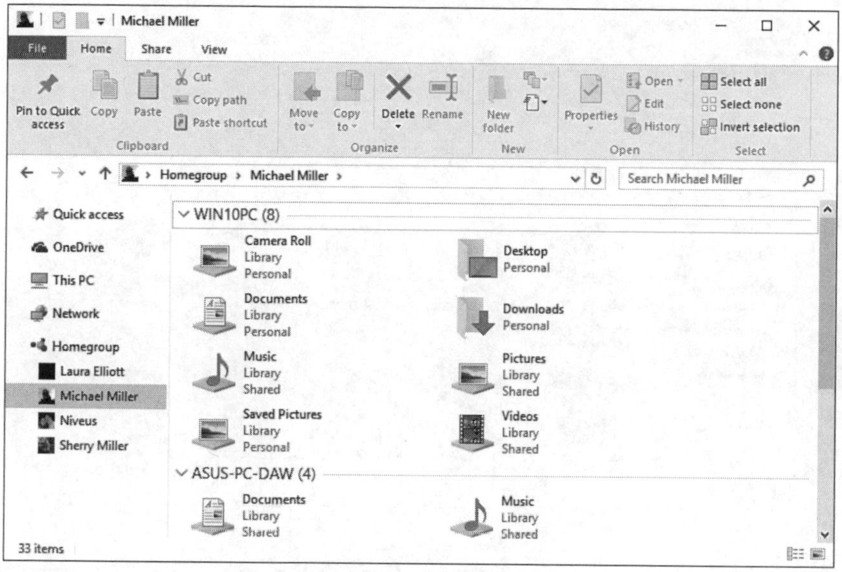

FIGURE 11.4

Viewing shared folders on a homegroup computer.

Accessing Other Computers on Your Network

A computer doesn't have to be connected to your HomeGroup for you to access its content. Windows enables you to access any computer connected to your home network—although you can only share content the computer's owner has configured as sharable.

To access other computers on your network, follow these steps:

1. Click the File Explorer icon on the taskbar.

2. Go to the Network section of the Navigation pane, as shown in Figure 11.5.

3. Click the computer you want to access.

4. Windows displays the shared folders on the selected computer; double-click or tap a folder to view that folder's content.

> **TIP** On most older computers, shared files are stored in the Public folder. Look in this folder first for the files you want.

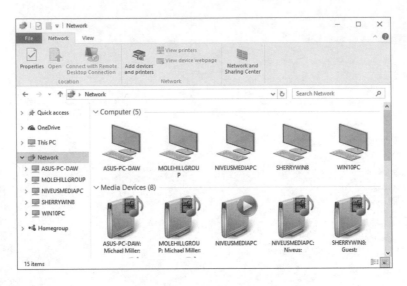

FIGURE 11.5

Viewing computers connected to your home network.

THE ABSOLUTE MINIMUM

Here are the key things to remember about creating a home network:

- To share information or hardware between two or more computers, as well as to share an Internet connection, you have to connect your computers in a network.

- There are two basic types of networks: wired and wireless (Wi-Fi).

- A wireless network uses a wireless router to serve as the hub for all connected devices.

- The easiest way to share content between connected computers is to create a homegroup.

- After you connect your computers in a network, you access other connected computers via File Explorer.

12

CONNECTING TO THE INTERNET—AT HOME AND AWAY

It used to be that most people bought personal computers to do serious work—word processing, spreadsheets, databases, the sort of programs that still make up the core of Microsoft Office. But today, people also buy PCs to access the Internet—to send and receive email, surf the Web, watch movies and listen to music, and socialize with other users on Facebook and other social networks.

To do this, of course, you first have to connect your computer to the Internet. Fortunately, Windows makes this easy to do.

Different Types of Connections in the Home

The first step in going online is establishing a connection between your computer and the Internet. When you connect from home, you need to sign up with an Internet service provider (ISP). This is a company that, as the name implies, provides your home with a connection to the Internet.

Although some of us might remember slow-as-molasses dial-up access, ISPs today offer various types of *broadband* access. Broadband is the fastest type of Internet connection available to homes today, and it comes in many flavors: cable, digital subscriber line (DSL), Fiber Optic Service (FiOS), and even satellite. You get the type of service that your chosen ISP offers.

Whichever ISP and type of broadband connection you choose, the Internet comes into your home via a wire or cable and connects to a device called a *modem*. This little black box then connects either directly to your computer or to a wireless router, so you can share the connection with all the computers and wireless devices in your home.

NOTE   Some ISPs provide a combination modem and router, sometimes called an Internet gateway device. If you get this combo box, you don't need a separate wireless router; the wireless networking functionality is built in.

Broadband DSL

DSL is a phone line-based technology that operates at broadband speeds. DSL service piggybacks onto the existing telephone line, turning it into a high-speed digital connection (768Kbps to 15Mbps, depending on your ISP). DSL connections are "always on" and independent of your regular phone service. Most providers offer DSL service for $30–$50 per month. Look for package deals that offer a discount when you subscribe to both Internet and phone services.

CAUTION   Many ISPs provide slower speeds for data uploaded from your computer. So you may see, for example, an offer of 50Mbps downstream (downloading to your PC) but just 8Mbps upstream (uploading from your PC). In addition, some ISPs employ "speed caps" for customers who download too much data, effectively throttling their use or charging extra for excessive data usage. It pays to check the fine print for these items before you sign up.

Broadband Cable

Another popular type of broadband connection is available from your local cable company. Broadband cable Internet piggybacks on your normal cable television line, providing speeds in the 6Mbps to 250Mbps range, depending on the provider. Most cable companies offer broadband cable Internet for $30–$50 per month, which is about the same as you pay for a similar DSL connection; some ISPs offer faster speeds at higher prices. As with DSL, look for package deals from your cable company, offering some sort of discount on a combination of Internet, cable, and (sometimes) digital phone service.

Fiber Broadband

The newest type of broadband connection is fiber, which in the United States you'll see most often offered under Verizon's FiOS or AT&T's U-verse brands. As the name implies, this type of service delivers an Internet connection over a fiber optic network.

Fiber connection speeds are similar to those of broadband cable, with different speeds available at different pricing tiers. Most ISPs offer download speeds between 3Mbps and 50Mbps. Pricing is also similar to broadband cable, in the $30/month to $50/month range.

In the home, the fiber line connects to a modem-like device called an optical network terminal (ONT) that can split the signal to provide a combination of Internet, television, and telephone services. You typically connect the ONT to your wireless router or PC via Ethernet.

Broadband Satellite

If you can't get DSL, cable, or FiOS Internet in your area, you have another option—connecting to the Internet via satellite. Any household or business with a clear line of sight to the southern sky can receive digital data signals from a geosynchronous satellite at speeds between 1Mbps and 52Mbps.

The largest provider of satellite Internet access is HughesNet. (Hughes also developed and markets the popular DIRECTV digital satellite system.) The HughesNet system (www.hughesnet.com) enables you to receive Internet signals via a small dish that you mount outside your house or on your roof. Fees range from $50 to $110 per month.

Sharing an Internet Connection

If you have more than one PC in your home, you can connect them to share a single high-speed Internet connection. That is, you don't have to bring in separate lines and modems for each of your PCs, nor do you have to pay for more than one connection.

You share an Internet connection by connecting your broadband modem to your home network. It doesn't matter whether you have a wired or a wireless network; the connection is similar in both instances. All you have to do is run an Ethernet cable from your broadband modem to your network router, and then Windows does the rest, connecting your modem to the network so that all your computers can access the connection.

To work through all the details of this type of connection, turn to Chapter 11, "Setting Up a Home Network." It's really quite easy!

Connecting to a Public Wi-Fi Hotspot

If you have a notebook or tablet PC, you can connect to the Internet when you're away from home. Many coffeehouses, restaurants, hotels, and public spaces offer wireless Wi-Fi Internet service, either free or for an hourly or daily fee. Assuming that your notebook has a built-in Wi-Fi adapter (which almost all do), connecting to a public Wi-Fi hotspot is a snap.

 NOTE A *hotspot* is a public place that offers wireless access to the Internet using Wi-Fi technology. Some hotspots are free for all to access; others require some sort of payment.

When you're near a Wi-Fi hotspot, your PC should automatically pick up the Wi-Fi signal. Make sure that your PC's Wi-Fi adapter is turned on (some notebooks have a switch for this, either on the front or on the side of the unit), and then follow these steps:

1. In the notification area of the taskbar, click the Connections icon. This icon is typically labeled Not Connected—Connections Are Available if no network is currently connected.

2. You now see a list of available Wi-Fi hotspots, as shown in Figure 12.1. Most public hotspots have a warning shield next to the wireless icon, indicating that the network is public and thus not secured. Locate the network you want to connect to, and then click that network. The panel for this network expands.

Connections icon

FIGURE 12.1

Choosing from available Wi-Fi hotspots.

3. Check the Connect Automatically box to connect automatically to this network in the future.

4. Click Connect.

After Windows connects to the selected hotspot, you can log on to the wireless network. Windows may do this automatically, prompting you that further input is required; if you see such a message, click it to display the hotspot's logon screen.

You may also have to do this manually. Open Microsoft Edge or another web browser and try to go to a website—any website. If the hotspot has free public access without any logon necessary, you'll see the website and be able to surf normally. If the hotspot requires a password, payment, or other logon procedure, it intercepts the request for your normal home page and instead displays its own login page, like the one in Figure 12.2. Enter the appropriate information, and you'll be surfing in no time!

FIGURE 12.2

Logging onto the Internet from a Starbucks coffee shop.

THE ABSOLUTE MINIMUM

When you configure your new PC system to connect to the Internet, remember these important points:

- You connect to the Internet through an Internet service provider, or ISP; you need to set up an account with an ISP before you can connect.

- There are three common types of broadband service available today: DSL, cable, and FiOS. (The more expensive satellite service is an option for rural areas.)

- If you have more than one computer at home, you can share your Internet connection by connecting your broadband modem to your home network.

- If you have a notebook PC, you can connect to the Internet wirelessly at any public Wi-Fi hotspot, such as those offered by Starbucks, Caribou Coffee, and similar establishments.

13

BROWSING AND SEARCHING THE WEB

Now that you've connected to the Internet, either at home or via a public wireless hotspot, it's time to get busy. The World Wide Web is a particular part of the Internet with all sorts of cool content and useful services, and you surf the Web with a piece of software called a *web browser*.

Windows includes its own web browser, called Microsoft Edge, but you can use other browsers if you like, such as the popular Google Chrome.

Understanding the Web

Before you can surf the Web, you need to understand a little bit about how it works.

Information on the World Wide Web is presented in *pages*. A web page is similar to a page in a book, made up of text and graphics. A web page differs from a book page, however, in that it can include other elements, such as audio and video, and links to other web pages.

It's this linking to other web pages that makes the Web such a dynamic way to present information. A *link* on a web page can point to another web page on the same site or to another site. Most links are included as part of a web page's text and are called *hypertext links*, or just *hyperlinks*. (If a link is part of a graphic, it's called a *graphic link*.) These links are usually in a different color from the rest of the text and often are underlined; when you click a link, you're taken directly to the linked page.

Web pages reside at a *website*. A website is nothing more than a collection of web pages (each in its own computer file) residing on a host computer. The host computer is connected full time to the Internet so that you can access the site— and its web pages—anytime you access the Internet. The main page at a website is called the *home page*, and it often serves as an opening screen that provides a brief overview and menu of everything you can find at that site. The address of a web page is called a *URL*, which stands for *uniform resource locator*. Most URLs start with http://, add a www., continue with the name of the site, and end with a .com, .org, or .net.

TIP   You can normally leave off the http:// when you enter an address into your web browser. In most cases, you can even leave off the www. and just start with the domain part of the address.

Using Microsoft Edge

Microsoft includes its own web browser in Windows 10. Microsoft Edge is a brand new browser in Windows 10; it replaces the Internet Explorer browser found in older versions of Windows.

NOTE   Technically Internet Explorer is still around, but it's fairly well buried in the Start menu. Unless you have a specific need for it, stick with Edge.

You launch Edge from the taskbar or Start menu. As shown in Figure 13.1, when you click at the top of the browser, you see an Address box, where you enter the address (URL) of the web page you want to visit. You can display multiple web pages on multiple tabs, and all your controls are located to the right of the Address box.

FIGURE 13.1

The Microsoft Edge browser in Windows 10.

Browsing the Web with Edge

Browsing the Web with Edge is easy. Just do the following:

1. To go to a specific web page, click to display the Address box; then enter that page's address and press Enter.

2. To return to the previous web page, click the Back (left arrow) button beside the Address box.

3. To reload or refresh the current page, click the Refresh button.

4. To jump to a linked-to page, click the hyperlink on the current page.

 NOTE If you've backed up several pages and want to return to the page you were on last, click the Forward button.

Revisiting History

What do you do if you remember visiting a page earlier in the day, or even in the past few days, but can't get there by clicking the Back button? Now's the time to revisit your browsing history—follow these steps:

1. Click the Hub button on the toolbar to display the Hub pane.

2. Click the History tab, as shown in Figure 13.2.

3. Click a day to display all pages visited that day.

4. Click a page to revisit it.

FIGURE 13.2

Revisiting browser history.

 TIP If you want to delete your browsing history—say you've visited a web page you don't want anyone to know you visited— you can do that, too. Open the Hub pane, select the History tab, and then click Clear All History. This displays the Clear Browsing Data pane; check those items you want to delete (typically Browsing Data, Cookies and Saved Website Data, and Cached Data and Files); then click the Clear button.

Opening Multiple Pages in Tabs

Microsoft Edge enables you to display multiple web pages as separate tabs in the browser, and thus easily switch between web pages—which is great when you want to reference different pages or want to run web-based applications in the background.

Here's how to work with tabs in Edge:

1. To switch to another open tab, click that tab.

2. To close an open tab, click the X on that tab.

3. To open a new tab, click the + next to the last open tab.

4. Click a tile on the new tab page or…

5. …enter a new web page address into the Address box.

 TIP   By default, Edge displays in the normal Light color scheme. To switch to the Dark scheme, which displays toolbars and tabs in black, click the More Actions button, click Settings, and then make a new selection from the Choose a Theme list.

Saving Your Favorite Pages

You can save your favorite pages in what Edge calls the Favorites list. Follow these steps:

1. Navigate to the web page you want to pin, and then click the Add to Favorites (star) button on the right side of the Address box.

2. Click the Favorites button to display the Favorites panel, as shown in Figure 13.3.

FIGURE 13.3

Adding a new web page to your Favorites list.

3. Confirm or enter a name for this page.

4. Pull down the Create In list, and select where you want to save it—in the general Favorites list, the Favorites Bar, or a new folder you've created.

5. Click the Add button.

 TIP You can organize your favorite pages into separate folders in the Favorites list. When the Favorites panel appears, click Create a New Folder, and then enter a name for the folder. The new folder now appears in the Create In list.

Returning to a Favorite Page

To return to a page you've saved as a favorite, follow these steps:

1. Click the Hub button to display the Hub pane, as shown in Figure 13.4.

2. Click the Favorites tab to display all your favorites.

3. Click to open any folder you've created.

4. Click the page you want to revisit.

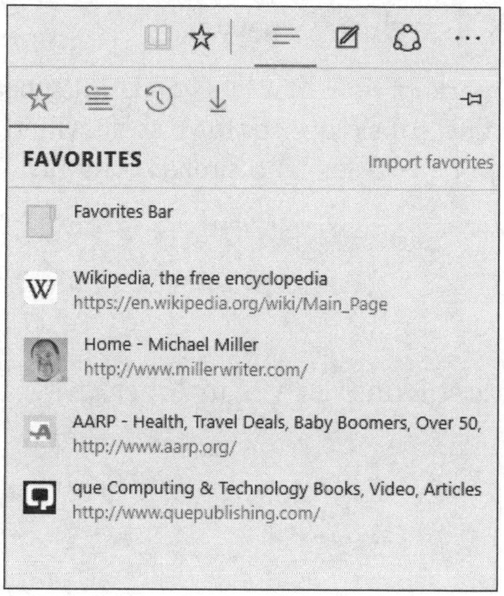

FIGURE 13.4

Revisiting favorite pages in the Favorites list.

Displaying the Favorites Bar

For even faster access to your favorite pages, display the Favorites bar at the top of the browser window, beneath the Address bar. You can then click any site on the Favorites bar to go directly to that site. Follow these steps:

1. Click the More Actions button.

2. Click Settings to display the Settings panel.

3. Click "on" the Show the Favorites Bar option.

TIP   If you have favorites or bookmarks saved in Internet Explorer, Google Chrome, or any other web browser, you can import those favorites into Edge. Open the Settings panel; then click Import Favorites from Another Browser. On the next page, select which browser(s) you want to import from, and then click the Import button.

Displaying a Page in Reading View

Edge offers a new reading view that lets you display certain web pages without ads or other distracting subsidiary content, as shown in Figure 13.5. This is great for reading news stories, articles, and similar content.

FIGURE 13.5

Reading a web article in reading view.

To switch to reading view, click the Reading View button on the right side of the Address box, or press Ctrl+Shift+R. Click the button again to return to normal web view. (Note that reading view is not available for all web pages.)

Browsing in Private

You may want to visit web pages that you'd rather your friends or family not know about. To that end, Edge lets you browse anonymously via the InPrivate Browsing mode. Here's how to activate it:

1. Click the More Actions button to display the menu of options.

2. Click New InPrivate Window.

This opens a new browser window with InPrivate Browsing turned on. You can now browse anonymously; the pages you visit will not be tracked.

Setting a Different Start Page

By default, Edge displays its own Start page when it launches. You can, however, specify a different page to display on launch. Follow these steps:

1. Click the More Actions button to display the menu of options.

2. Click Settings to display the Settings panel.

3. Scroll to the Open With section and select A Specific Page or Pages. A new list displays.

4. Click the list and select Custom.

5. Enter the URL (web address) of the page you want to open.

Using Google Chrome

Edge is a brand new, state-of-the-art web browser that rivals any other browser available today. You don't have to use it, however. There are several other third-party web browsers available, and some users prefer them for their simplicity and speed.

The most popular of these non-Microsoft web browsers include:

- Google Chrome (www.google.com/chrome/)

- Mozilla Firefox (www.mozilla.org/firefox/)

- Apple Safari (www.apple.com/safari/)

You can download these browsers for free from their respective web pages. (Yes, you can use Edge to go to another browser's web page.)

Of these browsers, Google Chrome is definitely the most popular. In fact, Chrome is the number-one browser in use today.

Figure 13.6 shows the Google Chrome browser. It looks a lot like IE, but with fewer obvious options. Google chooses to hide most of the "chrome"—buttons and icons and such—so that you can focus on viewing the selected web page, front and center.

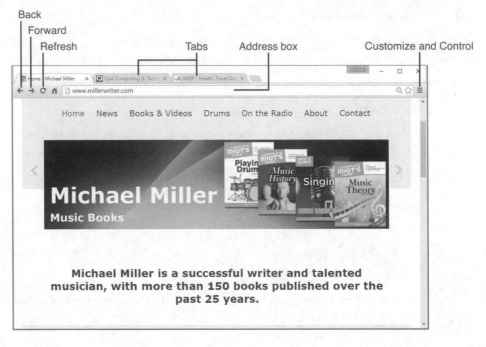

FIGURE 13.6

The Google Chrome web browser.

Using Chrome is pretty much like using Microsoft Edge. You have tabs for different web pages, forward and back buttons, a button for reloading the current web page, and an Address box for entering URLs. All the other controls are found by clicking the Customize and Control (three bar) button at the far right of the tabs; the resulting menu lets you access all Chrome's various configuration options.

Chromes "favorites" are called bookmarks. To bookmark a favorite page, click the star at the right side of that page's Address box. To access bookmarked pages, click the Customize button; then click Bookmarks. (You can also display a Bookmarks bar beneath the Address box; click the Customize button, select Bookmarks, and then click Show Bookmarks Bar.)

 TIP Chrome also has an anonymous browsing mode, dubbed Incognito mode. To open a page in Incognito mode, click the Customize menu and select New Incognito Window.

Searching the Web with Google

Now that you know how to surf the Web, how do you find the precise information you're looking for? Fortunately, there are numerous sites that help you search the Web for the specific information you want. Not surprisingly, these are among the most popular sites on the Internet.

Understanding Web Search

The sites you use to search the Web are commonly called Internet *search engines*. These sites, such as Google and Bing, employ special software programs (called *spiders* or *crawlers*) to roam the Web automatically, feeding what they find back to a massive bank of computers. These computers then build giant *indexes* of websites.

When you perform a search at a search engine site, your query is sent to the search engine's index. (You never actually search the Web itself; you only search the index that was created by the spiders crawling the Web.) The search engine then creates a list of pages in its index that match, to one degree or another, the query you entered.

Using Google Search

The most popular search engine today is Google (www.google.com). Google is easy to use, extremely fast, and returns highly relevant results. That's because it indexes more pages than any other site—billions and billions of pages, if you're counting.

Most users search Google several times a week, if not several times a day. The Google home page, as shown in Figure 13.7, is a marvel of simplicity and elegant web page design. All you have to do to start a search is enter one or more keywords into the search box and then press Enter or click the Google Search button. This returns a list of results ranked in order of relevance, such as the one shown in Figure 13.8. Click a results link to view that page.

FIGURE 13.7

Searching the Web with Google.

FIGURE 13.8

The results of a Google search.

 TIP Other popular search engines include Microsoft's Bing (www.bing.com), Yahoo! (www.yahoo.com), and Ask (www.ask.com).

Constructing a Query

When you search Google (or any search site), the quality of your results depends on the accuracy of your query. It's kind of a "garbage in, garbage out" thing; the better you describe what you're looking for, the more likely that Google will return the results you want.

It's important to focus on keywords because Google looks for these words when it processes your query. Your keywords are compared to the web pages that Google knows about; the more keywords found on a web page, the better the match.

Choose keywords that best describe the information you're looking for—using as many keywords as you need. Don't be afraid of using too many keywords; in fact, using too *few* keywords is a common fault of many novice searchers. The more words you use, the better idea the search engine has of what you're looking for.

 TIP You can use Google to display stock quotes (enter the stock ticker), answers to mathematical calculations (enter the equation), and measurement conversions (enter what you want to convert). Google can also track USPS, UPS, and FedEx packages (enter the tracking number), as well as the progress of airline flights (enter the airline and flight number).

Performing an Advanced Search

Google offers a variety of advanced search options to help you fine-tune your search. Click Search Tools at the top of the search results page to see these options, which are fine-tuned for specific types of searches. For example, you may have the option to filter your search results by time (Past 24 Hours, Past Week, and so on), reading level, and location (show nearby results only).

Additional options are found on the Advanced Search page, which you get to by clicking the Options (gear) button on any search results page and then selecting Advanced Search. To narrow your search results, all you have to do is make the appropriate selections from the options present.

Searching for Images

If you're looking for pictures or illustrations, Google can help with that, too. Just look for the list of categories at the top of the screen and click the Images link. You then see a page full of images that match your original query.

You can search directly for images from the Google Image Search site (images. google.com). Enter your query into this page's search box, press Enter, and you see only images that match what you're looking for, as shown in Figure 13.9. Click the Search Tools link to filter your results by image size, color, type, and so forth.

FIGURE 13.9

The results of a Google Image search.

Using Wikipedia for Research

Although many people use Google for research, searching the Web for just the right information can sometimes be like looking for a needle in a haystack; the information you get is totally unfiltered and not always accurate. A better way to research is to use a site designed primarily for research.

Such a site is Wikipedia (www.wikipedia.org), which is fast becoming the primary information site on the Web.

Understanding Wikipedia

Wikipedia is like a giant online encyclopedia—but with a twist. Unlike a traditional encyclopedia, Wikipedia's content is created solely by the site's users, resulting in the world's largest online collaboration.

At present, Wikipedia hosts more than 4 million English-language articles, with at least that many articles available in more than 250 different languages. The articles are written and revised by tens of thousands of individual contributors. These users volunteer their time and knowledge at no charge, for the good of the Wikipedia project.

You don't have to be an academic type to contribute to Wikipedia, and you don't have to be a student to use it. Anyone with specialized knowledge can write an article, and regular people like you and me can read them.

CAUTION Because Wikipedia content is provided by users, not professional editors, it may not always be 100% accurate. Use it at your own discretion.

Searching Wikipedia

Information on the Wikipedia site is compiled into a series of articles. You search Wikipedia to find the exact articles you need.

To find an article on a given topic, go to the Wikipedia home page, shown in Figure 13.10, enter your query into the search box, and then press Enter. If an article directly matches your query, Wikipedia now displays that article. If a number of articles might match your query, Wikipedia displays the list of articles, organized by type or topic. Click the article name to display the specific article.

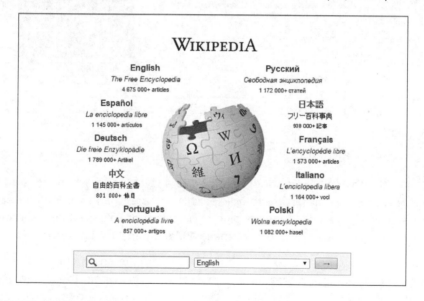

FIGURE 13.10

The Wikipedia home page.

For example, if you search Wikipedia for **john adams**, it displays the article on founding father John Adams. If, instead, you search only for **adams**, it displays a disambiguation page with sections for matching people and places bearing the name of "Adams." From there you can find the article on the second president, as well as lots of other articles.

Reading Wikipedia Articles

As you can see in Figure 13.11, each Wikipedia article is organized into a summary and subsidiary sections. Longer articles have a table of contents, located beneath the summary. Key information is sometimes presented in a sidebar at the top right of the article.

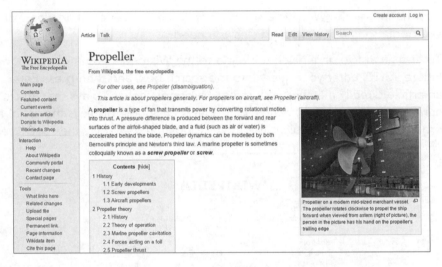

FIGURE 13.11

A typical Wikipedia article.

One of the things I liked about reading the encyclopedia when I was a kid was jumping around from article to article. This is easier than ever in Wikipedia, as the text of each article contains blue hypertext that links to related articles in the Wikipedia database. Click one of these links to jump to that article.

If you want to know the source for the information in an article, scroll to the bottom of the page, where the sources for key facts within the article are footnoted. Additional references and information about the topic also appear at the bottom of the page.

Searching—and More—with Cortana

New to Windows 10 is Cortana, a virtual personal assistant you can use to search the web and retrieve all kinds of relevant information. You can search Cortana from the Windows taskbar or from within the Edge browser.

Cortana is useful for searching for files on your computer, information on the Web, and more. You can even use Cortana to set reminders, display personalized news and weather, and perform conversions.

There are many ways to use Cortana's Web search capabilities (which use Microsoft's Bing search engine). You can query Cortana by typing into the search box on the taskbar, right-clicking words or terms on web pages, or with voice commands by speaking into your computer's microphone.

Search Cortana from the Taskbar

By default, Windows 10 displays an Ask Me Anything box on the left side of the taskbar, next to the Start button, as shown in Figure 13.12. Use this box to initiate Cortana searches.

FIGURE 13.12

The Cortana search box.

All you have to do is click within the Ask Me Anything box and begin typing your query. As you type, Cortana displays items that match your query in the new Cortana pane, as shown in Figure 13.13. The results may include apps and files on your computer, as well as results from the Web. Click an item to display or open it.

FIGURE 13.13

Search results in the Cortana pane.

Search Cortana from Microsoft Edge

If you browse the web with Microsoft Edge, you can use Cortana to extend the web content. There are a number of ways to do this.

First, if Cortana knows more about a particular site you're visiting, you see the round Cortana icon in the Address bar, along with text that tells you Cortana knows more. Click the Cortana icon to display a new Cortana pane with the additional information, as shown in Figure 13.14. (You're more likely to see this option when you visit business pages—restaurants, hotels, and the like.)

FIGURE 13.14

The Cortana pane in the Edge browser.

Second, you can search within any given web page for additional information. Simply highlight one or more words on the page, right-click, and then select Ask Cortana. You now see the Cortana pane on the right with information about the word(s) you selected.

Search Cortana by Voice

If your computer has a built-in microphone, or if you have a microphone connected to your computer, you can control Cortana with voice commands.

When voice control is activated, query Cortana by speaking "Hey, Cortana" into your computer's microphone, followed by whatever it is you're asking.

View News and Other Information

As Cortana learns about you (through the items you view and search for), it displays information it deems relevant—news items, stock prices, weather conditions, and such.

All you have to do is click within the Cortana search box to open the Cortana pane, with relevant items displayed, as shown in Figure 13.15. Click an item to view it in your Web browser.

FIGURE 13.15

Viewing personalized content in the Cortana pane.

To personalize the content Cortana displays, follow these steps:

1. Click within the Cortana search box to display the Cortana pane.

2. Click the Notebook icon on the left.

3. Click the type of content you want to display.

4. Click "on" the specific information you want to see.

Set a Reminder

You can also use Cortana to remind you of events and deadlines. Follow these steps:

1. Click within the Cortana search box to display the Cortana pane.

2. Click the Reminders icon on the left. All your current reminders now display, as shown in Figure 13.16.

FIGURE 13.16

Viewing reminders in Cortana.

3. Click the + (Add) button.

4. Enter the reminder where it says "Remember to."

5. To add a location to this reminder, click Place and then enter that location.

6. To set a time for this reminder, click Time and then enter the desired time.

7. Click the Remind button.

THE ABSOLUTE MINIMUM

Here are the key points to remember from this chapter:

- You surf the Web with a web browser, such as Microsoft Edge (the new browser in Windows 10) or Google Chrome.

- To go to a particular web page, enter the page's address in the Address box, and then press Enter. (You can also click or tap a hyperlink on a web page to jump to the linked page.)

- Microsoft Edge and Chrome both offer tabbed browsing, where you can open new web pages in additional tabs; click or tap a tab to switch to that web page.

- When you need to search for specific information on the Internet, you can use one of the Web's many search engine sites, such as Google.

- When you need to research specific topics, Wikipedia is a good source; it contains information written and edited by its large user base.

- Windows 10's Cortana virtual personal assistant lets you search your computer and the web for useful and relevant information.

SHOPPING AND SELLING ONLINE

Many users have discovered that the Internet is a great place to buy things—all kinds of things. All manner of online merchants make it easy to buy books, clothing, and other merchandise with the click of a mouse.

The Web isn't just for shopping, however. You can also use sites such as eBay and Craigslist to sell your own stuff online. It's a great way to get rid of all that old stuff cluttering your attic—or a few unwanted Christmas presents!

How to Shop Online

If you've never shopped online before, you're probably wondering just what to expect. Shopping over the Web is actually easy; all you need is your computer and a credit card—and a fast connection to the Internet!

Online shopping is pretty much the same, no matter which retailer website you visit. You proceed through a multiple-step process that goes like this:

1. **Find an online store** that sells the item you're shopping for.
2. **Find a product**, either by browsing or searching through the retailer's site.
3. **Examine the product** by viewing the photos and information on a product listing page.
4. **Order the product** by clicking a "purchase this" or "buy it now" button on the product listing page that puts the item in your online shopping cart.
5. **Check out** by entering your payment (credit card) and shipping information.
6. **Confirm the order** and wait for the merchant to ship your merchandise.

Let's look at each of these steps separately.

Step 1: Find an Online Store

The first step in online shopping is finding where you want to shop. Most major retailers, such as Target and Walmart, have their own websites you can use to shop online, as do most catalog merchants. In addition, there are online-only retailers that offer a variety of merchandise, such as Amazon.com. You should find no shortage of places to shop online.

You can also use a price comparison site to help find the best merchandise and pricing online. These sites let you search for specific products and then sort and filter the results in a number of different ways. Many of these sites include customer reviews of both the products and the available merchants; some even let you perform side-by-side comparisons of multiple products, which is great if you haven't yet made up your mind as to what you want to buy.

The most popular (and useful) of these price comparison sites include

- BizRate (www.bizrate.com)
- Google Shopping (www.google.com/shopping)
- mySimon (www.mysimon.com)
- NexTag (www.nextag.com)
- PriceGrabber (www.pricegrabber.com)

- Shopping.com (www.shopping.com), shown in Figure 14.1
- Yahoo! Shopping (shopping.yahoo.com)

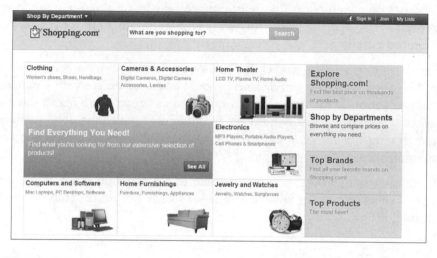

FIGURE 14.1

Comparing prices at Shopping.com

Step 2: Find a Product

After you determine where to shop, you need to browse through different product categories on that site or use the site's search feature to find a specific product.

Browsing product categories online is similar to browsing through the departments of a retail store. You typically click a link to access a major product category, and then click further links to view subcategories within the main category. For example, the main category might be Clothing; the subcategories might be Men's, Women's, and Children's clothing. If you click the Men's link, you might see a list of further subcategories: outerwear, shirts, pants, and the like. Just keep clicking until you reach the type of item that you're looking for.

Searching for products is often a faster way to find what you're looking for if you have something specific in mind. For example, if you're looking for a women's leather jacket, you can enter the words **women's leather jacket** into the site's search box and get a list of specific items that match those criteria.

The only problem with searching is that you might not know exactly what it is you're looking for; if this describes your situation, you're probably better off browsing. But if you *do* know what you want—and you don't want to deal with lots of irrelevant items—then searching is the faster option.

Step 3: Examine the Product

Whether you browse or search, you'll probably end up looking at a list of different products on a web page. These listings typically feature one-line descriptions of each item—in most cases, not nearly enough information for you to make an informed purchase.

The thing to do now is to click the link for the item you're particularly interested in. This should display a dedicated product page, complete with a picture and full description of the item. This is where you can read more about the item you selected. Some product pages include different views of the item, pictures of the item in different colors, links to additional information, and maybe even a list of optional accessories that go along with the item.

If you like what you see, you can proceed to the ordering stage. If you want to look at other items, just click your browser's Back button to return to the larger product listing.

Step 4: Order the Product

Somewhere on each product description page should be a button labeled Purchase, Buy Now, Add to Cart, or something similar. This is how you make the actual purchase: by clicking that Buy button. You don't order the product just by looking at the product description; you have to manually click the Buy button to place your order. (Figure 14.2 shows a product page on Amazon.com; click the Add to Cart button to purchase this item.)

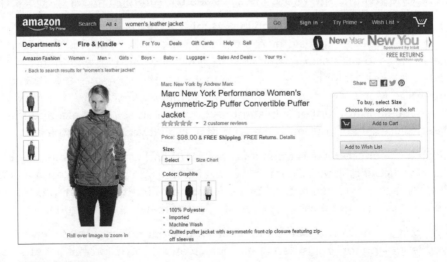

FIGURE 14.2

Getting ready to purchase a leather jacket on Amazon.com.

When you click the Buy button, that particular item is added to your *shopping cart*. That's right, the online retailer provides you with a virtual shopping cart that functions just like a real-world shopping cart. Each item you choose to purchase is added to your virtual shopping cart.

After you order a product and place it in your shopping cart, you can choose to shop for other products on that site or proceed to the site's checkout. It's important to note that when you place an item in your shopping cart, you haven't actually completed the purchase yet. You can keep shopping (and adding more items to your shopping cart) as long as you want.

You can even decide to abandon your shopping cart and not purchase anything at this time. All you have to do is leave the website, and you won't be charged for anything. It's the equivalent of leaving your shopping cart at a real-world retailer and walking out the front door; you don't actually buy anything until you walk through the checkout line. (Although, with some sites, the items remain in your shopping cart—so they'll be there waiting for you the next time you shop!)

Step 5: Check Out

To finalize your purchase, you have to visit the store's *checkout*. This is like the checkout line at a traditional retail store; you take your virtual shopping cart through the checkout, get your purchases totaled, and then pay for what you're buying.

The checkout at an online retailer typically consists of one or more web pages with forms you have to fill out. If you've visited the retailer before, the site might remember some of your personal information from your previous visit. Otherwise, you have to enter your name, address, and phone number, as well as the address you want to ship the merchandise to (if that's different from your billing address). You also have to pay for the merchandise, typically by entering a credit card number.

The checkout provides one last opportunity for you to change your order. You can delete items you decide not to buy or change quantities on any item. At some merchants you can even opt to have your items gift-wrapped and sent to someone as a present. You should find all these options somewhere in the checkout process.

You might also have the option of selecting different types of shipping for your order. Many merchants offer both regular and expedited shipping—the latter for an additional charge.

Another option at some retailers is to group all items for reduced shipping cost. (The alternative is to ship items individually as they become available.) Grouping items is attractive cost-wise, but you can get burned if one of the items is out of stock or not yet available; you could end up waiting weeks or months for those items that could have been shipped immediately.

 TIP   The better online retailers tell you either on the product description page or during the checkout process whether or not an item is in stock. Look for this information to help you decide how to group your items for shipment.

Step 6: Confirm the Order

After you enter all the appropriate information, you're asked to place your order. This typically means clicking a button that says Place Your Order or something similar. You might even see a second screen asking you whether you *really* want to place your order, just in case you have second thoughts.

After you place your order, you see a confirmation screen, typically displaying your order number. Write down this number or print this page; you need to refer to this number if you have to contact customer service. Most online merchants also send you a confirmation message, including this same information, via email.

That's all there is to it. You shop, examine the product, place an order, proceed to checkout, and then confirm your purchase. It's that easy!

How to Shop Safely

Shopping online is every bit as safe as shopping at a traditional brick-and-mortar retailer. The big online retailers are just as reputable as traditional retailers, offering safe payment, fast shipping, and responsive service.

How do you know that you're shopping at a reputable online retailer? Simple—look for the following features:

- **Payment by major credit card**—Credit cards offer ample consumer protection in case of fraud. Smaller merchants might accept credit cards via PayPal or a similar online payment service; this is also acceptable.

- **A *secure server* that encrypts your credit card information—and keeps online thieves from stealing your credit card numbers**—You know that you're using a secure site when the little lock icon appears in the lower-right corner of your web browser.

- **Good contact information—email address, street address, phone number, fax number, and so on**—You want to be able to physically contact the retailer if something goes wrong.

- **A stated returns policy and satisfaction guarantee**—You want to be assured that you'll be taken care of if you don't like whatever you ordered.

- **A stated privacy policy that protects your personal information**—You don't want the online retailer sharing your email address and purchasing information with other merchants—and potential spammers.

- **Information *before you finalize your order* that tells you whether the item is in stock and how long it will take to ship**—More feedback is better.

 TIP   Credit card purchases are protected by Federal law. In essence, you have the right to dispute certain charges, and your liability for unauthorized transactions is limited to $50. In addition, some card issuers offer a supplemental guarantee that says you're not responsible for *any* unauthorized charges made online. (Make sure that you read your card's statement of terms to determine the company's exact liability policy.)

Buying and Selling on eBay

Some of the best bargains on the Web come from other consumers, just like you, selling their own items online. The most popular website for individual sales is eBay, which is an online marketplace that facilitates transactions between people and businesses that have things to sell and customers who want to buy those things.

The sellers on eBay can opt to sell their products via traditional fixed-priced transactions, or via *online auctions*. An online auction is, quite simply, a Web-based version of a traditional auction. You find an item you'd like to own and then place a bid on it. Other users also place bids, and at the end of the auction— typically a 7-day period—the highest bidder wins.

How Does an eBay Auction Work?

If you've never used eBay before, you might be a little curious about what might be involved. Never fear; participating in an online auction is a piece of cake—something hundreds of millions of other users have done before you. That means you don't have to reinvent any wheels; the procedures you follow are well established and well documented.

An eBay auction is an Internet-based version of a traditional auction—you know, the type where a fast-talking auctioneer stands in the front of the room, trying to coax potential buyers into bidding *just a little bit more* for the piece of merchandise up for bid. The only difference is that there's no fast-talking auctioneer online (the bidding process is executed by special auction software on the auction site), and your fellow bidders aren't in the same room with you—in fact, they might be located anywhere in the world. Anyone who has Internet access and is registered with eBay can be a bidder. You do this from eBay's home page (www.ebay.com), shown in Figure 14.3.

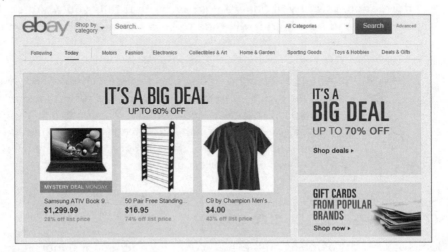

FIGURE 14.3

Where all the auction action starts—eBay's home page.

 NOTE There is no cost to register with eBay; although, if you want to sell items, you have to provide your credit card and checking account numbers. (eBay uses this information to help weed out potential scammers and to provide a billing option for the seller's eBay fees.)

When a buyer has something to sell, she creates an item listing. This is essentially a sale page for the item, with photos and a description and all that, as shown in Figure 14.4. In the case of an auction listing, the page includes a form for interested buyers to enter their bids.

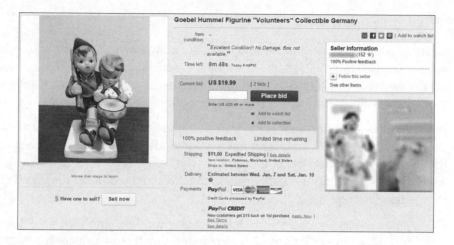

FIGURE 14.4

A typical eBay auction listing.

A potential buyer reads the item listing and makes a bid, specifying the maximum amount he will pay; this amount has to be equal to or greater than the seller's minimum bid, or higher than any other existing bids.

At this point, eBay's built-in bidding software automatically places a bid for the bidder that bests the current bid by a specified amount—but doesn't reveal the bidder's maximum bid. For example, the current bid on an item might be $25. A bidder is willing to pay up to $40 for the item and enters a maximum bid of $40. eBay's "proxy" software places a bid for the new bidder in the amount of $26—higher than the current bid, but less than the specified maximum bid. If there are no other bids, this bidder wins the auction with a $26 bid. Other potential buyers, however, can place additional bids; unless their maximum bids are more than the current bidder's $40 maximum, they are informed (by email) that they have been outbid—and the first bidder's current bid is automatically raised to match the new bids (up to the specified maximum bid price).

At the conclusion of an auction, eBay informs the high bidder of his winning bid. When the seller receives the buyer's payment (typically via PayPal), the seller then ships the merchandise directly to the buyer. eBay also bills the seller 10% of the final bid price as a final value fee.

Buying Fixed-Price Items

Tired of waiting around for the end of an auction, only to find out you didn't have the winning bid? Well, there's a way to actually *buy* some items you see for auction without going through the bidding process. All you have to do is look for those item listings that have a Buy It Now option.

Buy It Now is an option that some (but not all) sellers add to their auctions. With Buy It Now, the item is sold (and the auction ended) if a buyer opts to purchase the item for a specified price. (For this reason, some refer to Buy It Now auctions as "fixed-price" auctions—even though they're slightly different from eBay's *real* fixed-priced listings.)

Other eBay sellers choose to skip the auction process entirely and sell their items at a fixed price. These listings also display the Buy It Now button but without a bidding option. Fixed-priced listings are also common in eBay Stores, where larger sellers offer a constant supply of fixed-priced merchandise for sale all year round.

Buying a fixed-price item on eBay is really simple. If you see an item identified with a Buy It Now price, just click the Buy It Now button. You are immediately notified that you've purchased the item and are instructed to pay—typically via PayPal.

Protecting Yourself Against Fraudulent Sellers

When you bid for and buy items on eBay, you're pretty much in "buyer beware" territory. You agree to buy an item, almost sight unseen, from someone whom you know practically nothing about. You send that person a check and hope and pray that you get something shipped back in return—and that the thing that's shipped is the thing you thought you were buying, in good condition. If you don't like what you got—or if you received nothing at all—the seller has your money. And what recourse do you have?

The first line of defense against frauds and cheats is to intelligently choose the people you deal with. On eBay, the best way to do this is via the Feedback system.

Next to every seller's name is a number and percentage, which represents that seller's Feedback rating. You should always check a seller's Feedback rating before you bid. If the number is high with an overwhelmingly positive percentage, you can feel safer than if the seller has a lot of negative feedback. For even better protection, click the seller's name in the item listing to view his Member Profile, where you can read individual feedback comments. Be smart and avoid those sellers who have a history of delivering less than what was promised.

TIP If you're new to eBay, you can build up your feedback fast by purchasing a few low-cost items—preferably using the Buy It Now feature, so you get the transaction over quickly. It's good to have a Feedback rating of 20 or better before you start selling!

What do you do if you follow all this advice and still end up receiving unacceptable merchandise—or no merchandise at all? Fortunately, eBay offers a Money Back Guarantee for any auction transaction gone bad.

To file for a claim, go to eBay's Resolution Center (resolutioncenter.ebay.com). Follow the onscreen instructions from there. (You have 45 days to file a claim after you pay for the item.)

eBay Selling, Step-by-Step

Have some old stuff in your garage or attic that you want to get rid of? Consider selling it on eBay. Selling on eBay is a little more involved than bidding but can generate big bucks if you do it right.

NOTE eBay makes its money by charging sellers two types of fees. (Buyers don't pay fees to eBay.) *Insertion fees* are based on the minimum bid or reserve price of the item listed. *Final value fees* are charged when you sell an item, based on the item's final selling price. Fees are typically charged directly to the seller's credit card account.

Here's how selling works:

1. If you haven't registered for an eBay seller account yet, do so now. You need to provide eBay with your credit card and checking account number, for verification and billing purposes.

2. Before you list your first item, you need to do a little homework. That means determining what you're going to sell and for how much, as well as how you're going to describe the item. You need to prepare the information you need to write a full item description, as well as take a few digital photos of the item to include with the listing.

3. Homework out of the way, it's time to create the item listing. Start by clicking the Sell button on eBay's home page. As you can see in Figure 14.5, eBay walks you through the selling process step-by-step, describing what you need to enter to proceed. For many items you can just enter a UPC or ISBN to pull up standard information. In other cases, you need to select a category for your

item; enter a title and description; insert a photo of the item, if you have one; and determine whether you want to sell at a fixed price or via auction. You also need to enter the item's price (or, in the case of an auction, the minimum bid price).

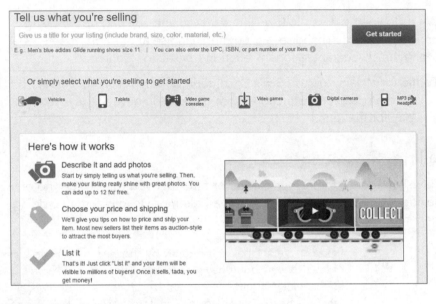

FIGURE 14.5

Creating a new eBay item listing.

4. After you enter all the information, eBay creates and displays a preliminary version of your listing. If you like what you see, click OK to go live or start the auction.

5. When the auction is over or the item is sold, eBay notifies you (via email) and provides the email address of the winning bidder.

6. Most buyers pay via credit card (using the PayPal service). When you receive notice of payment, pack the item and ship it out.

 TIP You can monitor the progress of all your current eBay activity from the My eBay page. Just click the My eBay link at the top of eBay's home page.

That's it—you've just become a successful eBay seller!

Buying and Selling on Craigslist

eBay isn't the only place to buy and sell items on the Web. When you want to buy or sell something locally, Craigslist is the place.

Craigslist is a network of local online classifieds sites. On Craigslist you pick your local site and then create a classified ad for what you're selling; potential buyers browse the ads, contact the seller, and pay for and pick up the items locally.

Understanding Online Classifieds

Like eBay, Craigslist is just a middleman, facilitating sales between individual buyers and sellers. Unlike eBay, all Craigslist sales are at a fixed cost; there's no bidding involved. Of course, as with traditional print-based classified ads, some sellers might accept lower prices than listed if you make an offer, or they might list an item at a fixed price or "best offer." All negotiations are between the seller and the buyer. Most sales are paid for with cash.

Another big difference between eBay and Craigslist is that eBay is a fairly full-featured marketplace; eBay offers a number of tools for both buyers and sellers that help to automate and take the guesswork out of the process. Not so with Craigslist, which resembles what eBay was like more than 10 years ago, before it became more sophisticated. Creating an ad is pretty much filling in a blank text box, with little help from Craigslist on how to do it. Craigslist doesn't even get involved in the selling process; buyers pay sellers directly, often in cash. There's no PayPal to deal with and no way to pay via credit card.

For that matter, Craigslist doesn't offer the buyer and seller protection plans that you find on eBay—which makes buying via a classified ad that much more risky. If a buyer pays with a bad check, there's not much the seller can do about it; if a seller gets an item home and finds out it doesn't work as promised, *caveat emptor*.

Browsing the Listings

As noted previously, Craigslist is actually a network of individual local sites. In fact, the Craigslist home page is nothing more than a listing of these local sites. So to use Craigslist, you first have to navigate to your specific local site; you do this by going to the national Craigslist home page and then clicking your city or state from the list.

When you're on your local Craigslist site, you see links to all the product and service categories offered by Craigslist in your area, as shown in Figure 14.6.

The categories available mirror those in a typical newspaper classifieds section, including Housing, Jobs, Personals, and the like.

| craigslist | minneapolis / st paul * | hnp | ram | ank | wsh | dak | csw |

| post to classifieds | | |
| my account | | |

search craigslist

event calendar						
S	M	T	W	T	F	S
4	5	6	7	8	9	10
11	12	13	14	15	16	17
18	19	20	21	22	23	24
25	26	27	28	29	30	31

help, faq, abuse, legal
avoid scams & fraud
personal safety tips
terms of use
privacy policy
system status

about craigslist
craigslist is hiring in sf
craigslist open source
craigslist blog
best-of-craigslist
craigslist TV
"craigslist joe"

community

activities	local news
artists	lost+found
childcare	musicians
classes	pets
events	politics
general	rideshare
groups	volunteers

personals

strictly platonic
women seek women
women seeking men
men seeking women
men seeking men
misc romance
casual encounters
missed connections
rants and raves

discussion forums

apple	help	photo
arts	history	p.o.c.
atheist	housing	politics
autos	jobs	psych
beauty	jokes	queer
bikes	kink	recover
celebs	legal	religion
comp	linux	romance
crafts	m4m	science
diet	manners	spirit
divorce	marriage	sports
dying	media	tax
eco	money	travel
educ	motocy	tv
feedbk	music	vegan
film	nonprofit	w4w

housing

apts / housing
housing swap
housing wanted
office / commercial
parking / storage
real estate for sale
rooms / shared
rooms wanted
sublets / temporary
vacation rentals

for sale

antiques	farm+garden
appliances	free
arts+crafts	furniture
atv/utv/sno	garage sale
auto parts	general
baby+kid	heavy equip
barter	household
beauty+hlth	jewelry
bikes	materials
boats	motorcycles
books	music instr
business	photo+video
cars+trucks	rvs+camp
cds/dvd/vhs	sporting
cell phones	tickets
clothes+acc	tools
collectibles	toys+games
computers	video gaming
electronics	wanted

services

jobs

accounting+finance
admin / office
arch / engineering
art / media / design
biotech / science
business / mgmt
customer service
education
food / bev / hosp
general labor
government
human resources
internet engineers
legal / paralegal
manufacturing
marketing / pr / ad
medical / health
nonprofit sector
real estate
retail / wholesale
sales / biz dev
salon / spa / fitness
security
skilled trade / craft
software / qa / dba
systems / network
technical support
transport
tv / film / video
web / info design
writing / editing
[ETC]
[part-time]

FIGURE 14.6

A local Craigslist site.

If you're looking for an item for sale, it's probably going to be in the For Sale category. If you're looking for something else, however, then the other categories might hold interest. It might surprise you to know that in many cities Craigslist is the largest marketplace for job wanted ads; it's also a big site for home and apartment listings. For that matter, Craigslist has a thriving personals section, in case that's what you're looking for.

Buying on Craigslist

If you want to buy a specific type of item, you need to browse Craigslist's For Sale listings. Within this major category there are additional subcategories, such as Computers, Furniture, Musical Instruments, Electronics, Tools, and the like. Click through to a subcategory to view the ads within that category.

As you can see in Figure 14.7, a typical Craigslist ad includes a title, a description of the item being sold, and one or more pictures of the item. Unlike with eBay, Craigslist offers no direct mechanism for contacting the seller or for purchasing directly from the listing page. Although some ads include the seller's phone number, most don't. Instead, you contact the seller by clicking the email link included in the ad.

FIGURE 14.7

A typical Craigslist For Sale ad.

So if you're interested in the item, contact the seller via email and express your interest. You can then arrange a time to view the item; if you like what you see, you can pay for it then and take it with you.

Listing an Item for Sale

If you're a seller, the big difference between eBay and Craigslist is that most listings on Craigslist are free. The site charges nothing to list most items for sale, and it charges no final value or commission fees. This makes Craigslist quite attractive to sellers; you can list anything you want and don't have to pay if it doesn't sell.

 NOTE   Although the vast majority of Craigslist ads are free, not all are. In particular, Craigslist charges for job listings in some major cities, brokered apartment listings in New York City, and all listings in the adult services category.

Listing an item for sale on Craigslist is similar to listing a fixed-price item on eBay. The differences are more in what you *don't* have to do; there are fewer "blanks" to fill in—and fewer options for your listing.

 TIP Selling on Craigslist is better than eBay when you have a big or bulky item that might be difficult to ship long distances. Local buyers can pick up the items they purchase.

To list an item for sale on the Craigslist site, follow these steps:

1. Navigate to the home page for your local Craigslist community.

2. Click the Post to Classifieds link on the left side of the page.

3. When the next page appears, click what type of posting this is —probably For Sale by Owner.

4. On the next page, select the appropriate category.

5. If prompted for your location, select it.

6. You now see the listing creation page, as shown in Figure 14.8. Enter information into the appropriate fields: Posting Title, Price, Specific Location, Posting Body, and the like. Click Continue to proceed.

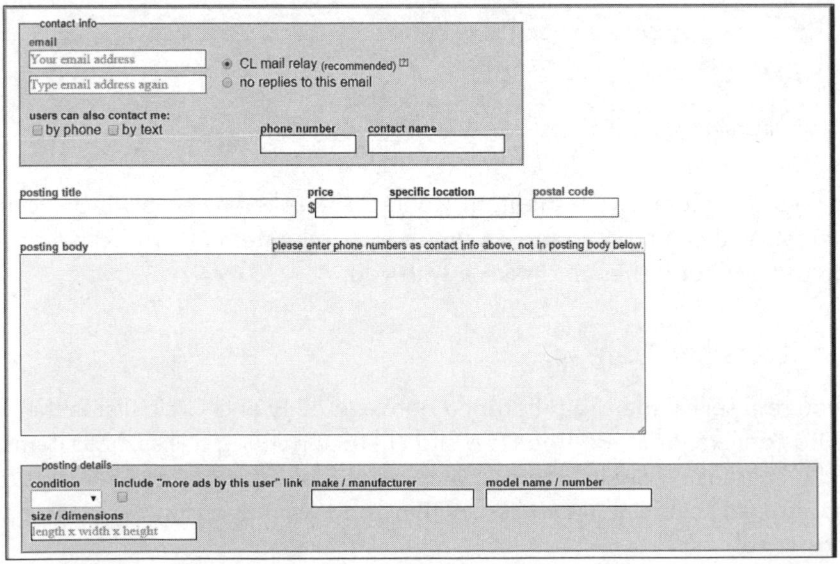

FIGURE 14.8

Creating a new Craigslist classified listing.

7. When the next page appears, click the Choose Files button to select any digital photos you want to include with the item. Click the Done with Images button when you're ready to proceed.

8. Craigslist now displays a preview of your listing. If you like what you see, click the Publish button. (If you don't like what you see, click the Edit Text or Edit Images button to make changes.) Your listing appears on the Craigslist site within the next 14 minutes or so.

For your protection, Craigslist displays an anonymized email address in your item listing. Buyers email this anonymous address, and the emails are forwarded to your real email address. That way you won't get email stalkers from your craigslist ads—in fact, no one will know exactly who is doing the posting!

Making the Sale

When someone replies to your listing, Craigslist forwards you that message via email. You can then reply to the potential buyer directly; in most instances, that means arranging a time for that person to come to your house to either view or purchase the item of interest.

Unlike eBay, where you have to ship the item to the buyer, Craigslist buyers more often than not pick up the items they purchase. That means you have to be at home for the buyer to visit, and you have to be comfortable with strangers visiting. You also have to be prepared to help the buyer load up whatever it is you're selling into her vehicle for the trip home—which can be a major issue if you're selling big stuff and you're a small person.

 CAUTION   If you're not comfortable with strangers visiting your house and you're selling something portable, arrange to meet at a neutral location. If you're selling a larger item, make sure another family member or friend is home when the buyer is supposed to visit.

As to payment, the vast majority of Craigslist purchases are made with cash. You might want to keep some ones and fives on hand to make change in case the buyer pays with larger bills.

For higher priced items, you might want to accept payment via cashier's check or money order. Just be sure that the check or money order is made out for the exact amount of the purchase; you don't want to give back cash as change for a money order purchase.

CAUTION Under no circumstances should you accept payment via personal check. It's far too easy for a shady buyer to write you a check and take off with the merchandise, only for you to discover a few days later that the check bounced. If you *must* accept a personal check, hold onto the merchandise for a full 10 working days to make sure the check clears; it's probably easier for all involved for the buyer to just get the cash.

THE ABSOLUTE MINIMUM

Here are the key points to remember from this chapter:

- You can find just about any type of item you want for sale somewhere on the Internet.

- Shopping online is a lot like shopping in a traditional store; you find the product you want, go through the checkout system, and make your payment.

- Internet shopping is very safe, especially if you buy from a major merchant that offers a secure server and a good returns policy.

- If you want to sell your own items online, try eBay, which lets you list items either at a fixed price or via online auction format.

- Another good place to sell items you own is Craigslist, which functions like a local classified advertising site.

SENDING AND RECEIVING EMAIL

Email is a modern way to communicate with friends, family, and colleagues. An email message is like a regular letter, except that it's composed electronically and delivered almost immediately via the Internet.

You can use a dedicated email program, such as Microsoft Outlook or Windows 10's own Mail app to send and receive email from your personal computer. If you prefer, you can use a web mail service such as Gmail or Yahoo! Mail to manage all your email from any web browser on any computer. Either approach is good and enables you to create, send, and read email messages from all your friends, family, and colleagues.

How Email Works

Email—short for "electronic mail"—is like traditional postal mail, except that you compose messages that are delivered electronically via the Internet. When you send an email message to another Internet user, that message travels from your PC to your recipient's PC through a series of Internet connections and servers, almost instantaneously. Email messages can be of any length and can include file attachments of various types.

To make sure your message goes to the right recipient, you have to use your recipient's *email address*. Every Internet user has a unique email address, composed of three parts:

- The user's name

- The **@** sign

- The user's domain name (usually the name of the Internet service provider, or ISP)

As an example, if you use Comcast as your Internet provider (with the domain name comcast.net) and your login name is jimbo, your email address is jimbo@comcast.net.

POP/IMAP Email Versus Web Mail

There are actually two different ways to send and receive email via the Internet.

The traditional way to send and receive email uses a protocol called the Post Office Protocol (POP). POP email requires use of a dedicated email software program and—at the ISP level—separate email servers to send and receive messages.

 NOTE   Many POP email providers also offer web-based access from any web browser.

Internet Message Access Protocol (IMAP) is a newer type of POP email. It works just like POP email through your ISP but offers a few more options for synchronizing messages between different devices.

In addition to POP/IMAP email services, the other way to send and receive email is via Web-based email services, also known as *web mail*. Unlike straight POP/IMAP email, you can access web mail from any computer, using any web browser; no special software is required.

POP/IMAP Email

POP/IMAP email is the standard type of email account you receive when you sign up with an ISP. You're assigned an email account, given an email address, and provided with the necessary information to configure your email program to access this account.

To use POP/IMAP email, you have to use a special email program, such as Microsoft Outlook (part of the Microsoft Office suite) or the Mail app included with Windows 10. That email program has to be configured to send email to your ISP's outgoing mail server (called an SMTP server) and to receive email from your ISP's incoming mail server (called a POP3 or IMAP server). If you want to access your email account from another computer, you have to use a similar email program and go through the entire configuration process all over again on the second computer.

Web Mail

You're not limited to using the "hard-wired" POP/IMAP email offered by your ISP; you can also send and receive email from web mail services, such as Google's Gmail and Yahoo! Mail. These web mail services enable you to access your email from any computer, using any web browser.

If you use a PC in multiple locations—in the office, at home, or on the road—this is a convenient way to check your email at any time of day, no matter where you are. You can also use web mail to check your email from your smartphone or tablet; the device you use doesn't matter.

With web mail, you don't have to go through the same sort of complicated configuration routine that you use with POP/IMAP email. All you have to do is go to the email service's website, enter your user ID and password, and you're ready to send and receive messages.

 TIP   Your ISP might offer web-based access to its traditional POP/IMAP email, which is convenient when you're away from home and need to check your email.

Most web mail services are completely free to use. Some services offer both free versions and paid versions, with paid subscriptions offering additional message storage and functionality.

The largest web mail services include the following:

- AOL Mail (mail.aol.com)
- Gmail (mail.google.com)

- Lycos Mail (mail.lycos.com)

- Mail.com (www.mail.com)

- Outlook.com (www.outlook.com)

- Yahoo! Mail (mail.yahoo.com)

Using Gmail

One of the largest web mail services today is Google's Gmail. It's the web mail service I use, and one I definitely recommend.

Navigating Gmail

You access the Gmail home page at mail.google.com. If you don't yet have a Google account, you're prompted to sign up for one. Do so now; signing up is free.

After you activate your Gmail account, you're assigned an email address (in the form of *name*@gmail.com), and you get access to the Gmail Inbox page.

The default view of the Gmail page is the Inbox, shown in Figure 15.1, which contains all your received messages. You can switch to other views by clicking the appropriate links on the left side of the page. For example, to view all your sent mail, simply click the Sent Mail link on the left.

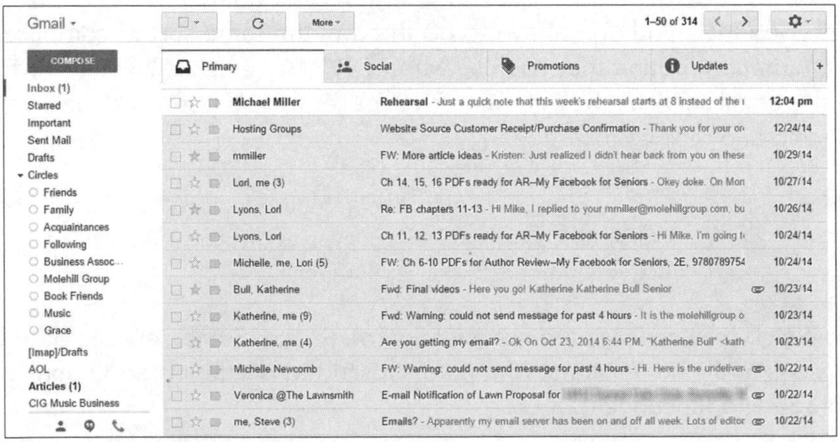

FIGURE 15.1

The Gmail Inbox.

Gmail attempts to organize your incoming mail by type and display each type of message on a separate tab. The Primary tab displays standard correspondence; the Social tab displays messages from Facebook, Google+, and other social networks; the Promotions tab displays advertising email; and the Updates tab displays messages from your bank, credit card company, and similar services you use on a regular basis. Click a tab to read all messages of a given type.

Each message is listed with the message's sender, the message's subject, a snippet from the message, and the date or time the message was sent. (The snippet typically is the first line of the message text.) Unread messages are listed in bold; after a message has been read, it's displayed in normal, unbold text with a shaded background. And if you've assigned a label to a message, the label appears before the message subject.

To perform an action on a message or group of messages, put a check mark by the message(s), and then click one of the buttons at the top of the list. Alternatively, you can click the More button to display a list of additional actions to perform.

Reading Messages

To read a message, all you have to do is click the message title in the Inbox. This displays the full text of the message on a new page, as shown in Figure 15.2.

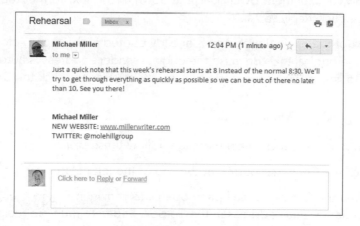

FIGURE 15.2

Reading a message in Gmail.

If you want to display this message in a new window, click the In New Window icon. To print the message, click the Print All icon. To return to the Inbox, click the Back to Inbox button.

Viewing Conversations

One of the unique things about Gmail is that all related email messages are grouped in what Google calls *conversations*. A conversation might be an initial message and all its replies (and replies to replies). A conversation might also be all the daily emails from a single source with a common subject, such as messages you receive from subscribed-to mailing lists.

A conversation is noted in the Inbox list by a number in parentheses after the sender name(s). If a conversation has replies from more than one person, more than one name is listed.

To view a conversation, simply click the message title; the most recent message displays in full. To view the text of any individual message in a conversation, click that message's subject. To expand *all* the messages in a conversation, click the Expand All link. All the messages in the conversation are stacked on top of each other, with the text of the newest message fully displayed.

Replying to a Message

Whether you're reading a single message or a conversation, it's easy enough to send a reply. In the original message, click the Reply button to expand the message to include a reply box. Or if a conversation has multiple participants, you can reply to all of them by clicking the down arrow next to the Reply button and then selecting Reply to All.

The text of the original message is already quoted in the reply. Add your new text above the original text. Because the original sender's address is automatically added to the To line, all you have to do to send the message is click the Send button.

Composing a New Message

To compose and send a new message, follow these steps:

1. Click the Compose button at the top of the left column on any Gmail page.

2. When the Compose Mail pane opens, as shown in Figure 15.3, enter the recipient's email address in the To box. Separate multiple recipients with commas.

3. Enter a subject for the message into the Subject box.

4. Enter the text of your message in the large text box. Click the Formatting Options button at the bottom of the pane to enhance your text with bold, italic, and other formats.

5. When you finish composing your message, click the Send button.

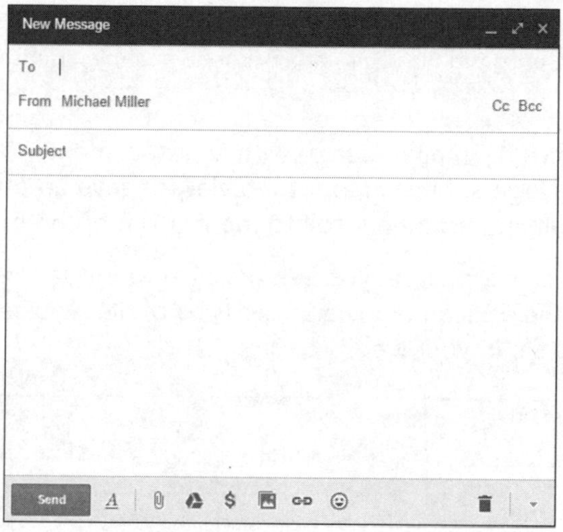

FIGURE 15.3

Composing a new Gmail message.

TIP   You can also carbon copy and blind carbon copy additional recipients by clicking the Cc and Bcc links. This expands the message to include Cc or Bcc boxes, into which you enter the recipients' addresses.

Sending and Receiving Photos and Other Files

When you need to send a digital photo or other file to a friend or colleague, you can do so via email. To send a file via email, you attach that file to a standard email message. When the message is sent, the *file attachment* travels along with it; when the message is received, the file is right there, waiting to be opened.

It's easy to send file attachments in Gmail. Just follow these steps:

1. Compose a new message, and then click the Attach Files (paperclip) button at the bottom of the pane.

2. When the Open dialog box appears, navigate to and select the file you want to attach, and then click the Open button.

3. The file you selected now appears under the Subject box on the new message page. Continue to compose, and then send your message as normal.

CAUTION Gmail blocks the transmittal of all executable program files (with an .EXE extension) in an attempt to prevent potential computer viruses.

When you receive a Gmail message with an attachment, you see a paper clip icon next to the message subject/snippet. To view or save an attachment, click the message to open it, and then scroll to the bottom of the message.

If the attachment is a picture, you see the picture in the message, as shown in Figure 15.4. If the attachment is another type of file, you see a View link; click this link to view the file in your web browser.

FIGURE 15.4

Viewing and downloading attachments to an email message.

To save the file to your hard disk, click the Download link. When you're asked if you want to open or save the file, click or tap the Save button. After a quick security scan, Windows saves the file and asks if you want to open it. Click the Open button to do so.

 CAUTION Email file attachments are the biggest source of computer virus and spyware infection. Malicious users attach viruses and spyware to email messages, oftentimes disguised as legitimate files; when a user clicks to open the file, his computer is infected with the virus or spyware. You should avoid opening any file sent to you from a user you don't know, or even from people you do know if you weren't expecting them. If you receive an email from a complete stranger with an unknown file attached, that's almost definitely a malicious file that you should not open. Instead, delete the entire message. Learn more about computer viruses and spyware in Chapter 25, "Protecting Your PC from Computer Attacks, Malware, and Spam."

Using the Windows 10 Mail App

Windows 10 includes a built-in Mail app for sending and receiving email messages. You open the Mail app from the Start screen.

By default, the Mail app manages email from the Outlook.com or Hotmail account linked to your Microsoft Account. This means you see Outlook.com and Hotmail messages in your Mail Inbox, and you can easily send emails from your Outlook.com account.

 NOTE   Microsoft's web-based email service used to be called Hotmail but recently was renamed to Outlook.com. All older accounts retain the @hotmail.com part of the email address; newer accounts have an @outlook.com address.

Checking Your Inbox

When you open the Mail app, resize the window so that it is wider than the default. When you do this, as you can see in Figure 15.5, you see three distinct panes in the Mail window.

The left pane app displays all the folders from the selected email account. Select a folder, such as your Inbox, and all the messages from that folder display in the center pane. To read a message, all you have to do is click or tap it; the message content then displays in the large right pane.

FIGURE 15.5

Viewing a message from your Inbox.

To reply to a message, follow these steps:

1. From an open message, click Reply at the top of screen. (If you want to respond to all recipients of a multi-recipient message, click Reply All instead.)

2. The content pane now changes into a reply message pane, as shown in Figure 15.6. Enter your reply at the top of the message; the bottom of the message "quotes" the original message.

3. Click Send when you're ready to send the message.

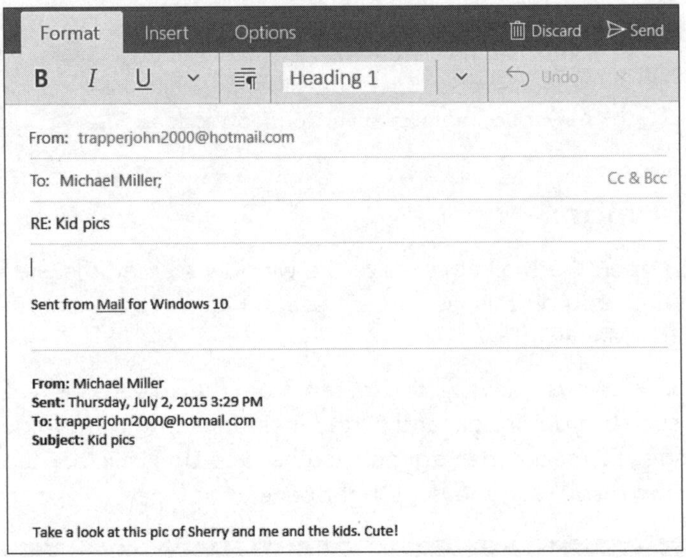

| Format | Insert | Options | | 🗑 Discard | ▷ Send |

B *I* U ⌄ | ≡¶ | Heading 1 | ⌄ | ↺ Undo

From: trapperjohn2000@hotmail.com

To: Michael Miller;   Cc & Bcc

RE: Kid pics

|

Sent from Mail for Windows 10

From: Michael Miller
Sent: Thursday, July 2, 2015 3:29 PM
To: trapperjohn2000@hotmail.com
Subject: Kid pics

Take a look at this pic of Sherry and me and the kids. Cute!

FIGURE 15.6

Replying to a message.

Sending New Messages

It's equally easy to create and send a new email message. Follow these steps:

1. Click New Mail in the navigation pane to display the new message pane, shown in Figure 15.7.

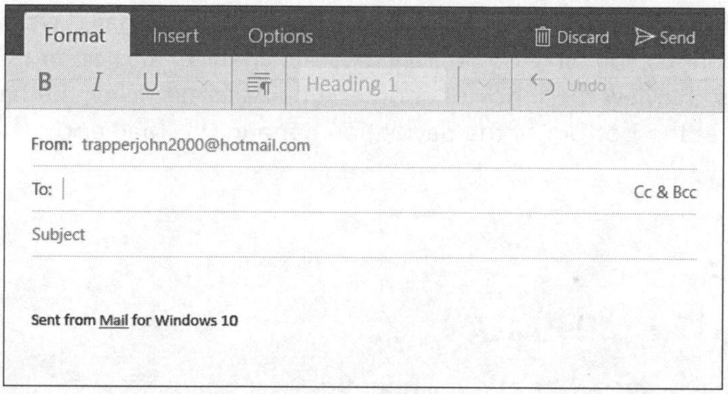

FIGURE 15.7

Creating a new email message.

2. Click within the To: field and begin entering the name or email address of the message's recipient. Mail displays a list of matching names from your contact list; select the person you want to email.

3. Click the Subject field and type a subject for this message.

4. To attach a file to this message, click the Insert tab and then click Attach. When the Open dialog box appears, navigate to and select the file you want to attach; then click the Open button.

5. When you're ready to send the email, click Send.

That's it. Windows now sends your message, using your default email account.

Adding Another Email Account

By default, the Mail app sends and receives messages from the email account associated with your Microsoft account. You can, however, configure Mail to work with other email accounts, if you have them. Follow these steps:

1. Click the Settings icon at the bottom of the navigation pane.

2. When the Settings pane appears, click Accounts.

3. When the Accounts pane appears, click Add Account.

4. When the Choose an Account window appears, click the type of account you want to add.

5. When the next pane appears, enter your email address and password, and then click the Sign In or Connect button.

The Mail app lets you add Outlook.com (including Hotmail, Live.com, and MSN Mail accounts), Gmail (Google), Microsoft Exchange, and other POP/IMAP email accounts. To view the Inbox of another email account, click the name of that account at the bottom of the navigation pane in the Mail app.

THE ABSOLUTE MINIMUM

Here are the key points to remember from this chapter:

- Email is a fast and easy way to send electronic letters over the Internet.

- There are two types of email: POP/IMAP email, which requires a separate email program, and web mail, which can be sent and received from any web browser.

- The most popular web mail services include Google's Gmail, Microsoft's Outlook.com, and Yahoo! Mail.

- You can use the Windows 10 Mail app to send and receive email from your default email account; the app also consolidates messages from other services you've connected to your account.

- Don't open unexpected files attached to incoming email messages; they might contain computer viruses!

16

SOCIAL NETWORKING WITH FACEBOOK AND OTHER SOCIAL MEDIA

Want to find out what your friends, family, and colleagues are up to? Want to let them know what you're doing today? Then you need to hop onboard the social networking train; it's how savvy online users connect today.

Social networking enables people to share experiences and opinions with each other via community-based websites. Whether you use Facebook, Twitter, Pinterest, or some other social networking site, it's a great way to keep up-to-date on what your friends and family are doing.

Using Facebook

No question about it, the number-one social network today is Facebook (www. facebook.com). Facebook has more than a billion active users worldwide; chances are, most of your friends and family are already on Facebook, just waiting for you to join in the fun.

 NOTE   Learn more about Facebook in my companion book *My Facebook for Seniors*, available at a bookstore near you.

Signing Up and Signing In with the Facebook App

You can access Facebook using Internet Explorer (or any web browser), at www. facebook.com.

If you're new to Facebook, use this page to create a new account for yourself. Enter your first and last name, email address, desired password, and birthday; then click Sign Up. Follow the rest of the steps to create your account and get started.

After you sign up for Facebook, you can log into your account by going to the same page and entering your email address and password into the boxes at the top of the page. Click the Log In button to proceed.

Getting to Know Facebook

You navigate the Facebook website from the navigation sidebar on the left side of the page. The middle of the screen displays the selected page or content, and the right column displays your list of friends and any group chats you've participated in.

 NOTE   Facebook is constantly upgrading its feature set, so what you see might differ somewhat from what is described here.

The default selection in the navigation sidebar is your News Feed, and for good reason; as you can see in Figure 16.1, this is where all the status updates from your friends display. Scroll down the page to view more updates.

FIGURE 16.1

The Facebook Home page—complete with News Feed of your friends' status updates.

You can also navigate the Facebook website from the toolbar at the top of the page. In addition to the big Search box, which you use to search for people and things on the Facebook site, the toolbar enables you to click to see friend requests, private messages, and notifications.

Finding Friends

Social networking is all about keeping in touch with friends, and the easiest way to find friends on Facebook is to let Facebook find them for you—based on the information you provided for your personal profile. The more Facebook knows about you, especially in terms of where you've worked and gone to school, the more friends it can find.

To find new friends on Facebook follow these steps:

1. Click the Friends button on the toolbar to display the pull-down menu, shown in Figure 16.2. This menu lists any friend requests you've received and offers a number of friend suggestions from Facebook ("People You May Know"). To add one of these people to your friends list, click the Add Friend button.

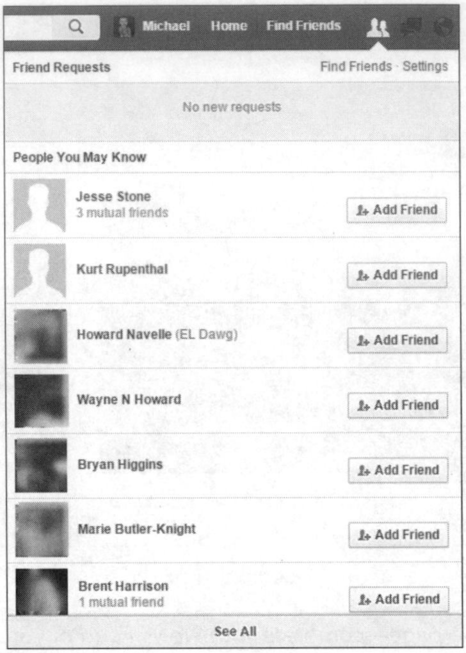

FIGURE 16.2

Finding friends on the Facebook website.

NOTE The people Facebook suggests as friends are typically people who went to the same schools you did, worked at the same companies you did, or are friends of your current friends.

2. To continue searching for friends, click See All at the bottom of this menu to display your Friends page.

3. Scroll down the page to view other suggested friends from Facebook in the People You May Know section. Click the Add Friend button for any person you'd like to add as a friend.

4. To find people in your email contacts list who are also members of Facebook, scroll to the top of the Friends page. Click the Find Friends link for the email service you use, and then enter any requested information (typically your email address and password). Facebook lists all matching contacts.

5. Check the people you'd like to add as a friend, and then click the Send Invites button.

NOTE Facebook doesn't automatically add a person to your friends list. Instead, that person receives an invitation to be your friend; she can accept or reject the invitation. To accept or reject any friend requests you've received, click the Friend Request button on the Facebook toolbar. (And don't worry; if you reject a request, that person won't be notified.)

Searching for Friends

You can also search directly for any old friends who might be on Facebook by entering a person's name into the Search box on the Facebook website or in the Facebook app. As you type, Facebook displays a list of suggestions beneath the search box; if the person you want is listed, click that person's name to see her Timeline page.

If you're searching from the Facebook website, you can fine-tune your search by clicking See More at the bottom of the initial search suggestions. The next page displays the detailed results of your search. You can adjust the results using the controls in the Refine This Search box. For example, you can filter the results by gender, current city, hometown, and school. If your friend is listed, click the Add Friend button to send him a friend request.

Viewing a Friend's Timeline Page

After you add some folks to your Facebook friends list, you can easily see what they've been up to by visiting their Timeline pages. A Facebook Timeline page is essentially a person's profile page on Facebook.

A Timeline page, like the one shown in Figure 16.3, displays all that person's status updates and activities on the Facebook site, in the form of a timeline. But that's not all that's there.

To view detailed personal information about your friend, click the About box. To view the pictures this person has uploaded, click Photos, and to see a list of this person's friends, click Friends.

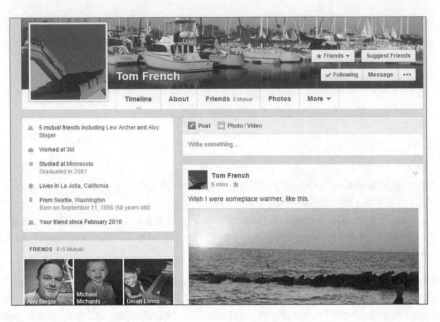

FIGURE 16.3

A typical Facebook Timeline page in the Facebook app.

Posting Status Updates

We've talked a lot about Facebook being the perfect place to update your friends and family on what you're up to—things you're doing, thoughts you're thinking, accomplishments you're accomplishing, you name it. The easiest way to let people know what's what is to post what Facebook calls a *status update*.

Every status update you make is broadcast to everyone on your friends list, displayed in the News Feed on their Home pages. This way everyone who cares enough about you to make you a friend knows everything you post about. And that can be quite a lot—from simple text posts to photos and videos and even links to other web pages.

Facebook makes it extremely easy to post a status update. Here's how you do it:

1. Click Home in the Facebook toolbar to display the News Feed.

2. Go to the Publisher box (labeled What's On Your Mind?) at the top of the page. Note that the Update Status tab is selected by default.

3. Type your message into the What's On Your Mind? box. The Publisher box expands to display a series of option buttons at the bottom, as shown in Figure 16.4.

> Update Status   Add Photos/Video   Create Photo Album
>
> What's on your mind?
>
> Public ▾   Post

FIGURE 16.4

Posting a new status update.

4. To include a photograph in your status update, click the Add Photos to Your Post button beneath the Publisher box; this opens the Choose File to Upload or Open dialog box. (Which dialog box displays depends on which web browser you use.) Navigate to and select the photo(s) you want to upload; then click the Open button.

5. To include a link to a web page, enter the URL (web address) for that page into the Publisher box. Facebook should recognize the link and display a Link panel, complete with a thumbnail image from the page. Click the left and right arrows to select one of multiple thumbnail images to accompany the link.

6. To include your location in this status update, click the Add a Location to Post button beneath the Publisher box. If Facebook can tell your location automatically, it displays a list of options. Otherwise, start entering your location manually; as you type, Facebook displays a list of suggested locations, along with a map of the current selection. Click the correct location from the resulting list.

 CAUTION You might not want to identify your location on every post you make. If you post while you're away from home, you're letting potential burglars know that your house is empty. You're also telling potential stalkers where they can find you. For these reasons, use caution when posting your location in your status updates.

7. To "tag" a friend in your status update, click the Tag People in Your Post button beneath the Publisher box. Enter the name of the person you want to tag. As you type, Facebook displays a drop-down list with matching names from your Facebook friends list. Select the friend from the list.

8. Click the Post button to post your status update to the Facebook site.

Determine Who Can—or Can't—See a Status Update

By default, everyone on Facebook can read every post you make. If you'd rather send a given post to a more select group of people, you can change the privacy settings for any individual post. This enables only selected people to see that post; other people on your friends list won't see it at all.

Here's how to do it:

1. Enter the text of your status update, or any photos you want to upload, into the Publisher box as normal.

2. Click the Privacy button (the second button from the right beneath the post) to display a list of privacy options, as shown in Figure 16.5.

FIGURE 16.5

Selecting privacy options for a status update.

3. Click Public to let everyone on Facebook see the post.

4. Select Friends to make a post visible only to people on your friends list.

5. Click More Options to view more privacy options, including sending to specific friends lists you've created.

6. With the privacy settings selected, click the Post button to send this status update to those people you've selected.

Viewing Friends' Updates in Your News Feed

The posts you make display in your friends' News Feeds. Conversely, your News Feed displays all the status updates posted by people on your friends list.

Here's how to read, like, and comment on posts in the News Feed:

1. Click News Feed in the navigation sidebar to display your News Feed.

2. Your friends' posts display in the News Feed in the middle of the page. The newest posts are at the top; scroll down through the list to read older posts. (Figure 16.6 shows a typical post with photo.)

FIGURE 16.6

A typical Facebook post. (Throwback Thursday—or TBT—is a big deal.)

3. To leave a comment about a post, click Comment and then enter your text into the resulting Write a Comment box.

4. To "like" a post, click Like.

5. If a post includes one or more photos, click the photo to view a larger version of that photo.

6. If a post includes a video (which is indicated by a Play icon in the middle of the thumbnail), click the video thumbnail to begin playback.

7. If a post includes a link to another web page, that link appears beneath the post, along with a brief description of the page. Click the link to open the other page in your web browser.

Uploading Photos to Facebook

Facebook is a social network, and one of the ways we connect socially is through pictures. We track our progress through life as a series of pictures. We document events small and large, from picnics in the backyard and family vacations to births, graduations, weddings, and everything else that transpires.

Facebook enables you to upload and store photos in virtual photo albums. You can upload new photos to an existing album or create a new album for newly uploaded photos. Just follow these steps:

1. Click your name in the Facebook toolbar to display your Timeline page.

2. Click Photos to display your Photos page.

3. Click the Create Album button to display the Open dialog box. Then select the photos you want to upload, and click the Open button.

4. You now see the Create Album page, with thumbnails of your photos displayed, as shown in Figure 16.7. You want to give this album a name, so click Untitled Album and enter the desired album name.

FIGURE 16.7

Uploading photos to a new photo album.

5. Click Say Something About This Album and enter an album description.

6. To enter a geographic location for all the photos in this album, go to the Where Were These Taken box and enter a location.

7. To add a date to all the photos in this album, click Use Date from Photos. (Alternatively, you can add custom dates by clicking Pick a Date.)

NOTE All the information you can add to a photo album is entirely optional; you can add as much or as little as you like. You don't even have to add a title. (If you don't, Facebook uses the title Untitled Album.)

8. To enter information about a specific picture, enter a description in the Say Something About This Photo box.

9. To tag a person who appears in a given photo, click that person's face and enter his name when prompted.

NOTE You identify people in your photos by *tagging* them. That is, you click on a person in the photo and then assign a friend's name to that part of the photo. You can then find photos where a given person appears by searching for that person's tag.

10. To determine who can view the photos in this album, click the Privacy button and make a selection.

11. Click the Post button when done.

TIP To achieve the best possible picture quality for anyone downloading or printing your photos, check the High Quality option to upload and store your photos at their original resolution. Note, however, that it takes longer to upload high-quality photos than those in standard quality.

After you create a photo album, you can easily upload more photos to that album; you don't have to create a new album every time you want to upload new photos.

To upload pictures to an existing album, go to your Photos page and click Albums to display your photo albums. Click to open the album to which you want to add new photos; then click Add Photos and select the photos to upload.

The photos you selected are now added to the album page. Add descriptions and tag anyone you need to tag; then click any information you want about a given photo—location, date, information, and the like. You can also tag people in each photo. Click the Post button when you finish.

Viewing Photos

Viewing a friend's photos is as easy as going to that person's Timeline page and clicking Photos. This displays your friend's Photos page, as shown in Figure 16.8. Click Albums to view your friend's photo albums; click a given album to view that album's contents.

FIGURE 16.8

Viewing a friend's Photos page in the Facebook app.

Click the thumbnail of the picture you want to view. The picture now displays in a *lightbox* superimposed on top of the previous page. You move to the next photo in the album by clicking the right arrow or pressing the right arrow on your keyboard; there's no need to close the photo before moving to the next one. Keep clicking the right arrow to move through all the photos in the album; click the left arrow to go back through the previously viewed photos. To close the viewer and get back to the photo album, just click the X (close) button at the top right of the lightbox.

FIGURE 16.9

Viewing a photo lightbox.

Managing Your Privacy on Facebook

Facebook is all about connecting users to one another. That's how the site functions, after all, by encouraging "friends" and all sorts of public sharing of information.

The problem is that Facebook, by default, shares all your information with just about everybody. Not just your friends or friends of your friends, but the entire membership of the site. And not just with Facebook members, either; Facebook also shares your information with third-party applications and games and with other sites on the Web.

Fortunately, you can configure Facebook to be much less public than it is by default. If you value your privacy, this might be worth doing.

With that in mind, here's how to configure Facebook's default privacy settings.

1. Click the Privacy Shortcuts button on the Facebook toolbar to display the pull-down menu.

2. Click the down arrow next to Who Can See My Stuff to expand the menu, as shown in Figure 16.10.

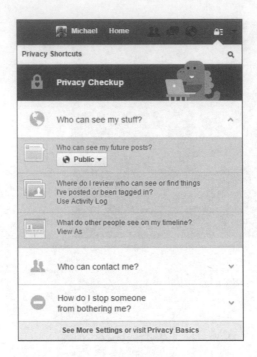

FIGURE 16.10

Configuring Facebook's default privacy options.

3. Go to the Who Can See My Future Posts? section, click the down arrow, and select one of the resulting options.

4. Click Public to let anyone on Facebook see your posts.

5. Click Friends to restrict viewing to only people on your Facebook friends list.

6. Click Only Me to keep your posts totally private—that is, to keep anyone from seeing them.

There are many other privacy settings available on the Privacy Shortcuts menu. You should investigate these options—or click the Privacy Checkup option to let Facebook lead you through what's available.

 NOTE   As discussed previously, you can change the privacy settings for any individual status update you post. The changes you make for that update are then saved as your new default settings.

Using Pinterest

Facebook might be the biggest social network on the Web today, but it's not the only one. There are several other social networks that help you keep in touch with friends and family—and, in some cases, focus on specific types of users or interests.

We'll start our examination of these social networks by looking at Pinterest, which is kind of a visual version of Facebook that's become increasingly popular among average, nontechnical users. The user base includes a fairly large number of women aged 30 and older who like to share pictures of clothing, DIY projects, and the like.

 NOTE Learn more about Pinterest in my companion book *My Pinterest*, available at a bookstore near you or at http://www. quepublishing.com.

What Pinterest Is and What It Does

Unlike Facebook, which lets you post text-based status updates, Pinterest is all about images. The site consists of a collection of virtual online "pinboards" that people use to share pictures they find interesting. Users "pin" photos and other images to their personal boards and then share their pins with online friends.

Here's how it works. You start by finding an image on a web page that you like and want to share. You then "pin" that image to one of your boards, which are like old-fashioned corkboards, except online.

A Pinterest board becomes a place where you can create and share collections of those things you like or find interesting. You can have as many boards as you like, organized by category or topic.

Friends who follow you see the images you pin, and you see the ones they pin. You can also "like" other people's pins and repin their items to your boards, thus repeating the original pin. It's a visual way to share things you like online.

Joining Pinterest is free; in fact, you can sign up using your Facebook username and password. (Or with your email address, of course.) Go to www.pinterest.com to get started.

Navigating the Pinterest Site

Pinterest is a relatively easy website to get around. After you log on, it's a simple matter of displaying certain types of pins from certain users and then knowing how to get back to the main page.

The Pinterest home page, shown in Figure 16.11, consists of a toolbar of sorts at the top, with individual pins filling the bulk of the page beneath that. You use the toolbar to navigate the site.

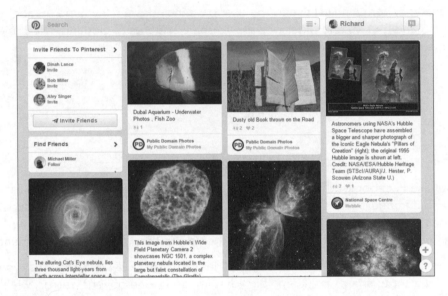

FIGURE 16.11

Pinterest's home page.

To search for pins about a particular topic, enter your query into the search box and press Enter. To browse pins by category, click the Category (three line) button on the right side of the search box, and select a category from the resulting list.

Viewing Boards and Pins

A user's presence on Pinterest is defined by her boards and the pins posted there. To view a friend's board and its contents, all you have to do is click that friend's name anywhere on the Pinterest site and your friend's personal Pinterest page displays with thumbnails of her boards, as shown in Figure 16.12.

FIGURE 16.12

Viewing a Pinterest profile page.

To open a board, click the board's thumbnail image. This displays all the pins for the selected board. Each pin consists of the pinned image, descriptive text (supplied by the user who pinned the item), and the URL for the website where this image was found. To view the web page where the image originally appeared, click the pin.

Following Other Users

When you find someone who posts a lot of things you're interested in, you can follow that person on Pinterest. When you follow a person, all that person's new pins display on your Pinterest home page.

You can find people to follow by using Pinterest's search box to search by name or interest. After you locate a person you want to follow, just go to that person's personal Pinterest page, and click the Follow All button.

You can also opt to follow a specific board, rather than all of that person's pins. From the person's personal page, click the Follow Board button for the board you want to follow.

Pinning Items

Pinterest is all about pinning items of interest—hence the name, a combination of "pin" and "interest." To fully participate in the Pinterest community, you have to learn how to pin items to your boards. There are several ways to do this.

The simplest way to create a pin is from the Pinterest site. To do this, you first need to know the address (URL) of the web page you want to pin. With that URL in hand, follow these steps:

1. Click the + button in the lower-right corner of the Pinterest window, and then select Pin from a website.

2. This displays the Pin from a Website dialog box. Enter the URL of the page you want to pin into the text box, and then click the Find Images button.

3. Pinterest displays a page with images from that web page on the top and previously pinned items below, as shown in Figure 16.13. Mouse over the item you want to pin and click the red Pin It button.

FIGURE 16.13

Selecting an image to pin.

4. You now see the Pick a Board dialog box, shown in Figure 16.14. Select the board to which you'd like to pin this image.

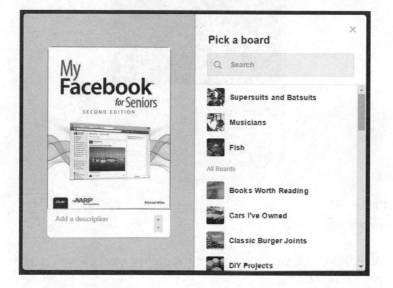

FIGURE 16.14

Creating a new pin.

5. Enter a short (500 characters or less) text description of or comment on this image into the Description box.

6. Click the red Pin It button when done.

Repinning Existing Items

You can also "repin" items that other users have previously pinned. This adds the pinned item to one of your pinboards. To repin an item from its thumbnail image, follow these steps:

1. Mouse over the item you want to repin, and then click the Pin It button, as shown in Figure 16.15.

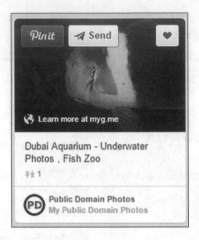

FIGURE 16.15

Repinning an item.

2. When the Pick a Board dialog box appears, select which board you want to pin this item to.

3. Accept the previous user's description or add your own into the Description box.

4. Click the red Pin It button to repin the item.

Creating New Board

You can create as many different boards as you like, each focusing on a specific topic. Create individual boards to match your own interests and hobbies.

To create a new board, follow these steps:

1. Click your name at the top-right corner of any page to open your profile page.

2. Click the Create a Board tile.

3. When the Create a Board dialog box appears, enter a name for this board into the Name box.

4. Enter a short description of the board's contents into the Description box.

5. Pull down the Category list and select a category for this board.

6. Make sure the Keep It a Secret option is turned off. (Turn it on if you want to create a private board that no one but you can see.)

7. Click the red Create Board button.

Pinterest creates the board and displays the page for this board. (It's currently empty.) You can now start pinning items to the board!

Using LinkedIn

LinkedIn is a different kind of social network—not necessarily in how it works but in whom it appeals to. Whereas Facebook and Pinterest are aimed at a general audience, LinkedIn is targeted at business professionals. As such, you can use LinkedIn to network with others in your industry or profession or even to hunt for a new position at another firm. (Figure 16.16 shows the LinkedIn home page—with a definite business slant.)

FIGURE 16.16

The LinkedIn home page.

LinkedIn membership is free. To join the LinkedIn network, go to www.linkedin.com and enter your first and last names, email address, and desired password. Click the Join Now button, and you are prompted to enter information to complete your personal profile—employment status, company, title, and so forth. Follow the onscreen instructions to complete the process.

TIP   Use the menu bar at the top of each page to find your way around the LinkedIn site. The menu bar contains links to the LinkedIn home page, your personal profile, your LinkedIn contacts, groups you belong to, LinkedIn's job search features, and your message Inbox.

Personalizing Your Profile

Each LinkedIn member has his own personal profile page. This profile page is what other LinkedIn users see when they search for you on the site; it's where you make your initial impression to potential employers and people with whom you want to make contact.

Because your profile page serves as your *de facto* resume on the LinkedIn site, you want to control the information you display to others. Presenting only selected information can help you present yourself in the best possible light.

Fortunately, your LinkedIn profile is fully customizable; you can select which content others see. This content can include a snapshot of your personal information (shown in Figure 16.17), your contact info, summaries of your professional experience and education, recommendations from other users, and more.

FIGURE 16.17

Snapshot information on a LinkedIn profile page.

To edit your profile page, click Profile on the menu bar and then select Edit Profile. When the Edit My Profile page appears, click the Edit button for the section(s) you want to edit.

Finding New Connections

LinkedIn's equivalent of Facebook friends is called *connections*. These are business or professional contacts you know and trust. Anyone on the LinkedIn site can become a connection; you can also invite people who are not yet LinkedIn members to join your connections list.

You can search for LinkedIn members in your email contacts list. (LinkedIn searches AOL Mail, Gmail, Outlook, Yahoo! Mail, and other email programs and services.) In addition, LinkedIn can search for members who've gone to the same schools or worked for the same employers that you have. You can also invite non-LinkedIn members to be new connections.

To add new connections, click the Connections menu and select Add Connections. From there you can add connections from your email contacts lists, invite others to join your LinkedIn network, and see who LinkedIn recommends as connections.

Contacting Other LinkedIn Members

Networking on LinkedIn involves a lot of personal contact, using LinkedIn's own internal email system. This system enables you to send messages to and receive messages from people on your connections list and anyone else who is a member of the LinkedIn site.

To send a new message, click the Messages button on the toolbar to display your Inbox page, and then click the New button. When the Message page appears, enter the recipient's name or email address into the To box. Type the subject of the message into the Subject box, type your message into the large text box, and then click the Send Message button.

To view messages you've received, click the Messages button on the toolbar. This displays all messages you've received. The newest messages are listed first; unread messages are in bold. To read a message, all you have to do is click the message header.

Using Twitter

Then there's Twitter. Unlike Facebook, Pinterest, and LinkedIn, Twitter isn't a fully featured social network per se. Instead, Twitter is a kind of microblogging service that enables you to create short (up to 140 characters) text posts—called *tweets*—that your followers receive and read.

 NOTE Most people use Twitter to follow other users rather than to tweet themselves. The most popular tweeters include celebrities, companies and brands, and news organizations and reporters.

Joining Twitter

You access Twitter from the Twitter website (www.twitter.com), using Internet Explorer or another web browser. When you first access the site, you're prompted to either sign in or sign up.

If you're new to Twitter, go to the Sign Up pane and enter your name, email address, and desired password. Click the Sign Up for Twitter button to complete the process.

If you're already a Twitter user, go to the Log In pane, enter your email address or Twitter username, enter your password, and then click the Log In button.

Navigating Twitter

After you register and signed in, you see the Twitter home page, shown in Figure 16.18. The left side of the page displays your personal information, along with recommendations of people to follow and the latest trending topics. The main part of the home page displays the most recent tweets from the users you're following, newest first. You can click any links in a tweet to go to the mentioned web page or view an embedded photo.

Click to compose new tweet

FIGURE 16.18

Twitter's home page.

The toolbar at the top of the page enables you to navigate to other sections of the Twitter site. Click Notifications to view tweets that have mentioned you, or click Messages to view private tweets from other users. Click Home to return to the home page.

You can also search for specific topics in others' tweets. Enter your query into the search box at the top of the page; then press Enter to see the results.

Tweeting with Twitter

To compose and send a tweet, start by clicking the Tweet button at the top-right corner of any screen. This displays the Compose New Tweet pane, shown in Figure 16.19. Enter your text at the blinking cursor, up to 140 characters long. (Spaces count as characters, by the way.) You can also include your location by clicking the Add Location button, or you can attach a photo by clicking the Add Photo button. When you finish, click the Tweet button to send your message on its way.

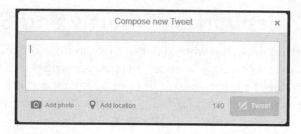

FIGURE 16.19

Composing a new tweet.

 TIP Because space is limited, many tweeters use abbreviations in their tweets. You can mention a hot topic (and make the term searchable) by preceding it with a hashtag (#), like this: #hottopic. To mention a given user in a tweet, put an @ sign in front of his username, like this: @username.

Following Other Users

If friends or family members are on Twitter, you can follow their activities by "following" their tweets.

The easiest way to do this is to use Twitter's search function. Enter the person's name, Twitter username, or email address into the search box at the top of the page, and then press Enter.

If the person you want is listed in the search results, click that person's name to display his profile page. Click the Follow button, and all tweets from that user start appearing on your Twitter home page.

 CAUTION Some users protect their profiles so that strangers can't follow them without their permission. When you click the Follow button for these users, they have to register their approval before you can follow them.

Customizing Your Profile

As you've just seen, every Twitter user has his own personal profile page on the site. To view your profile page, click your picture or name in the toolbar, and then select View Profile.

From there, click the Edit Profile button to begin editing. You can edit any of the information on this page, and you can even change the profile picture that others see.

Using Social Networks—Smartly and Safely

Social networking puts your whole life out there in front of your friends and family—and, in some cases, just about anyone perusing a network's profiles. With so much personal information displayed publicly, how do you protect yourself against those who might want to do harm to you or your children?

Protecting Your Children

Given that social networks are so popular among teenagers and preteens, many parents worry about their children being cyberstalked on these sites. That worry is not ill founded, especially given the amount of personal information that most users post on their social networking profiles.

It's important to note that all social networking sites try to police themselves, typically by limiting access for younger users. In addition, sites such as Facebook work hard to keep known sex offenders off their sites by monitoring lists of known sex offenders and culling those users from their sites.

That said, the best way to protect your children on social networking sites is to monitor what they do on those sites. As such, you need to become "friends" with your children on Facebook, follow their Twitter feeds, and visit their profile pages on a regular basis. You might be surprised what you find there.

It's an unfortunate fact that not all teens and preteens are wise about what they put online. It's not unusual to find provocative pictures posted on their social networking profiles; you probably don't want your children exposing themselves in this fashion.

You also need to warn your kids that not everyone on Facebook or Twitter is truly a "friend." They should be circumspect about the information they make public and with whom they communicate. It's also worth noting that kids shouldn't arrange to meet in person strangers who they're "friends" with online; it's not unheard of for unsavory adults to use social networks as a stalking ground.

In other words, teach your kids to be careful. Hanging out on a site like Facebook is normally no more dangerous than hanging out at the mall, but even malls aren't completely safe. Caution and common sense are always called for.

Protecting Yourself

The advice you give to your children regarding social networks also applies to yourself. Think twice before posting personal information or incriminating photographs, and don't broadcast your every move on your profile page. Also, don't automatically accept friend requests from people you don't know.

Most important, don't view Facebook and similar sites as online dating services. Yes, you might meet new friends on these social networks, but use caution about transferring online friendships into the physical world. If you decide to meet an online friend offline, do so in a public place and perhaps with another friend along. Don't put yourself at risk when meeting strangers—and remember that until you get to know them in person, anyone you correspond with online remains a stranger.

THE ABSOLUTE MINIMUM

Here are the key points to remember from this chapter:

- Social networking sites enable you to keep in touch with what your friends and family are doing.

- The largest social networking site today is Facebook, with more than one billion users.

- On Facebook, view your friends' activity in the News Feed and let others know what you're doing by posting your own status updates.

- Pinterest is a popular social network among regular users, a way to share interesting images with friends.

- LinkedIn is a social network for business professionals.

- Twitter is a way to broadcast short text messages to your followers—and to follow others who tweet.

- Whichever social networking sites you use, be smart about the information you post; some personal information is best not made public.

17

VIDEO CHATTING WITH FRIENDS AND FAMILY

Not everyone lives close to family and friends. Even if you do have a close-knit local community, you may miss loved ones when you travel. Just because you're far away, however, doesn't mean that you can't stay in touch—on a face-to-face basis.

When you want to talk to your family members and other loved ones, nothing beats a video call. All you need is a webcam built into or connected to your PC and a service that lets you make face-to-face calls. The three most popular video calling services on the Internet are Skype, Facebook, and Google; they all let you talk via video to the people you love.

Video Chatting with Skype

Skype is a service that enables subscribers to connect with one another over the Internet in real time. You can use Skype to conduct one-on-one text chats, audio conversations, and video chats. You can even use Skype to make Internet-based phone calls from your PC to landlines or mobile phones (for a fee).

To use Skype for video calling, both you and the person you want to talk to must have webcams built into or connected to your PCs. In addition, you both must be connected to the Internet for the duration of the call.

 NOTE Most notebook PCs have webcams built in, which you can use to make video calls with Skype. If your PC doesn't have a built-in webcam, you can purchase and connect an external webcam to make video calls. Webcams are manufactured and sold by Logitech and other companies and connect to your PC via USB. They're inexpensive (as low as $30 or so) and sit on top of your monitor. After you connect it, just smile into the webcam and start talking.

To use Skype, you have to install the free Skype desktop application. This is available from www.skype.com, or by clicking Get Skype on Windows Start (All Apps) menu. After you have the app installed, you can then create your own Skype account. (You can also sign into Skype with your Microsoft account.)

The basic Skype service is free and enables you to make one-on-one voice and video calls to other Skype users. Skype also offers a Premium service, from $2.99/ month, which offers the capability of group video chats with up to 10 participants. You can also use Skype to call landline and mobile (non-Skype) phones, for 2.3 cents/minute; monthly subscriptions are also available if you do a lot of non-Skype calling.

Adding Contacts

Before you call someone with Skype, you have to add that person to your Skype contacts list. Here's how to do it:

1. From within the Skype app, type into the search box (in the top-left column) the actual name or Skype username of the person you want to locate, and then press Enter or click the Search Skype button.

2. When the search results appear, as shown in Figure 17.1, click the name of the person you want to add.

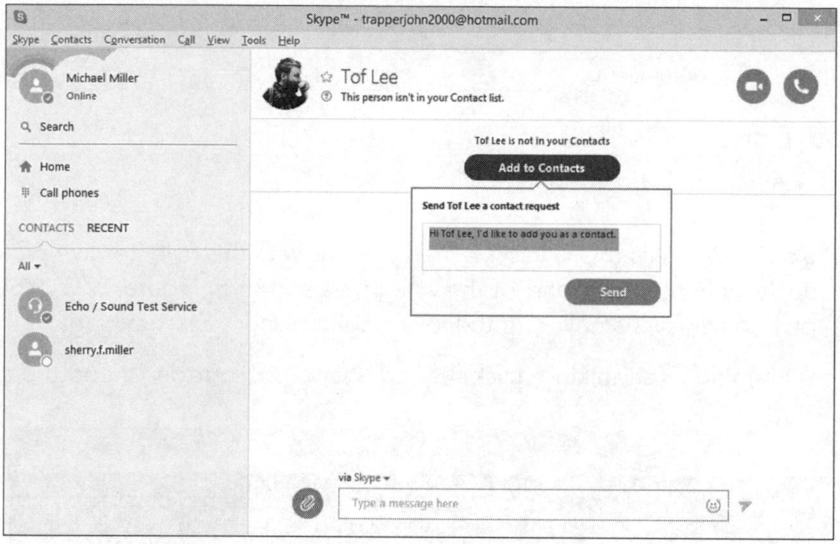

FIGURE 17.1

Adding a Skype contact.

3. Click the Add to Contacts button.

4. You now have to send a contact request to this person; if he accepts your request, you'll be added to each other's contact lists. Enter a short message into the text box, or accept the default message.

5. Click Send.

Making a Video Call

The whole point of Skype is to let you talk to friends and family. You can use Skype to make voice-only calls or to make video calls—which are great for seeing your loved ones, face to face.

If both you and the person you want to talk to have webcams built into or attached to your PCs, and if you're both online at the same time, it's easy to use Skype to initiate a one-to-one video call. Follow these steps:

1. From within the Skype app, scroll to the People section, and click the name of the person you want to call. (People who are online and ready to chat have green dots next to their names.)

2. Click the Video Call (camera) button at the top-right corner of the window, as shown in Figure 17.2. (To make a voice call, click the Call or telephone button instead.)

FIGURE 17.2

Click the Camera button to video call this person.

3. Skype now calls this person. When she answers the call, her live picture appears in the main part of the screen, as shown in Figure 17.3. (Your live picture appears smaller, in the lower-right corner.) Start talking!

4. When you finish talking, click the red "hang up" button to end the call.

FIGURE 17.3

A Skype video call, in progress.

Video Chatting in Facebook

If you're on Facebook, you also have video chat available to you through that social network. You can video chat with any of your Facebook friends, as long as they're online and have webcams.

 NOTE Interestingly, Facebook's video chat feature is powered by Skype. In fact, you can connect your Facebook and Skype accounts so that your Facebook friends appear as Skype contacts.

When you want to chat with someone on Facebook, open your web browser, log in to your Facebook account, and follow these steps:

1. Click the Chat gadget at the bottom-right corner of any Facebook page to display the full Chat panel.

2. Click the name of the friend you want to chat with to open an individual Chat panel with the selected friend.

3. If your friend has a webcam and is available to chat, you see a camera icon at the top of the Chat panel, as shown in Figure 17.4. Click this Start a Video Call button to initiate the video chat.

Click to start video chat

● Tom French

Tom called you.

about a minute ago

Hello Tom

Hi Mike

You up for a video call?

Sure. Give me a minute

FIGURE 17.4

Getting ready to video chat on Facebook.

4. When your friend answers the call, Facebook displays the video chat window. Your friend appears in the main part of the window; your picture is in a smaller window at the top left. All you have to do is talk.

5. When you're ready to close the chat, hover over the chat window, and then click the X at the top-right corner.

NOTE   The first time you use Facebook's video chat, you are prompted to download and install the necessary background chat applet on your computer. Follow the onscreen instructions to do so.

Video Chatting in Google Hangouts

Not to be outdone by Microsoft (which owns Skype) and Facebook, tech giant Google also offers video chatting. Google Hangouts are real-time video chats you can participate in either one-on-one or with a group of people.

Google Hangouts are part of the Google+ social network. We didn't talk about Google+ in Chapter 16, "Social Networking with Facebook and Other Social Media," because as a whole it's a lot less popular than Facebook or Twitter. But the Hangouts feature is definitely worth using, even if you need to have a Google+ account to do so.

The good news is that you probably already have a Google+ account and don't know it. That's because Google automatically signs up anyone with a general Google Account to Google+. So it's just a matter of signing onto Google+ with your Google Account and firing up a Hangout from there.

To log into Google Plus, point your web browser at plus.google.com and, if you're not already signed in, sign in with your Google Account. Now you're ready to start a Hangout:

1. Click the Hangouts (quotes) button at the top-right corner of the screen to display the Hangouts panel, shown in Figure 17.5. All your previous Hangouts are listed here.

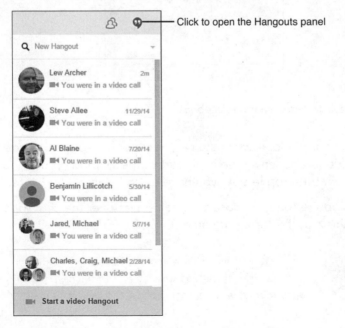

Click to open the Hangouts panel

FIGURE 17.5

Starting a new Hangout.

2. To resume a previous video call, click that Hangout in the list.

3. To start a new video call, click within the New Hangout box at the top of the panel, and enter the name of the person you want to call.

4. Google displays a list of matching names. Click a name to select that person.

5. Repeat steps 3 and 4 to add other people to this video call.

6. Click the Video Call button.

7. A new Hangouts window opens on your desktop, and Google calls the person or people you selected. When your friend answers the call, his picture appears large in the Hangout window, as shown in Figure 17.6. Your picture appears smaller, at the bottom. Start chatting.

8. To exit the Hangout, click the Leave Call button at the top of the window.

FIGURE 17.6

Video chatting in a Google Hangout.

THE ABSOLUTE MINIMUM

Here are the key points to remember from this chapter:

- If you have a webcam built into or connected to your PC, you can video chat with friends and family members over the Internet.

- The three most popular video calling services are Skype, Facebook, and Google Hangouts.

- Initiating a video call is as simple as selecting the other person's name for a list and inviting him to chat.

18

USING APPLICATIONS ON THE DESKTOP

When you want to do something on your computer, you need to use the appropriate applications. *Applications*—more commonly called *apps*—are software programs that perform one or more functions. Some apps are work-related; others provide useful information; still others are more entertaining in nature. But whatever it is you want to do, you need to launch the right app.

Managing Applications in Windows 10

You can run all sorts of applications in Windows. These include apps developed by Microsoft and by third-party software companies. We'll learn more about purchasing new apps in Chapter 19, "Finding and Installing New Applications;" for now, let's focus on finding, launching, and managing those apps from within Windows.

Finding Installed Apps

Each new application you install on your computer should automatically place a reference to itself on the Start menu. To browse through all installed apps, follow these steps:

1. Click the Start button to display the Start menu.

2. Click All Apps.

3. This displays a list of all the apps installed on your computer, as shown in Figure 18.1. Most of these apps are listed alphabetically; some are organized into folders by product or company name.

4. Click an app to open it.

FIGURE 18.1

Browsing through all installed apps on the Start menu.

If you have a lot of apps installed on your PC, browsing in this fashion might be cumbersome. You can instead search for specific apps, using the Cortana virtual personal assistant. Follow these steps:

1. Click within the Cortana search (Ask Me Anything) box and start typing the name of the app you're looking for.

2. As you type, Cortana Windows suggests apps (and other items) that match your query, as shown in Figure 18.2. If the app you want is listed here, click it to launch it.

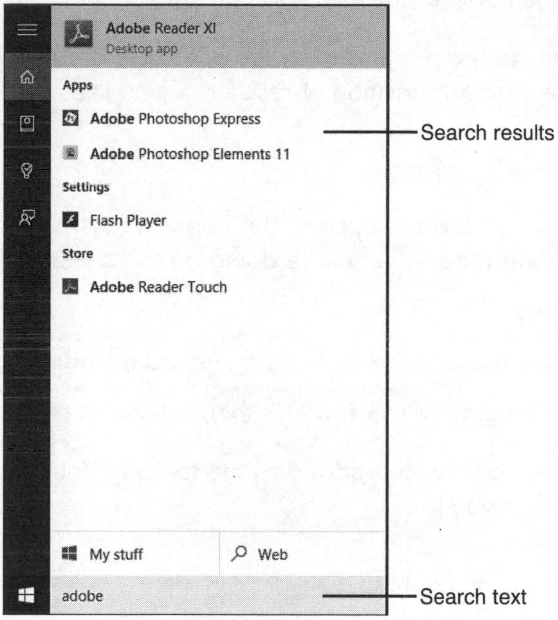

FIGURE 18.2

Searching for apps with Cortana.

3. If Cortana doesn't suggest the app you want, finish entering your query, and then click or tap the magnifying glass button to start the search.

Cortana now displays apps, files, and web pages that match your query. Click or tap an app to launch it.

Pinning Apps to the Start Menu

You might find that it's easier to launch a frequently used app by adding it to the Windows Start menu—what's known as "pinning" the app. When you pin an app to the Start menu, you create a tile for the app; you can click or tap the tile to launch the app.

To pin an app to the Start menu, follow these steps:

1. From the Start menu, click All Apps and scroll to the app you want to pin.

2. Right-click the name of the app and then select Pin to Start.

A tile for the selected app is added to the right side of the Start menu. You can then drag it to a different position or resize it, if you like.

Pinning Apps to the Taskbar

You can also pin your favorite apps to the Windows taskbar. This way they can be easily accessed no matter what you're doing on the desktop.

Follow these steps:

1. From the Start menu, click All Apps and scroll to the app you want to pin.

2. Right-click the name of the app and then select Pin to Taskbar.

An icon for the selected app is added to the taskbar. You can then drag it to a different position, if you like.

Adding App Shortcuts to the Desktop

You can also add shortcuts to your favorite apps directly to the Windows desktop. These shortcuts appear as small icons on the desktop.

To create a desktop shortcut, follow these steps:

1. Click the Show Desktop button at the far right side of the taskbar to minimize all windows on the desktop.

2. From the Start menu, click All Apps and scroll to the app you want to add to the desktop.

3. Click and drag the app from the Start menu onto the desktop.

The menu item remains on the Start menu, but a shortcut to that item is placed on the desktop. (This shortcut may be labeled Shortcut or Copy, or just have the name of the app.) You can then drag the shortcut to whatever position you want on the desktop.

Working with Applications

Most of the software programs that you purchase in a retail store or online are traditional desktop applications, designed to run both on Windows 10 and on older versions of Windows. These include popular programs such as Microsoft Word (and the entire Office suite), Adobe Photoshop Elements, and even Apple's iTunes media player.

These traditional desktop applications share many onscreen elements, so if you know how to use one program, you can probably use others. We'll look at the more common elements next.

Using Menus

Many software apps use a set of pull-down *menus* to store all the commands and operations you can perform. The menus are aligned across the top of the window, just below the title bar, in what is called a *menu bar*.

You open (or pull down) a menu by clicking the menu's name with your mouse. The full menu then appears just below the menu bar, as shown in Figure 18.3. You activate a command or select a menu item by clicking it with your mouse.

Untitled - Notepad				
File	Edit	Format	View	Help

New	Ctrl+N
Open...	Ctrl+O
Save	Ctrl+S
Save As...	
Page Setup...	
Print...	Ctrl+P
Exit	

FIGURE 18.3

Navigating the menu system in the Notepad app.

Some menu items have a little black arrow to the right of the label. This indicates that additional choices are available, displayed on a *submenu*. Click the menu item or the arrow to display the submenu.

 TIP   If an item in a menu, toolbar, or dialog box is dimmed (or grayed), that means it isn't available for the current task.

Other menu items have three little dots (called an ellipsis) to the right of the label. This indicates that additional choices are available, displayed in a dialog box. Click the menu item to display the dialog box.

The nice thing is, after you get the hang of this menu thing in one program, the menus should be similar in all the other programs you use. For example, many apps have a File menu that, when clicked, displays a pull-down menu of common file-oriented operations. Although each program has menus and menu items specific to its own needs, these common menus make it easy to get up and running when you install new software programs on your system.

Using Toolbars and Ribbons

Some apps put the most frequently used operations on one or more *toolbars*, typically located just below the menu bar. (Figure 18.4 shows a typical toolbar.) A toolbar looks like a row of buttons, each with a small picture (called an *icon*) and maybe a bit of text. You activate the associated command or operation by clicking the button with your mouse.

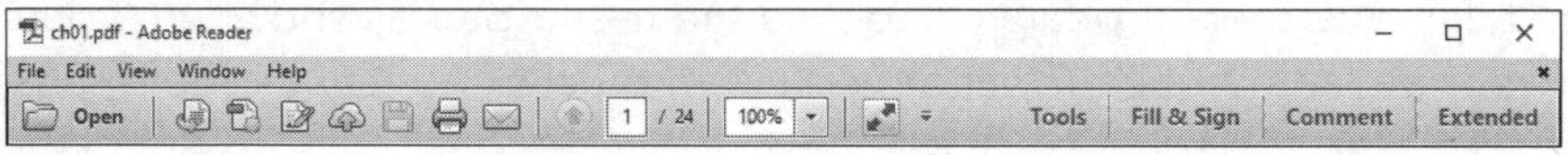

FIGURE 18.4

A typical toolbar in Adobe Reader app.

TIP If the toolbar is too long to display fully on your screen, you see a right arrow at the far-right side of the toolbar. Click this arrow to display the buttons that aren't currently visible.

Other programs substitute a *Ribbon* for the toolbar. For example, all the apps in Microsoft Office have Ribbons that contain buttons or controls for the most-used operations. As you can see in Figure 18.5, each Ribbon has different tabs, each containing a unique collection of buttons. Click the tab to see the Ribbon buttons for that particular type of operation.

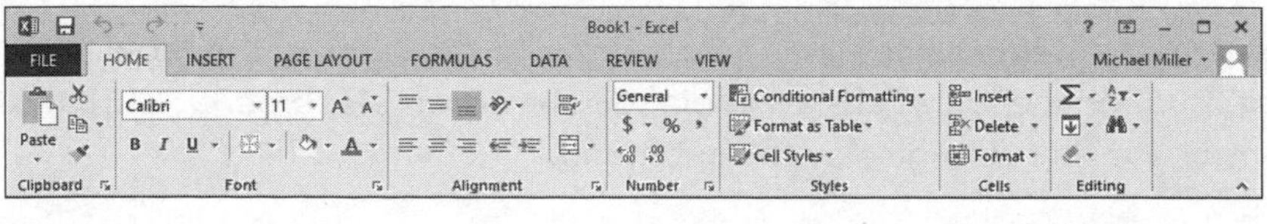

FIGURE 18.5

A Ribbon with tabs for different types of operations in Microsoft Excel.

TIP   If you're not sure which button does what on a toolbar or Ribbon, you can mouse over the button to display a ToolTip. A *ToolTip* is a small text box that displays the button's label or other useful information.

Closing an Open App

When you're working with a desktop app, you should close it when you're done. The easiest way to do this is to click the X at the top-right corner of the window, as shown in Figure 18.6. You might also pull down the app's File menu and select Exit, or click the File tab and click Exit from there.

FIGURE 18.6

Click the X to close the app.

Working with Universal Apps

In addition to traditional desktop apps, Microsoft introduced what it now calls Universal apps. These apps are subtly different from older software programs.

 NOTE   Universal is the latest name for what Microsoft has variously called Metro, Modern, and Windows Store apps. (They also call them Windows apps.)

In Windows 8 and 8.1, these apps ran full-screen, not on the desktop, and were designed for touch-first operation; although, you could still use them with a mouse and keyboard. With Windows 10, however, Microsoft enabled these apps to run on the traditional desktop, in normal windows and with better optimization for a mouse and keyboard. That means you can run these apps in their own windows and operate them with your computer's mouse and keyboard; although, touch still works just fine if you have a touch-enabled display.

Many of these Universal apps require you to configure some basic options for optimal operation. For example, in the Weather app that comes bundled with Windows 10, you need to select your current location so it can deliver the proper weather reports; in the News app, you can select what news categories and sources you want to read.

To configure a Universal app, click the App Commands button at the top-left corner of the window and select Settings. This opens a Settings panel for that app, which should contain all the settings you need to configure things. (Figure 18.7 shows the Settings panel for the Windows Weather app.)

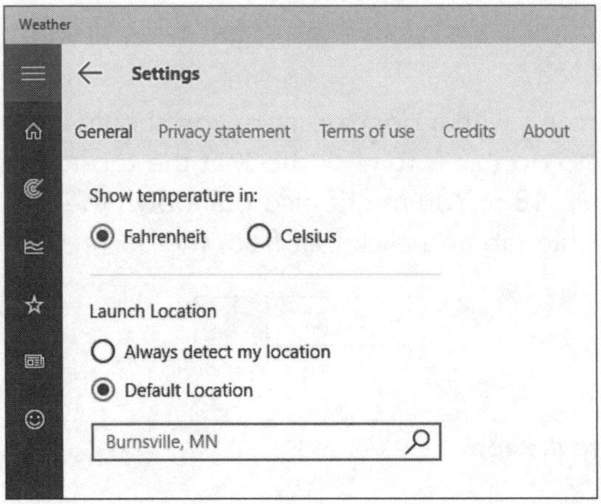

FIGURE 18.7

Configuring the Windows Weather app.

Exploring Windows 10's Built-In Apps and Utilities

Windows 10 comes with a variety of Universal apps you can start using as soon as you log onto your system. Table 18.1 details these apps.

TABLE 18.1 Windows 10 Apps

Name	Description
Alarms & Clock	Functions as an alarm clock, timer, and stopwatch.
Calculator	Functions as both a standard and a scientific calculator and offers popular conversions of various measures.
Calendar	Manages schedules and appointments.
Camera	Controls your PC's webcam (if it has one) to take still photos and videos.
Get Skype	Download the Skype app, enabling video and voice calling over the Internet.
Groove Music	Plays music stored on your PC and downloads new music from the Web.
Mail	Sends and receives email.
Maps	Displays street maps and driving directions.
Microsoft Edge	Microsoft's web browser.
Money	Serves as a hub for financial news and information.

Name	Description
Movies & TV	Enables you to view movies and TV shows from the Web or view your own videos stored on your PC.
News	Displays the latest news headlines; customizable to your personal news preferences.
OneDrive	Cloud-based document storage and online apps.
People	Serves as a contact manager program and consolidates posts from all your friends across multiple social networks.
Photos	Displays and edits digital photos stored on your PC.
Reading List	Lets you bookmark web content for later reading.
Scan	Manages document and photo scanning (if you have a scanner connected to your PC).
Sports	Displays the latest sports headlines and scores; customizable for your favorite sports and teams.
Store	Accesses the Windows Store so you can purchase and download new Universal apps.
Weather	Displays local weather conditions and forecasts.
Xbox	Offers access to various gaming related features and connects to your Xbox live account, enabling you to interact with your Xbox One game console, including streaming Xbox One games to your Windows 10 computer.

In addition, Windows 10 includes a number of apps (dubbed *accessories*) that add extra functionality to the basic operating system. Most of these apps run on the traditional desktop; Table 18.2 details these accessory programs.

TABLE 18.2 Windows 10 Accessories

Name	Description
Character Map	Enables you to insert all manner of special characters into your word processing and other documents.
Math Input Panel	Enables you to create handwritten equations (on a tablet or touchscreen PC) that are converted into digital format.
Notepad	Serves as a basic word processor.
Paint	Serves as a basic illustration/coloring tool.
Remote Desktop Connection	Enables you to remotely control other PCs as if you were using them directly—great for accessing your home PC when you're on the road.
Snipping Tool	Enables you to take snapshots of the current computer screen.
Steps Recorder	Typically used for troubleshooting system problems; records a series of screenshots used in performing a given operation.
Sticky Notes	Enables you to create virtual sticky notes on the traditional desktop.
Windows Fax and Scan	Enables you to send and receive faxes, as well as scan printed documents into digital files.

TABLE 18.2 Continued

Name	Description
Windows Journal	Enables you to create handwritten notes (on a tablet or touchscreen PC) that are converted into digital format.
Windows Media Player	Serves as a full-featured music and video player.
WordPad	Offers a slightly more fully featured word processor than Notepad (but still not as fully featured as Microsoft Word).
XPS Viewer	Enables you to view XPS-format files.

If you have difficulty seeing what's on the computer screen or typing on a traditional keyboard, Windows 10 includes four useful utilities for improved ease of access. Table 18.3 details these utility programs.

TABLE 18.3 Windows 10 Ease of Access Utilities

Name	Description
Magnifier	Enlarges all or part of the screen for the visually impaired.
Narrator	"Reads" onscreen text out loud for the visually impaired.
On-Screen Keyboard	Displays a fully functioning onscreen keyboard, like the one shown in Figure 18.8. It's ideal for tablets or other touchscreen devices without a traditional keyboard.
Windows Speech Recognition	Converts speech to digital text, which is ideal for the visually impaired.

FIGURE 18.8

Windows 10's onscreen keyboard—for when tablet users need to type.

Finally, Windows 10 includes a number of utility programs that help you better manage your computer and the Windows environment. Table 18.4 details these system utilities.

TABLE 18.4 Windows 10 System Utilities

Name	Description
Command Prompt	Opens a "DOS window" with a prompt where you can enter system commands.
Control Panel	Enables you to configure various Windows system settings.
Default Programs	Enables you to select which programs Windows uses by default to open specific types of files.
File Explorer	Enables you to manage files on your system.
Help and Support	Accesses Windows 10's help system.
This PC	Opens File Explorer with This PC selected, which enables you to access the different devices connected to your computer. You can then drill down to the folders, subfolders, and files stored on each device.
Run	Displays the Run box, which you can use to open programs directly (by entering their program name or filename).
Task Manager	Displays the Task Manager, which details current system resource usage and enables you to close frozen programs.
Windows Defender	Installed on PCs that do not have other malware protection options; protects your system against computer viruses and spyware.
Windows PowerShell	For developers, an environment for creating scripts and batch files.

To display all available apps and utilities, open the Start menu and select All Apps. This displays a list of all apps and utilities installed on your system.

Exploring Windows 10's Universal Apps

To give you a quick idea of how some of Windows 10 built-in apps work, let's take a quick look at some of the more popular Universal apps—what they do and how they work.

Weather

Windows 10's Weather app is one of the better-looking apps available. It's also quite useful.

The functionality starts before you ever launch the app. If you have this app pinned to the Start menu, its tile displays current weather conditions, "live" right on the Start menu. (Make the tile larger to display more information.) Click or tap the tile to launch the app.

Figure 18.9 shows what the Weather app itself looks like. The background image represents current conditions; for example, a sunny spring day is represented by a beautiful image of fresh leaves in the sunlight. Current conditions are on the left—temperature, wind, humidity, and the like. The rest of the screen is devoted to a 5-day forecast.

FIGURE 18.9

Viewing current conditions and a 5-day forecast in the Weather app.

Scroll right to view additional weather information, including an hourly forecast, various weather maps, and a graph for historical weather in your location. Click any item to view it.

Maps

The Windows 10 Maps app lets you create street maps and driving directions. It's based on Bing Maps, which is Microsoft's web-based mapping service.

The first thing you see when you launch the Maps app is a street map of your current location, with controls at the left and right side of the screen, as shown in Figure 18.10. (You can also display a local street map by clicking the Show My Location button, or by pressing Ctrl+Home.)

FIGURE 18.10

Viewing a street map with the Maps app.

You can click and drag your mouse to move the map in any direction. You can zoom in and out of the map by using the + and - zoom controls at the right. On a touchscreen device, you can zoom out by pinching the screen with your fingers, or you can zoom in by expanding your fingers on the screen.

To show current traffic conditions (green is smooth flowing; yellow and red, less so), click the Map Views button and select Traffic. To change from a traditional street map to a satellite map, click the Map Views button and select Aerial. To switch back to the traditional map, click the Map Views button and select Road.

To generate driving directions, click Directions on the left to display the Directions panel. Enter the destination address or location into the second (B) box, and then press Enter. You now see the directions onscreen, as shown in Figure 18.11. Click Go to display turn-by-turn directions.

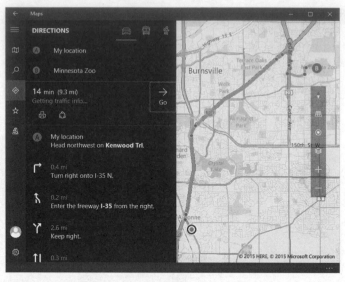

FIGURE 18.11

Generating turn-by-turn driving directions.

News

When you want to read the latest headlines, use the Windows 10 News app. When you launch the app, you see the All page, like the one shown in Figure 18.12. To view specific types of stories, click the appropriate tab (US, World, Crime, and so forth). To read a story, click the story tile.

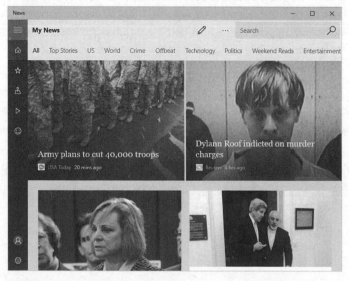

FIGURE 18.12

Viewing today's stories in the Windows 10 News app.

Sports

You can use the Windows 10 Sports app to read the latest headlines from the world of sports, as well as follow your favorite sports and teams. When you launch the Sports app you see the top stories of the day. Click to read a complete story, or scroll down to view more stories, headlines, and videos.

The Sports app makes it easy to follow a particular sport or league (NFL, NBA, MLB, NHA, and so forth). Just click the icon for that sport on the left side of the window, and you see stories, standings, scores, and stats from that league, as shown in Figure 18.13.

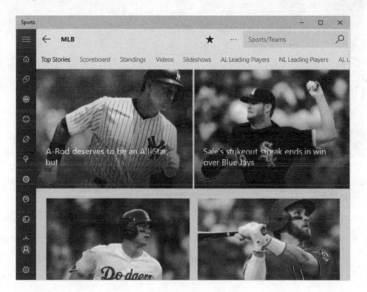

FIGURE 18.13

Viewing Major League Baseball news and stats.

Money

Windows 10's Money app is the perfect way to stay up-to-date on the latest financial news, as well as keep track of your personal investments. Scroll past the top stories of the day to view current market information, or click the Watchlist icon on the left to view your own Watchlist—those stocks you want to track. Click a stock's tile to view more information about that stock, as shown in Figure 18.14.

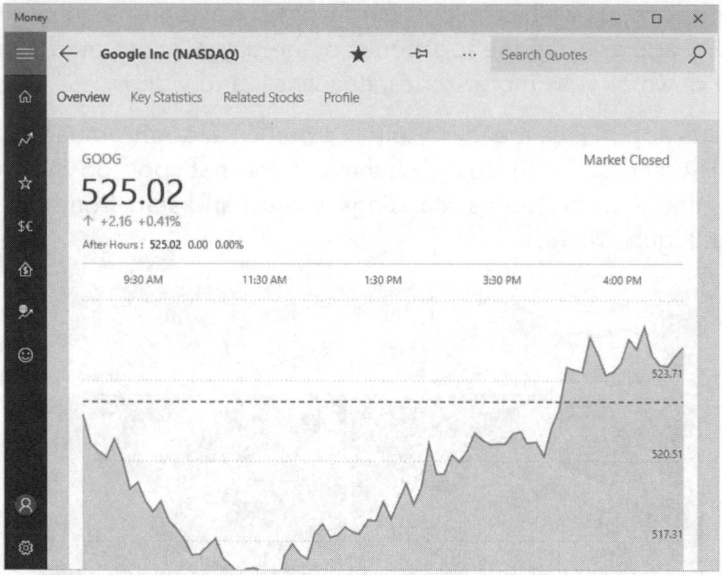

FIGURE 18.14

Viewing detailed stock information in the Windows 10 Money app.

To add a new stock to your Watch List, click the + button in the toolbar. When the Add to Watchlist panel appears, enter the name or symbol of the stock and then press Enter.

Alarms & Clock

The Alarms & Clock app turns your computer into a digital alarm clock. It also includes timer and stopwatch functions.

To set an alarm in the app, click Alarm to enter the alarm function, shown in Figure 18.15, and then click or tap the + button. Enter a name for the alarm and then the time you want the alarm to sound. If you want the alarm to repeat, pull down the Repeats list and select those days you want the alarm to go off. Pull down the Sound list to set the alarm sound, and pull down the Snooze Time list if you want a little extra time to wake up in the morning. Click the Save button to save the alarm.

To use the app's timer function, click Timer. To use the app as a stopwatch, click Stopwatch.

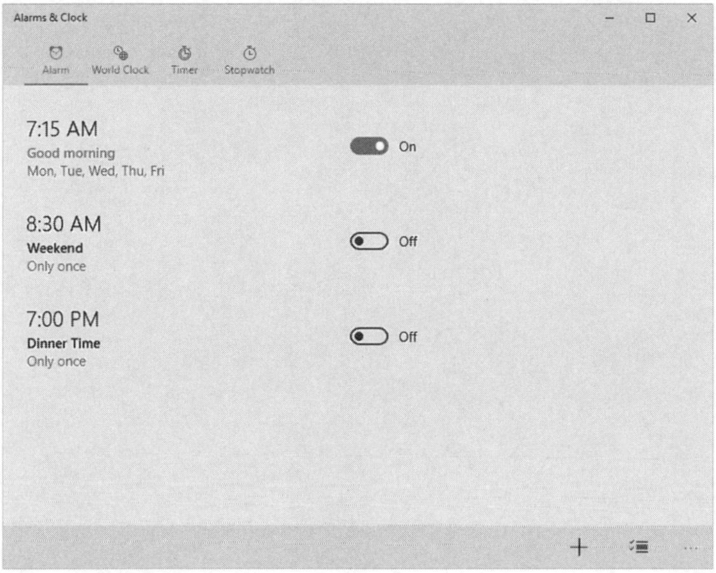

Alarms & Clock   — □ ✕

Alarm   World Clock   Timer   Stopwatch

7:15 AM
Good morning   On
Mon, Tue, Wed, Thu, Fri

8:30 AM
Weekend   Off
Only once

7:00 PM
Dinner Time   Off
Only once

+   ☑   ...

FIGURE 18.15

Setting an alarm in the Alarms & Clock app.

THE ABSOLUTE MINIMUM

Here are the key points to remember from this chapter:

- An application, or app, is a software program that performs a specific function.

- Browse all installed apps by opening the Start menu and selecting All Apps.

- You can also search for apps by using the Cortana virtual personal assistant.

- Apps can be pinned to the Start menu or taskbar, or have shortcuts added to the desktop.

- To switch between open apps, press Alt+Tab.

- Most apps use some combination of pull-down menus, toolbars, and ribbons.

- Microsoft includes a variety of Universal and traditional apps and utilities in Windows 10 that offer a variety of useful functions.

19

FINDING AND INSTALLING NEW APPS

Your new computer system probably came with a bunch of programs preinstalled on its hard disk. Some of these are the apps that come with Windows 10 that we discussed in the previous chapter, some are preview or limited-use versions provided by the PC manufacturer (included in the hope you'll purchase the full version if you like what you see), and some are real, honest-to-goodness fully functional applications. The more the merrier.

As useful as some of these programs might be, at some point you're going to want to add something new. Maybe you want to install the full version of Microsoft Office or purchase a full-featured photo editing program, such as Adobe Photoshop Elements. Maybe you want to add some educational apps for the kids or a productivity program for yourself. Maybe you just want to play some new computer games.

Whatever type of app you're considering, installing it on your computer system is easy. In fact, you might find just what you're looking for in the Microsoft Windows Store. Wherever you find a new app, however, installing it on your system is relatively easy, as you'll soon discover.

Finding and Installing Apps from the Windows Store

With Windows 8, and continued in Windows 10, Microsoft plunged headfirst into the app model popularized by Apple's iPhone and Google's Android smartphones. In this model, applications are designed specifically for the given operating system and sold through a central "app store." You search or browse the app store for the apps you want and then purchase and download them directly to your device.

This new app model is consumer-friendly, especially when it comes to pricing. A traditional computer software program can cost hundreds of dollars, whereas most apps cost just a few bucks—and many are free. In addition, you can download and install the apps you want without ever leaving home; you install apps directly from the app store to your device.

Opening the Windows Store

Along these lines, Microsoft runs its own Windows Store offering Universal apps from a variety of publishers. You access the Windows Store from the Start menu.

As you can see in Figure 19.1, the Windows Store offers all manner of free and paid apps. You see a selection of spotlighted apps first (click the right arrow to view more), but you can then scroll down to view other offerings—Picks for You, Top Free Apps, Best-Rated Apps, New and Rising Apps, and the like.

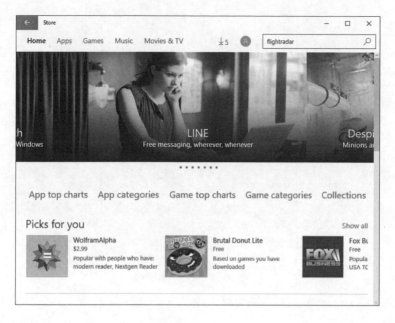

FIGURE 19.1

Shopping for apps in the Windows Store.

In addition, the Windows Store offers the following "departments":

- App Top Charts
- App Categories
- Game Top Charts
- Game Categories
- Collections

Click a department header to view more similar selections.

Browsing the Windows Store

To browse the Windows Store by category, click App Categories. This displays, on the left side of the window, a list of all available app categories, as shown in Figure 19.2. Click a category to view apps within that category.

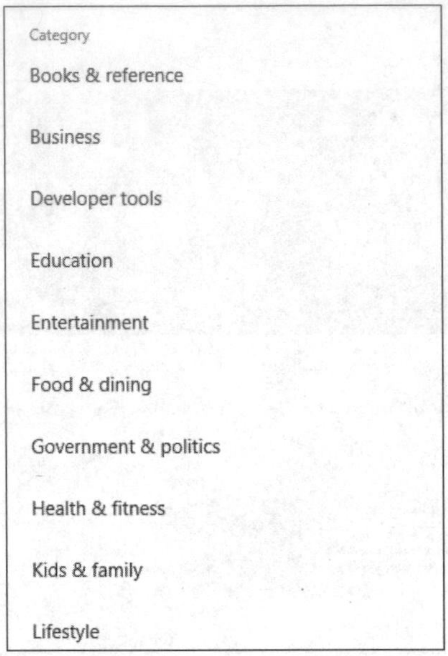

Category

Books & reference

Business

Developer tools

Education

Entertainment

Food & dining

Government & politics

Health & fitness

Kids & family

Lifestyle

FIGURE 19.2

Browsing apps by category.

Within a category, apps are organized by Top Free, New and Rising, Top Grossing, Top Paid, and Best Rated. Click the See All link to view all apps with that description. Apps can then be filtered by price (free or paid) and sorted by noteworthy, newest, lowest price, or highest price.

Searching the Windows Store

If you know the app you're looking for, the easiest way to find it is to use the Store's search function. Just enter the name or description of the app into the search box at the top-right corner of the screen, and press Enter. The app you're looking for should be somewhere on the search results screen.

Downloading an App

When you find an app you want, click or tap it to view the app's page in the Store, like the one shown in Figure 19.3. Scroll right to read more about the app, as well as view consumer reviews.

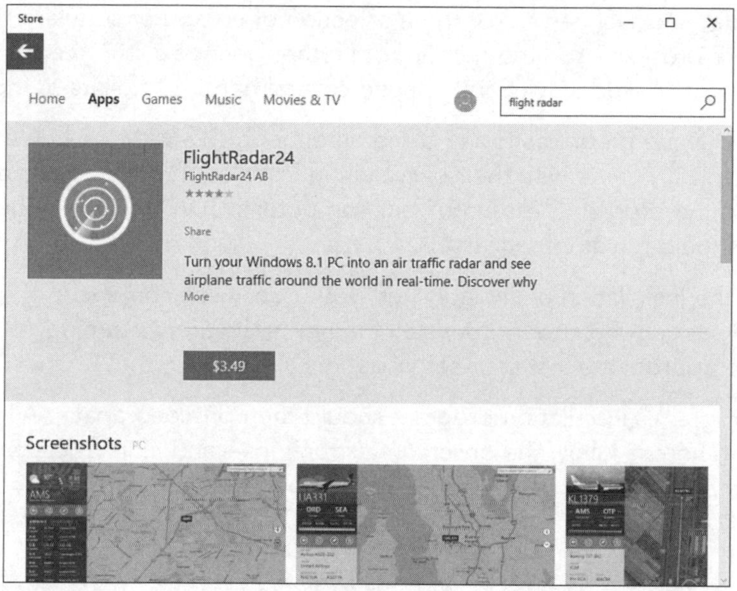

FIGURE 19.3

Getting ready to download and install a new app from the Windows Store.

If it's a free app, click or tap the Free button to download it to your computer. If it's a paid app, click or tap the price button to purchase that app. You'll be prompted for your payment information; then you're good to go.

Your new app will be automatically downloaded and installed to your PC. You'll see a notification pop-up when the installation is complete, and many apps launch automatically after this initial install. Otherwise, look for your new app in the All Apps pane of the Start menu.

Finding and Installing Apps from Your Local Retailer

The majority of apps in the Windows Store are Universal apps, optimized for use with Windows 8, 8.1, and 10. However, there are a great many more traditional software programs available that work just fine with your version of Windows—as well as with older versions, too.

You can find these software programs at just about any consumer electronics store, office store, or computer store. (For that matter, mass merchants such as Target and Walmart also carry a selection of computer software.) Traditional software programs run the gamut from rather generic sub-$10 apps to more sophisticated productivity apps priced several hundred dollars or more.

Most software programs today come on either a CD-ROM or a DVD disc; these disks typically come with their own built-in installation utilities. All you have to do is insert the program's disc into your computer's CD/DVD drive. The installation utility should run automatically.

When the installation utility launches, you usually see some sort of notification window asking if you want to install the new software. Assuming you do, click or tap the appropriate install or setup option.

The program's installation program should then proceed apace. All you have to do from here is follow the onscreen instructions—and, if instructed, reboot your computer at the end of the installation process.

Finding and Installing Apps Online

Nowadays, many software publishers make their products available via download from the Internet. Some users like this because they can get their new programs immediately without having to make a trip to the store.

When you download a program from a major software publisher, the process is generally easy to follow. You probably have to read a page of do's and don'ts, agree to the publisher's licensing agreements, and then click a button to start the download. If you purchase a commercial program online, you also need to provide your credit card information, of course. Then, after you specify where (which folder on your hard disk) you want to save the downloaded file, the download begins.

When the download is complete, you should be notified via an onscreen dialog box. When prompted, choose to run the program you just downloaded. Follow the onscreen instructions from there.

 CAUTION   Limit your software downloads to reputable download sites and software publisher sites. Programs downloaded from unofficial sites might contain computer viruses or spyware, which can damage your computer. Learn more in Chapter 25, "Protecting Your PC from Computer Attacks, Malware, and Spam."

Understanding Cloud Computing Apps

There is another type of app that's becoming increasingly popular. You don't actually install this type of app on your computer; instead, it runs over the Web from what we call the *cloud*.

In essence, the cloud is that nebulous assemblage of computers and servers on the Internet. Cloud-based computing involves storing your files on and running apps from the cloud. The apps aren't located on your PC; they're located in the cloud, and you run them from within Internet Explorer or a similar web browser.

Because of this, cloud apps are sometimes called web-based apps. They're just like traditional software-based apps, except they run over the Internet.

With traditional software applications, you have to install a copy of the application on each computer you own; the more computers you use, the more expensive that gets. Web-based applications, however, are typically free to use. That's always appealing.

Then there's the issue of the documents you create. With traditional software applications, your documents are stored on the computer on which they were created. If you want to edit a work document at home, you have to transfer that document from one computer to another—and then manage all the different "versions" you create.

 TIP Cloud apps are also great for group collaboration. Multiple users from different locations can access the same document over the Internet, in real time.

Document management is different with a web-based application. That's because your documents aren't stored on your computer; instead, they're stored on the Internet, just like the applications are. You can access your web-based documents from any computer, wherever you might be. So it's a lot easier to edit that work document at home or access your home budget while on the road.

Some other advantages of cloud apps are that they can run on any computer at any location, and they don't take up hard disk space. This is especially important if you have a device without traditional hard disk storage, such as a tablet, ultrabook, or smartphone. Just point your web browser to the cloud app and start running—no installation required.

It isn't all positive, however. The primary downside of running cloud apps is that you need a stable Internet connection to do so. If you can't connect to the

Internet, you can't access the cloud, and you can't run any apps. So if you plan on getting work done on your next plane trip, cloud apps might not be the way to go.

For most other uses, however, cloud apps represent a viable alternative to traditional hard disk-based computer programs. Most cloud apps are low cost or free to use, and they offer much the same functionality as their more traditional software cousins.

What types of cloud apps are available? Some of the more popular apps are traditional office apps in the cloud, such as Google Docs, Sheets, and Slides (docs.google.com), and similar apps from Zoho (www.zoho.com). For that matter, Microsoft Office Online (www.office.com) offers free web-based versions of Microsoft's popular Office applications (Word, Excel, PowerPoint, and the like).

But there's more than that out there. So if you're into universal document access and online collaboration, keep an eye open!

THE ABSOLUTE MINIMUM

Here are the key points to remember from this chapter:

- You can purchase, download, and install Universal-style apps from Microsoft's Windows Store.

- Traditional software apps come on either CD or DVD and install automatically when you insert the installation disc into your computer's CD/DVD drive.

- You can download many software apps from the Internet just by clicking a button (and providing your credit card number).

- Web-based or cloud apps don't install on your PC; instead, they run over the Internet within your web browser.

20

DOING OFFICE WORK

To do office work—writing letters and reports, crunching budgets, and creating presentations—you need a particular type of app called an *office suite*. In reality, an office suite is a combination of different programs, each designed to perform a specific task.

The most common office suite components are a *word processor* (for writing letters and memos), a *spreadsheet* (for crunching your numbers), and a *presentation program* (for creating and giving presentations to small and large groups). With these office apps installed on your computer, you're ready to do just about anything you might be asked to do in the workplace.

What kind of office suite should you use? It all depends on how often and for what purposes you'll be using it.

Getting to Know Microsoft Office

The most popular office suite today is Microsoft Office, which comes to you from the same folks who produce Microsoft Windows. Microsoft Office is available as traditional desktop software for purchase, as desktop software available on a subscription plan (kind of like leasing it), and as web-based apps. The web-based version, dubbed Microsoft Office Online, is available for free but isn't as fully featured as the desktop versions.

Microsoft Office contains several productivity applications; which apps are included depends on the version of Office you have. All versions include Word (word processing), Excel (spreadsheet), PowerPoint (presentations), and OneNote (note taking). Some versions also include Outlook (email), Access (database), and Publisher (desktop publishing).

You can learn more about Office at products.office.com. You can even purchase and subscribe to Office there.

Using Office on the Desktop

The version of Office that reigns supreme is the traditional desktop software version—whether purchased outright or leased on a subscription basis. This is a software program—actually, a group of programs—that you install on your computer, either from a physical installation DVD or over the Internet. (The online installation is definitely the most convenient.)

There are several different editions of the Microsoft Office suite, each containing its own unique bundle of programs. Which Office programs you get depends on the edition of Office you have. Table 20.1 details the different editions for the current version, Microsoft Office 2013.

TABLE 20.1 Microsoft Office 2013 Editions

Edition	Applications Included	Description	Price
Office 365 Personal (one PC)	Word Excel PowerPoint OneNote Outlook Access Publisher	Subscription model for a single PC (plus one tablet and one smartphone), apps installed on your PC but downloaded and continuously updated over the Internet, includes 1TB of OneDrive online storage	$69.99/year or $6.99/month subscription

Edition	Applications Included	Description	Price
Office 365 Home (up to five PCs)	Word Excel PowerPoint OneNote Outlook Access Publisher	Subscription model for up to five PCs (plus five tablets and five smartphones), apps installed on your PC but downloaded and continuously updated over the Internet, includes 1TB of OneDrive online storage	$99.99/year or $9.99/month subscription
Office Home and Student 2013	Word Excel PowerPoint OneNote	Traditional software model with no online updates; designed for casual home and student users	$139.99 one-time purchase
Office Home and Business 2013	Word Excel PowerPoint OneNote Outlook	Traditional software model with no online updates; similar to Home and Student but with Outlook added	$219.99 one-time purchase
Office Professional 2013	Word Excel PowerPoint OneNote Outlook Access Publisher	Traditional software model with no online updates; includes full suite of applications	$399.99 one-time purchase

Microsoft is really pushing the Office 365 subscriptions, and I think they're the best deal going. You spend less money upfront, get 1TB (terabyte) of online storage, and end up with software that constantly calls into the mothership to keep itself continuously updated. If you have just a single PC in your house, go with the Office 365 Personal version at $69.99/year. If you have more than one PC, you can't beat the Office 365 Home version, which enables you to install the software on up to five PCs for just $99.99/year.

 NOTE Many new PCs come with a trial version of Office preinstalled. You can use this version for 90 days at no charge; at that point, you have the option of purchasing the software or having the trial version deactivated.

Using Office Online

If you don't want to go to all the trouble of purchasing and installing an expensive piece of software, you can still use Microsoft Office Online. This is a web-based version of Microsoft Office that can run on any computer, over the Internet.

Microsoft Office Online is free, which is always appealing. The individual apps, however, don't come with all the sophisticated functionality of the software versions, so there's a trade-off. Bottom line: If you're not a power user, you might get by with the free apps in Office Online instead of purchasing and installing the traditional software version of Office.

You access Office Online from within Internet Explorer or any other web browser. Launch your web browser and go to www.office.com, as shown in Figure 20.1. Click an app tile to launch that online app.

FIGURE 20.1

The web-based applications in Microsoft Office Online.

The home page for each app lists your most recently created files in the navigation pane on the left, as shown in Figure 20.2. You can open an existing file or click the appropriate tile to create a new file.

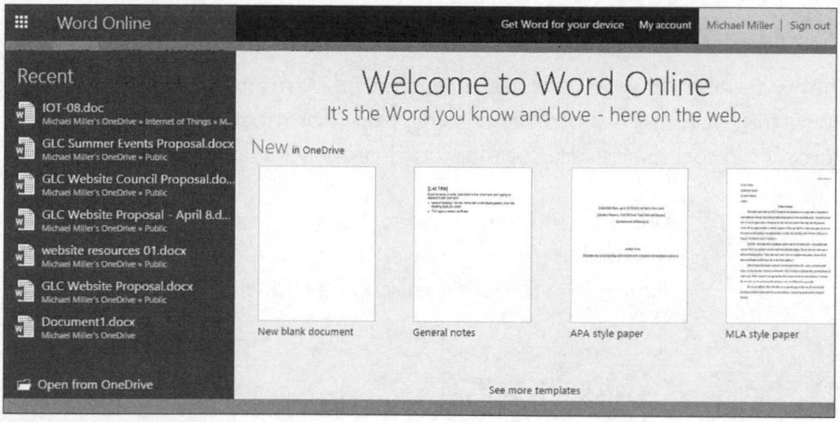

FIGURE 20.2

Using Microsoft Word Online.

TIP   You can also open and edit existing documents from Microsoft OneDrive. Go to www.onedrive.com to view your online files; click a file to open it in the corresponding online app.

Which Version of Office Should You Use?

Given the choice of a free web-based version of Microsoft Office or a somewhat expensive desktop version, many users choose the web-based Office Online. There's a good argument for that—free is always more attractive than paid.

For Office Online, what you get is kind of a basic version of the full-featured Office you can buy in a store. For most users, Office Online offers all the features they need; it's great for doing letters and memos, home budgets and planning, and even basic presentations. There's the added plus that you can run Office Online on any Windows-based PC or tablet without having to install anything. Getting up and running is as quick and easy as clicking a few buttons.

If your needs are more sophisticated, however, a paid desktop version of Office is the way to go. There are so many advanced functions in the Office software that it's unlikely you'll ever use them all. But if your work involves creating brochures or newsletters, fancy comparison spreadsheets, or sophisticated presentations with animations and such, you have to go the Office software route; you just can't do some of this stuff in the web-based version.

Word Processing with Microsoft Word Online

When you want to write a letter, fire off a quick memo, create a report, or create a newsletter, you use a word processing app. For most computer users, that means Microsoft Word, the most popular word processing program of the past decade.

 NOTE In these next sections we examine the online versions of Word, Excel, and PowerPoint. The desktop versions differ slightly in terms of layout and functionality.

Exploring the Word Workspace

Before we get started, let's take a quick tour of the Word workspace—so you know what's what and what's where.

If you use the web-based version of Word, dubbed Word Online, you see the screen shown in Figure 20.3. At the top of the screen is the Ribbon, which provides all the buttons and controls you need to create and edit a document. Different tabs on the Ribbon display different collections of functions; click a tab, such as File, Home, Insert, or View, to access commands associated with that particular operation.

Beneath the Ribbon is the document itself. Begin typing at the cursor.

FIGURE 20.3

The Word Online workspace—all functions are on the Ribbon.

Click a tab on the Ribbon to access all the related commands. For example, the File tab contains basic file opening and saving operations; the Home tab contains most of the editing and formatting functions you use on a daily basis; the Insert tab contains commands to add images and tables to a document; and the View tab contains commands that enable you to change how a document is viewed or displayed.

 TIP If you're not sure just what button on a Ribbon or toolbar does what, you're not alone—those little graphics are sometimes difficult to decipher. To display the name of any specific button, just hover your cursor over the button until the descriptive *ScreenTip* appears.

Working with Documents

Anything you create with Word is called a *document*. A document is nothing more than a computer file that can be copied, moved, and deleted—or edited—from within Word.

To create a new document with Word Online, go to the main Word Online page, and click one of the templates on the right for the type of document you want to create. If you don't want to use one of these templates, click New Blank Document.

Word now opens a new blank document, ready for editing. You'll want to give this document a name by clicking the File tab and then clicking Save As.

Opening an existing document is just as easy. Just go to the main Word Online page, scroll through the list of recent documents on the left, and then click the one you want to open.

After you make changes to a document, you'll want to save those changes. With the desktop versions of Word, you have to save your changes manually. (Click File, Save.) With Word online, however, the app saves your work automatically, in the cloud. You don't have to manually save a thing.

Entering Text

You enter text in a Word document at the *insertion point*, which appears onscreen as a blinking cursor. When you start typing on your keyboard, the new text is added at the insertion point.

You move the insertion point with your mouse by clicking a new position in your text. You move the insertion point with your keyboard by using your keyboard's arrow keys.

Editing Text

After you enter your text, it's time to edit. With Word you can delete, cut, copy, and paste text—or graphics—to and from anywhere in your document, or between documents.

Before you can edit text, though, you have to *select* the text to edit. The easiest way to select text is with your mouse; just hold down your mouse button and drag the cursor over the text you want to select. You also can select text using your keyboard; use the Shift key—in combination with other keys—to highlight blocks of text. For example, Shift+left arrow selects one character to the left; Shift+End selects all text to the end of the current line.

Any text you select appears as white text against a black highlight. After you select a block of text, you can then edit it in a number of ways, as detailed in Table 20.2.

TABLE 20.2 Word Editing Operations

Operation	Keystroke
Delete	Del
Copy	Ctrl+Ins or Ctrl+C
Cut	Shift+Del or Ctrl+X
Paste	Shift+Ins or Ctrl+V

Formatting Text

After your text is entered and edited, you can use Word's numerous formatting options to add some pizzazz to your document. Fortunately, formatting text is easy.

When you want to format your text, select the Home tab on the Ribbon. This tab includes buttons for bold, italic, and underline, as well as font, font size, and font color. To format a block of text, highlight the text, and then click the desired format button.

Checking Spelling and Grammar

If you're not a great speller, you'll appreciate Word's automatic spell checking. You can see it right onscreen; just deliberately misspell a word, and you see a squiggly red line under the misspelling. That's Word telling you you've made a spelling error.

When you see that squiggly red line, position your cursor on top of the misspelled word, and then right-click your mouse. Word displays a pop-up menu with its suggestions for spelling corrections. You can choose a replacement word from the list or return to your document and manually change the misspelling.

Sometimes Word meets a word it doesn't recognize, even though the word is spelled correctly. In these instances, you can add the new word to Word's spelling dictionary by right-clicking the word and selecting Add from the pop-up menu.

Printing Your Document

When you finish editing your document, you can instruct Word to send a copy to your printer. To print a document, select the File tab, click Print, and then click the Print button. You now see the Print page or dialog box for your web browser; select the printer you want to use, and then click the Print button.

Number Crunching with Microsoft Excel

When you're on your computer and want to crunch some numbers, you use a program called a *spreadsheet*. Microsoft Excel is the spreadsheet program in the Microsoft Office suite, and it's available in both web-based and traditional desktop versions.

Exploring the Excel Workspace

A spreadsheet is nothing more than a giant list. Your list can contain just about any type of data you can think of—text, numbers, and even dates. You can take any of the numbers on your list and use them to calculate new numbers. You can sort the items on your list, pretty them up, and print the important points in a report. You can even graph your numbers in a pie, line, or bar chart!

In a spreadsheet, everything is stored in little boxes called *cells*. Your spreadsheet is divided into a lot of these cells, each located in a specific location on a giant grid made of *rows* and *columns*. Each cell represents the intersection of a particular row and column.

As you can see in Figure 20.4, each column has an alphabetic label (A, B, C, and so on). Each row, however, has a numeric label (1, 2, 3, and so on). The location of each cell is the combination of its column and row locations. For example, the cell in the upper-left corner of the spreadsheet is in column A and row 1; therefore, its location is signified as A1. The cell to the right of it is B1, and the cell below A1 is A2.

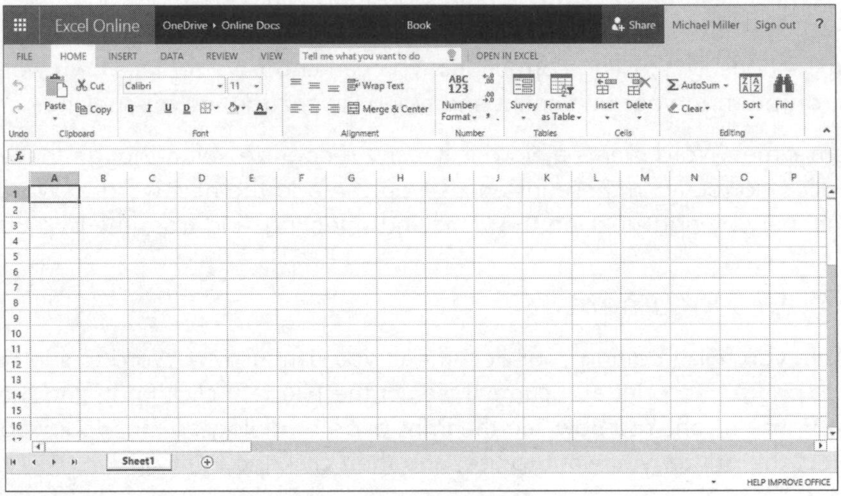

FIGURE 20.4

An Excel spreadsheet—divided into many rows and columns.

Entering Data

Entering text or numbers into a spreadsheet is easy. Just remember that data is entered into each cell individually—then you can fill up a spreadsheet with hundreds or thousands of cells filled with their own data.

To enter data into a specific cell, follow these steps:

1. Select the cell you want to enter data into.

2. Type your text or numbers into the cell; what you type is echoed in the Formula bar at the top of the screen.

3. When you finish typing data into the cell, press Enter.

TIP You can enter numbers and text directly into the selected cell or into the Formula bar at the top of the spreadsheet. The Formula bar echoes the contents of the active cell.

Inserting and Deleting Rows and Columns

Sometimes you need to go back to an existing spreadsheet and insert some new information.

To insert a new row or column in the middle of your spreadsheet, follow these steps:

1. Click the row or column header *after* where you want to make the insertion.

2. Select the Home tab on the Ribbon, and click the down arrow below the Insert button; then select either Insert Rows or Insert Columns.

Excel now inserts a new row or column either above or to the left of the row or column you selected.

To delete an existing row or column, follow these steps:

1. Click the header for the row or column you want to delete.

2. Select the Home tab on the Ribbon, and click the Delete button.

The row or column you selected is deleted, and all other rows or columns move up or over to fill the space.

Adjusting Column Width

If the data you enter into a cell is too long, you see only the first part of that data—there'll be a bit to the right that looks cut off. It's not cut off, of course; it just can't be seen because it's longer than the current column is wide.

You can fix this problem by adjusting the column width. Wider columns allow more data to be shown; with narrow columns you can display more columns per page.

To change the column width, move your cursor to the column header, and position it on the dividing line on the right side of the column you want to adjust. When the cursor changes shape, click the left button on your mouse and drag the column divider to the right (to make a wider column) or to the left (to make a smaller column). Release the mouse button when the column is the desired width.

 TIP To make a column the exact width for the longest amount of data entered, position your cursor over the dividing line to the right of the column header, and double-click your mouse. This makes the column width automatically "fit" your current data.

Calculating with Formulas

Excel enables you to enter just about any type of algebraic formula into any cell. You can use these formulas to add, subtract, multiply, divide, and perform any nested combination of those operations.

Excel knows that you're entering a formula when you type an equal sign (**=**) into any cell. You start your formula with the equal sign and enter your operations *after* the equal sign.

For example, if you want to add 1 plus 2, enter this formula into a cell: **=1+2**. When you press Enter, the formula disappears from the cell—and the result, or *value*, displays.

Table 20.3 shows the algebraic operators you can use in Excel formulas.

TABLE 20.3   Excel Operators

Operation	Operator
Add	+
Subtract	−
Multiply	*
Divide	/

So if you want to multiply 10 by 5, enter **=10*5**. If you want to divide 10 by 5, enter **=10/5**.

Including Other Cells in a Formula

If all you're doing is adding and subtracting numbers, you might as well use a calculator. Where a spreadsheet becomes truly useful is when you use it to perform operations based on the contents of specific cells.

To perform calculations using values from cells in your spreadsheet, you enter the cell location into the formula. For example, if you want to add cells A1 and A2, enter this formula: **=A1+A2**. And if the numbers in either cell A1 or A2 change, the total automatically changes, as well.

An even easier way to perform operations involving spreadsheet cells is to select them with your mouse while you're entering the formula. To do this, follow these steps:

1. Select the cell that will contain the formula.

2. Type **=**.

3. Click the first cell you want to include in your formula; that cell location is automatically entered in your formula.

4. Type an algebraic operator, such as +, −, *, or /.

5. Click the second cell you want to include in your formula.

6. Repeat steps 4 and 5 to include other cells in your formula.

7. Press Enter when your formula is complete.

Quick Addition with AutoSum

The most common operation in any spreadsheet is the addition of a group of numbers. Excel makes summing up a row or column of numbers easy via the AutoSum function.

All you have to do is follow these steps:

1. Select the cell at the end of a row or column of numbers, where you want the total to appear.

2. Select the Home tab on the Ribbon, and click the AutoSum button.

Excel automatically sums all the preceding numbers and places the total in the selected cell.

Excel's AutoSum also includes a few other automatic calculations. When you click the down arrow on the bottom of the AutoSum button, you can perform the following operations:

- **Sum**, which totals the values in the selected cells

- **Average**, which calculates the average of the selected cells

- **Count Numbers**, which counts the number of selected cells

- **Max**, which returns the largest value in the selected cells

- **Min**, which returns the smallest value in the selected cells

 TIP   When you reference consecutive cells in a formula, you can just enter the first and last number of the series separated by a colon. For example, cells A1 through A4 can be entered as A1:A4.

Using Functions

In addition to the basic algebraic operators previously discussed, Excel includes a variety of *functions* that replace the complex steps present in many formulas. For example, if you want to total all the cells in column A, you could enter the formula **=A1+A2+A3+A4**. Or you could use the SUM function, which enables you to sum a column or row of numbers without having to type every cell into the formula. (And when you use AutoSum, it's simply applying the SUM function.)

In short, a function is a type of prebuilt formula.

You enter a function in the following format: **=function(argument)**, where **function** is the name of the function and **argument** is the range of cells or other data you want to calculate. Using the last example, to sum cells A1 through A4, you'd use the following function-based formula: **=sum(A1,A2,A3,A4)**.

Excel includes hundreds of functions. You can access and insert any of Excel's functions by following these steps:

1. Select the cell where you want to insert the function.

2. Select the Home tab on the Ribbon. Then click the down arrow beneath the AutoSum button, and select More Functions.

3. When the Insert Function dialog box appears, pull down the Select a Category list to display the functions of a particular type.

4. Click the function you want to insert.

5. If the function has related arguments, a Function Arguments dialog box displays; enter the arguments and click OK.

6. The function you selected is inserted into the current cell. You can manually enter the cells or numbers into the function's argument.

 TIP   In the desktop version of Excel, you can access more functions directly from the Formula tab on the Ribbon.

Formatting Your Spreadsheet

You don't have to settle for boring-looking spreadsheets. You can format the way the data appears in your spreadsheet—including the format of any numbers you enter.

When you enter a number into a cell, Excel applies what it calls a "general" format to the number—it just displays the number, right-aligned, with no commas or dollar signs. You can, however, select a specific number format to apply to any cells in your spreadsheet that contain numbers.

All of Excel's number formatting options are in the Number section of the Home tab. Click the Dollar Sign button to choose an accounting format, the Percent button to choose a percentage format, the Comma button to choose a comma format, or the General button to choose from all available formats. You can also click the Increase Decimal and Decrease Decimal buttons to move the decimal point left or right.

In addition, you can apply a variety of other formatting options to the contents of your cells. You can make your text bold or italic, change the font type or size, or even add shading or borders to selected cells.

These formatting options are found in the Font and Alignment sections of the Home tab. Just select the cell(s) you want to format; then click the appropriate formatting button.

Creating a Chart

Numbers are fine, but sometimes the story behind the numbers can be better told with a picture. The way you take a picture of numbers is with a *chart*, such as the one shown in Figure 20.5.

FIGURE 20.5

Some numbers are better represented via a chart.

You create a chart based on numbers you've previously entered into your Excel spreadsheet. It works like this:

1. Select the range of cells you want to include in your chart. (If the range has a header row or column, include that row or column when selecting the cells.)

2. Select the Insert tab on the ribbon..

3. In the Charts section of the Insert tab, click the button for the type of chart you want to create.

4. Excel displays a variety of charts within that general category. Select the type of chart you want.

5. When the chart appears in your worksheet, select the Design tab on the Ribbon to edit the chart's type, layout, and style.

Giving Presentations with Microsoft PowerPoint

When you need to present information to a group of people, the hip way to do it is with a PowerPoint presentation. Microsoft PowerPoint is a presentation program—that is, an app you can use to both create and give presentations.

If you work in an office, you probably see at least one PowerPoint presentation a week—if not one a day. Teachers use PowerPoint to present lesson materials in class. Kids even use PowerPoint to prepare what used to be oral reports.

So get with the program—and learn how to create your own great-looking presentations with PowerPoint!

Exploring the PowerPoint Workspace

As you can see in Figure 20.6, PowerPoint Online looks a lot like the other Office Online apps. The workspace is dominated by the Ribbon at the top of the screen, with the current slide displayed in the middle.

On the left side of the workspace is something unique to PowerPoint—the Slides pane, which displays all the slides in your presentation, one after another. Below the current slide is a Notes pane, which enables you to enter presentation notes.

FIGURE 20.6

The PowerPoint workspace.

Applying a Theme

You don't have to reinvent the wheel to design the look of your presentation. PowerPoint includes a number of slide *themes* that you can apply to any presentation, blank or otherwise. A theme specifies the color scheme, fonts, layout, and background for each slide you create in your presentation.

 NOTE In the desktop version of PowerPoint, themes are located on the Design tab.

To apply a new theme to your current presentation, select the Design tab on the Ribbon. Available themes display in the Themes section; click a theme to apply it to your presentation.

It's that simple. All the colors, fonts, and everything else from the theme are automatically applied to all the slides in your presentation—and every new slide you add carries the selected design.

 NOTE Don't confuse the slide *layout*, which defines which elements appear on the slide, with the slide *template*, which defines the colors and fonts used.

Inserting New Slides

When you create a new presentation, PowerPoint starts with a single slide—the *title slide*. Naturally, you need to insert additional slides to create a complete presentation. PowerPoint enables you to insert different types of slides, with different types of layouts for different types of information.

To insert a new slide, all you have to do is select the Home tab on the Ribbon and click the New Slide button. This displays the New Slide dialog box; select the slide layout you want, and then click the Add Slide button.

Adding and Formatting Text

You can enter text for a slide directly into that slide. When PowerPoint creates a new slide, the areas for text entry are designated with boilerplate text—"Click to add title" (for the slide's title) or "Click to add text" (for regular text or bullet points). Adding text is as easy as clicking the boilerplate text and then entering your own words and numbers. Press Enter to move to a new line or bullet. To enter a subbullet, press the Tab key first; to back up a level, press Shift+Tab.

Formatting text on a slide is just like formatting text in a word processing document. Select the text you want to format, and then click the appropriate button in the Font section of the Home tab.

 TIP   You can add transitions between slides and animate objects on a slide. Use the Transitions tab on the Ribbon to apply transitions and the Animations tab to apply animation effects.

Start the Show!

To run your slideshow, select the View tab and click the Slide Show button. To move from one slide to the next, all you have to do is click your mouse.

Exploring Google Docs, Sheets, and Slides

There used to be a lot of office suites on the market, but Microsoft Office pretty much obliterated the competition. Until recently, that is.

Google Docs, Sheets, and Slides are web-based applications that are giving Microsoft Office a run for its money. These apps are completely free, offer much the same functionality as Microsoft Office, and run on any computer or mobile device, in any web browser. All you need is an Internet connection (and a Google Account, of course), and you're good to go.

You access all these apps by pointing your web browser to docs.google.com. As you can see in Figure 20.7, this opens a dashboard to all your online documents, with your word processing documents front and center. To switch to documents from another app, click the Menu (three bar) button at the top left and select either Sheets or Slides.

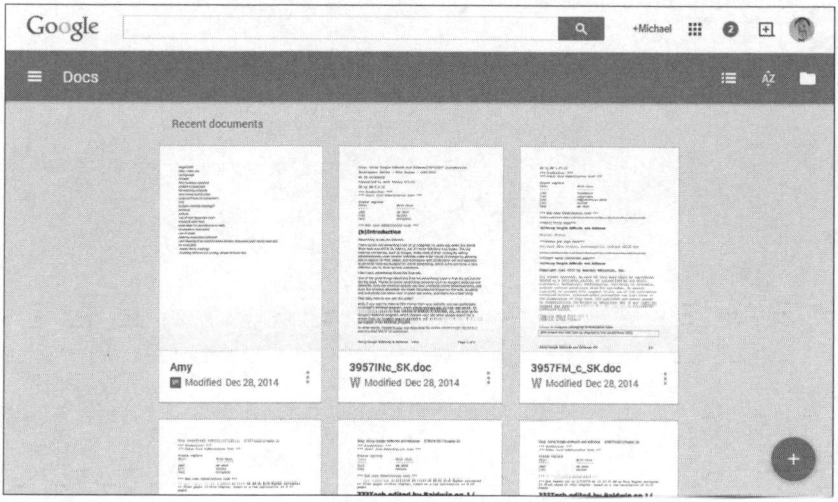

FIGURE 20.7

The Google Docs dashboard.

NOTE   All your Google Docs, Sheets, and Slides documents are stored online in Google Drive, Google's cloud-based storage service. You can also access your documents by going direct to Google Drive at drive.google.com.

To open an existing document, simply click its thumbnail. To create a new document of any type, first switch to the dashboard page for that app. Then click the round + button at the bottom-right corner of the window. This opens a new untitled document of the chosen type. To give this document a name, click the Untitled box at the top of the page, and enter a new name. You don't have to do any further saving; Google saves all your changes online, automatically.

Using Google Docs

Google Docs is the word processing app in the Google suite. It works pretty much like Microsoft Word, and you use it for similar tasks—creating memos, letters, newsletters, and the like.

As you can see in Figure 20.8, the Google Docs workspace consists of the document you're working on, with a toolbar and series of pull-down menus above that. Start typing at the cursor, and then use the controls on the toolbar (or the appropriate pull-down menu) to edit and format your text. Click the Print button to print your work.

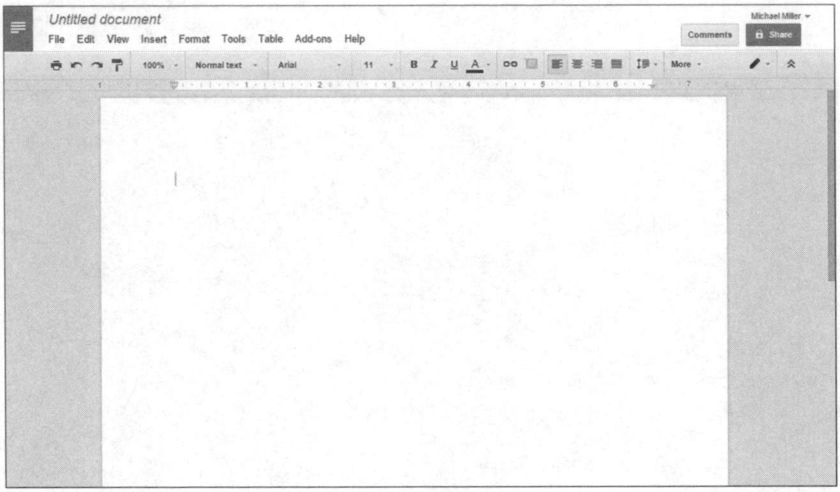

FIGURE 20.8

The Google Docs workspace.

Google Docs offers much of the same functionality as Microsoft Word. About the only major features missing are the ability to do multiple-column formatting and a lack of styles and features for more scholarly documents. Beyond that, Docs will do a great job with your day-to-day word processing tasks.

Using Google Sheets

Google Sheets is the spreadsheet app in the Google suite. It offers most of the features and functionality found in Microsoft Excel, including charts, formulas, and a full complement of functions.

Figure 20.9 shows the Google Sheets workspace. The spreadsheet itself takes up the bulk of the workspace, with a toolbar and pull-down menus above that. Individual sheets within the main sheet are accessed via tabs at the bottom of the window.

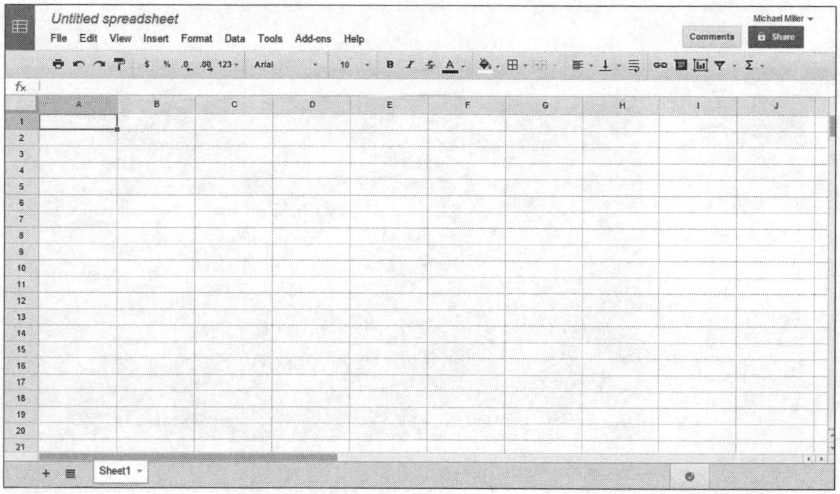

FIGURE 20.9

The Google Sheets workspace.

Using Google Slides

Google Slides is the presentation app in the Google suite. It compares with PowerPoint in its capability to create and give professional-looking presentations.

Figure 20.10 shows the Google Slides workspace. The slide sorter is on the left, the current slide is big in the middle, and there's a notes pane beneath that. All functions are accessible from the toolbar and pull-down menus; when you're ready to give a presentation, click the Present button above the toolbar.

FIGURE 20.10

The Google Slides workspace.

THE ABSOLUTE MINIMUM

Here are the key points to remember from this chapter:

- To perform common work-related tasks, you need the individual apps that make up an office suite.

- The most popular office suite today is Microsoft Office, which is available in either web-based or traditional desktop software versions.

- Microsoft Word is the word processor in Microsoft Office, used to write letters and reports.

- Microsoft Excel is Office's spreadsheet program, used for budgets and other number crunching.

- Microsoft PowerPoint is used to create and give presentations.

- Google Docs, Sheets, and Slides are free cloud-based apps that compete directly with Microsoft Word, Excel, and PowerPoint.

21

STAYING ORGANIZED

In today's hectic world, you need to stay organized. Fortunately, you can use your new computer to help you plan your schedule—to track appointments, manage your to-do list, and such. It's all a matter of entering the proper information into the appropriate app and letting your computer do its thing.

There are a number of different ways to use your computer to organize your day. Windows 10 includes a pretty good Calendar app that a lot of people like; there are also various web-based calendars and task management apps you might find worthwhile.

Using the Windows Calendar App

Let's start with the Calendar app included with Windows 10. Like most Universal Windows apps, it's integrated well into the operating system.

This integration starts on the Start menu. If you pin this app to the Start menu, the Calendar tile is "live"—that is, it displays a scrolling list of upcoming appointments. This way you can see what's coming up, without even having to launch the app.

Displaying Different Views

As you can see in Figure 21.1, the left side of the Calendar app displays a mini monthly calendar, a list of the various calendars available to display, and navigational icons at the bottom. On the right side of the app, you see the current calendar in the selected view.

By default, the Calendar app displays a traditional monthly calendar (the Month view). To display a different view—Day, Work Week, or Week—click that option above the calendar. To move from month to month (or week to week), click the up or down arrows above the calendar. To recenter the calendar on the current day, click Today.

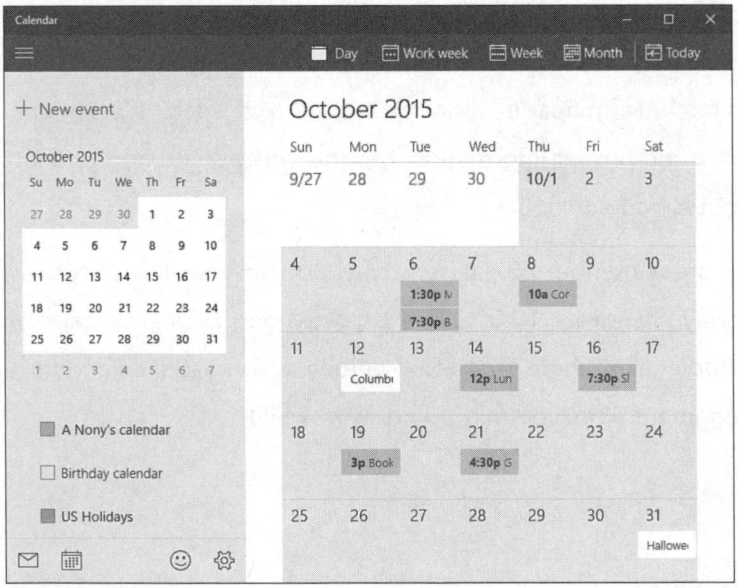

FIGURE 21.1

The Calendar app in monthly view.

You can also display your calendar in weekly or daily views. Right-click anywhere on the screen to display the Options bar, and then click the desired view—Day, Work Week, Week, Month, or What's Next.

To view more details about an appointment, click the item. The appointment screen opens; you can then edit anything about the appointment. Click the Save button to save your changes.

Creating a New Appointment

To create a new appointment, click New Event in the left column to display the new event pane, shown in Figure 21.2. In this pane, enter the name of the event into the Event Name field and the location in the Location field. Enter starting and ending dates and times—unless it's an all-day event, in which instance you check the All Day option.

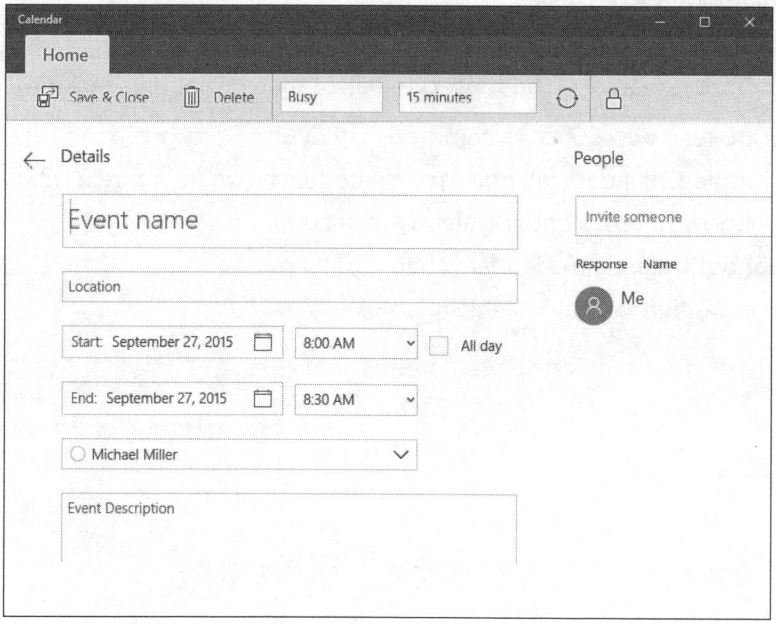

FIGURE 21.2

Creating a new appointment.

You can also use this window to create a recurring event, as well as invite others to this event. To keep this event private, check the Private button.

When you finish entering information about this event, click the Save & Close button.

Using Web-Based Calendars

It's one thing to keep a private schedule on a single PC, as you can with the Windows Calendar app, but most of us have schedules that include a lot of public or shared events. In addition, if you keep a personal calendar on your home PC, you can't reference it from work or when you travel. That limits the calculator program's usefulness.

This is why, instead of using a calendar that's wedded to a single computer, many users prefer web-based calendars. A web-based calendar stores your appointments on the Internet, where you can access them from any computer or device that has an Internet connection. This enables you to check your schedule when you're on the road, even if your assistant in the office or your spouse at home has added new appointments since you left. Web-based calendars are also extremely easy to share with other users in any location, which make them great for collaborative projects.

Most web-based calendars are free and offer similar online sharing and collaboration features. The most popular of these calendars include

- 30Boxes (www.30boxes.com)
- Google Calendar (calendar.google.com), shown in Figure 21.3.
- Windows Live Calendar (calendar.live.com)
- Yahoo! Calendar (calendar.yahoo.com)
- Zoho Calendar (calendar.zoho.com)

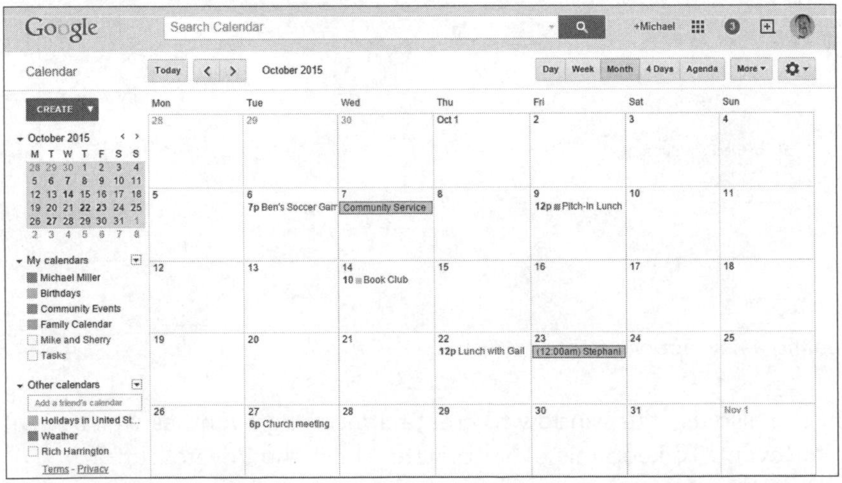

FIGURE 21.3

Google Calendar—one of the most popular web-based calendars.

Using Web-Based To-Do Lists

Just as you can track your appointments with a web-based calendar, you can track your to-do lists with web-based to-do lists. These apps enable you to manage everything from simple to-do lists to complex group tasks, and you can do it over the Internet so that you can collaborate with other users.

The most popular of these web-based task management applications include the following:

- Bla-bla List (www.blablalist.com)

- HiTask (www.hitask.com)

- iPrioritize (www.iprioritize.com)

- Remember the Milk (www.rememberthemilk.com)

- Vitalist (www.vitalist.com)

- voo2do (www.voo2do.com)

 TIP Some web-based calendars, such as Google Calendar, also offer task management and to-do list functions.

THE ABSOLUTE MINIMUM

Here are the key points to remember from this chapter:

- The Windows Calendar app is a good, basic way to manage your schedule and appointments.

- Web-based calendars, such as Google Calendar, enable you to access your schedule from any computer, and you can collaborate with others on public calendars.

- Web-based task management services help you manage your to-do lists.

VIEWING AND SHARING DIGITAL PHOTOS

In the old days, if you wanted to share your photos with friends and family, you had to have extra prints made and then hand them out or mail them off, as appropriate. This approach is not only time-consuming, but it's costly; you have to pay money for each extra print you make.

In today's age of digital photography, it's a lot easier to view and share your photos on your computer, over the Internet. In fact, you can even edit your digital photos to eliminate red-eye and such before you share them. It's a whole new digital world out there. All you need is a digital camera (or smartphone or tablet with built-in camera) and a computer.

Transferring Pictures from Your Camera, Smartphone, or Tablet

If you want to edit or print your digital photos, you need to connect your digital camera or smartphone or tablet to your PC—which is relatively easy to do. You can transfer digital photos directly from your camera's memory card, download pictures from your camera via a USB connection, or even scan existing photo prints.

Connecting via USB

Connecting a digital camera or smartphone or tablet to your PC is easy. All you have to do is connect a cable from your device to a USB port on your computer. With this type of setup, Windows recognizes your camera (or phone or tablet) as soon as you plug it in and installs the appropriate drivers automatically.

If you connect a digital camera to your PC, Windows should recognize it and ask what you want to do when this device is connected. If you answer that you want to have Windows import your pictures, that's exactly what it will do. (Connecting a smartphone or tablet is another matter, which we'll address in a moment.)

Some digital cameras come with their own proprietary picture management programs. If you've installed such a program on your PC, this is the program that probably launches when you connect your camera to your computer. If this program launches and asks to download the pictures from your camera, follow the onscreen instructions to proceed.

You might also have installed a third-party photo editing program, such as Adobe Photoshop Elements. If so, this might be the program that launches when you connect your camera to your PC. Again, just follow the onscreen instructions to proceed.

 CAUTION Depending on the apps you have installed on your system, you might get multiple prompts to download photos when you connect your camera. If this happens, pick the program you'd prefer to work with and close the other dialog boxes.

Transferring Pictures from a Memory Card

Copying digital pictures via USB cable is nice—if your camera supports this method. For many users, an easier approach is to use a memory card reader. Many PCs have memory card readers built in; if yours doesn't, you can always add a low-cost external memory reader via USB. You then insert the memory card from your digital camera into the memory card reader, and your PC recognizes the card as if it were another hard disk.

In many cases Windows recognizes a memory card full of photos and asks if you want to download them. If not, you can use File Explorer to copy files from the memory card to your computer. Just open File Explorer and click the drive icon for the memory card. This displays the card's contents, typically in a subfolder labeled DCIM. You can then move, copy, and delete the photos stored on the card, as you would with any other type of file in Windows.

Transferring Photos from a Smartphone or Tablet

If you're like my wife and daughter-in-law, you take more pictures with your smartphone than you do with your digital camera. There's a good reason why more and more people are ditching dedicated digital cameras and instead taking pictures with the cameras built into their smartphones and tablets—it's a lot more convenient to whip out your phone or tablet to take a quick picture than it is to lug around a digital camera everywhere you go.

If you have an iPhone or iPad, you can configure your device to use Apple's iCloud service to back up your photos and other data. With iPhone backup enabled, the photos you take will automatically be transferred from your device to your home computer whenever your device is connected to your home Wi-Fi network.

You can also manually transfer photos from your iPhone or iPad to your PC, using Apple's standard connection cable. Just connect your iOS device to your computer, using the appropriate Apple-approved cable, and then launch File Explorer on your PC. Click the This PC icon in the Navigation pane, select the iPhone or iPad icon, the Internal Storage folder, and then select the DCIM folder to display one or more subfolders that contain your device's pictures. Double-click each of these folders to display their contents.

Now hold down the Ctrl key and click each photo you want to transfer. Select the Home tab, click the Move To button, and then click Pictures. All the photos you've selected will be moved from your iPhone or iPad to the Pictures folder on your PC.

If you have an Android phone or tablet, use this same method to move pictures from your mobile device to your PC. Just connect your device, open File Explorer, navigate to the DCIM or Camera folder, and start moving.

Scanning a Picture

If your photos are of the old-fashioned print variety, you can still turn them into digital files using a flatbed scanner. The scanning starts automatically when you press the Scan button on your scanner. Your print photo is saved as a digital file for future use.

Note that some third-party software programs, such as Adobe Photoshop Elements, also enables you to scan photos from the program. In most instances, scanning via one of these programs offers more options than scanning via Windows; you can change the resolution (in dots per inch) of the scanned image, crop the image, and even adjust brightness and contrast if you want. If you're scanning a lot of old, washed-out prints, this approach might produce better results.

 NOTE   By default, Windows stores all your pictures in the Pictures folder, which you can access from File Explorer. This folder includes a number of features specific to the management of picture files, as well as all the normal file-related tasks, such as copying, moving, or even deleting your photos.

Viewing Your Photos with the Windows 10 Photos App

Viewing photos in Windows 10 is a snap. All you have to do is open the Photos app included with Windows 10. You can use this Universal-style app to both view and edit your digital photos.

As you can see in Figure 22.1, the Photos app displays all the photos and folders stored on your computer. Select Collection in the navigation pane and your photos display by date. Select Albums and the app organizes your pictures into folder-like photo albums. To view photos stored in a specific album, click the tile for that folder.

FIGURE 22.1

Viewing your photo collection in the Photos app.

Click through until you find a photo you want to view, and then click that photo to view in the full window, as shown in Figure 22.2. To move to the next picture in the folder, click the right arrow onscreen or press the right arrow key on your keyboard. To return to the previous picture, click the left arrow onscreen or press the left arrow key on your keyboard.

FIGURE 22.2

Viewing a single photo.

To enlarge the picture, click the + button at the lower-right corner of the screen. To make a picture smaller, click the – button.

To delete a photo, mouse over that photo and then check the box in the upper-right corner. This selects the photo and displays a handful of icons at the bottom of the app. Click the Delete (trashcan) icon to delete the selected photo.

 TIP   To use the current picture as the image on the Windows Lock screen, display the photo full screen, click the Options button at the top right, and then click Set As Lock Screen.

Editing Your Photos with the Photos App

Not all the digital photos you take turn out perfectly. Some pictures are too light, whereas others are too dark. Some have bad color, and some need to be cropped to highlight the important area.

Fortunately, the Photos app enables you to do this sort of basic photo editing. A better-looking photo is only a click or a tap away!

All the Photos app's editing controls are available when you double-click a thumbnail to open the photo, as shown in Figure 22.3.

FIGURE 22.3

Basic editing controls in the Photos app.

Automatically Enhancing a Photo

When you want to quickly touch up a photo, use the Photos app's Enhance tool. This applies some common fixes to your photo that, in many cases, are just what you need.

Here's how to use the Enhance tool:

1. From within the Photos app, navigate to and display the photo you want to edit.

2. Click the Enhance (magic wand) button.

3. If you don't like the enhancements, click Enhance again to return to the original version of the photo.

Rotating a Photo

Is your picture sidewise? To turn a portrait into a landscape or vice versa, use the Photos app's Rotate control. Follow these steps:

1. From within the Photos app, navigate to and display the photo you want to edit.

2. Click the Rotate button to rotate the picture 90 degrees clockwise.

3. Continue clicking to further rotate the picture.

Cropping a Photo

Sometimes you don't get close enough to the subject for the best effect. When you want to zoom in, use the Photos app's Crop control to remove the edges you don't want.

Here's how it works:

1. From within the Photos app, navigate to and display the photo you want to edit.

2. Click the Edit (pencil) button to display the editing screen.

3. Make sure Basic Fixes is selected on the left side of the screen.

4. Click Crop to display crop lines around the picture, as shown in Figure 22.4.

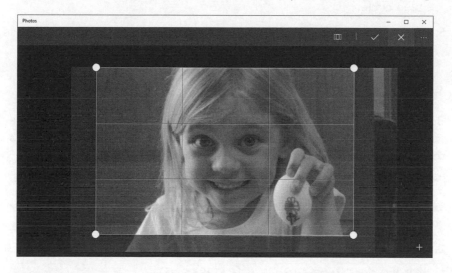

FIGURE 22.4

Cropping a photo.

5. Use your mouse to drag the corners of the white border until the picture appears as you like.

6. Click the check mark button to accept the cropping, or click the X to reject.

 NOTE   By default, Windows maintains the original aspect ratio when you crop a photo. To crop to a different aspect ratio, click the Aspect Ratio button and make a new selection.

Removing Red-Eye

Red-eye is caused when a camera's flash causes the subject's eyes to appear a devilish red. The Photos app enables you to remove the red-eye effect by changing the red color to black in the edited photo.

To remove red-eye from a photo, follow these steps:

1. From within the Photos app, navigate to and display the photo you want to edit.

2. Click the Edit button to display the editing screen.

3. Click Basic Fixes on the left side of the screen.

4. Click Red Eye on the right side of the screen; the cursor changes to a blue circle.

5. Move the circle to the eye(s) you want to fix, and then click the mouse button to remove the red eye effect.

Retouching a Photo

Does someone in your photo have a blemish or a loose hair, or is there a rough or scratched area in the photo you want to get rid of? Use the Photos app's Retouch control to smooth out or remove blemishes from your photos.

Follow these steps:

1. From within the Photos app, navigate to and display the photo you want to edit.

2. Click the Edit button to display the editing screen.

3. Click Basic Fixes on the left side of the screen.

4. Click Retouch on the right side of the screen; the cursor changes to a blue circle.

5. Move the circle to the area you want to repair, and then click the mouse button to do so.

Applying Filters

The Photos app includes several built-in filters you can apply to your pictures. Use filters to quickly and easily apply interesting effects to a photo.

1. From within the Photos app, navigate to and display the photo you want to edit.

2. Click the Edit button to display the editing screen.

3. Click Filters on the left side of the screen. Available filters now display on the right side of the screen.

4. Click a filter to apply it to your photo.

Adjusting Brightness and Contrast

When a photo is too dark or too light, use the Photos app's Light controls. There are four controls available:

- **Brightness** makes the picture lighter or darker.

- **Contrast** increases or decreases the difference between the photo's darkest and lightest areas.

- **Highlights** brings out or hides detail in too-bright highlights.

- **Shadows** brings out or hides detail in too-dark shadows.

Follow these steps to use these controls:

1. From within the Photos app, navigate to and display the photo you want to edit.

2. Click the Edit button to display the editing screen.

3. Click Light on the left side of the screen.

4. Click the control you want to adjust: Brightness, Contrast, Highlights, or Shadows.

5. The selected control changes to a circular control, as shown in Figure 22.5. Click/tap and drag the control clockwise to increase the effect or counterclockwise to decrease the effect.

FIGURE 22.5

Adjusting a photo's brightness levels.

Adjusting Color and Tint

The Photos app lets you adjust various color-related settings. There are four color controls available:

- **Temperature** affects the color characteristics of lighting; you can adjust a photo so that it looks warmer (reddish) or cooler (bluish).

- **Tint** affects the shade of the color.

- **Saturation** affects the amount of color in the photo; completely desaturating a photo makes it black and white.

- **Color Boost** enables you to increase the color saturation of selected areas of the photo.

Follow these steps to adjust a photo's color controls:

1. From within the Photos app, navigate to and display the photo you want to edit.

2. Click the Edit button to display the editing screen.

3. Click Color on the left side of the screen.

4. Click the control you want to adjust: Temperature, Tint, Saturation, or Color Boost.

5. The selected control changes to a circular control. Click/tap and drag the control clockwise to increase the effect or counterclockwise to decrease the effect.

 NOTE   If, when you edit a photo, you decide you don't want to keep the changes you make, simply click the Cancel Changes (X) button at the top of the window.

Applying Special Effects

You can also use the Photos app to apply various vignette and selective focus effects to a picture. Follow these steps:

1. From within the Photos app, navigate to and display the photo you want to edit.

2. Click the Edit button to display the editing screen.

3. Click Effects on the left side of the screen.

4. To apply a vignette to your photo, click Vignette on the right side of the screen, and then rotate the control clockwise for a dark (positive) vignette or counterclockwise for a light (negative) vignette.

5. To apply a selective focus effect, like the one shown in Figure 22.6, click Selective Focus. On the next screen, use your mouse to move or resize the circle in the middle of the screen; the center of this circle will be in focus,

whereas the area outside the circle will be blurred. To change the strength of the selective focus effect, click Strength and select a new value, from Minimum to Maximum.

6. Click the Apply (check mark) button to apply the effect.

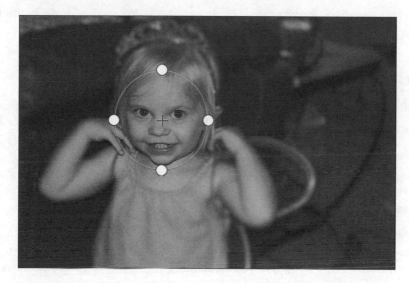

FIGURE 22.6

Applying a selective focus effect.

Using Other Photo-Editing Programs

When it comes to editing your digital photos, you're not limited to the Windows Photos app. In fact, there are many photo-editing apps available that provide more powerful editing tools.

If you're looking for an alternative photo editor, you can choose from low-priced, consumer-oriented programs to high-priced programs targeted at professional photographers. For most users, the low-priced programs do everything you need. The most popular of these include the following:

- Adobe Photoshop Elements (www.adobe.com), $99.99

- Paint Shop Pro (www.corel.com), $79.99

- Photo Explosion Deluxe (www.novadevelopment.com), $49.95

- Picasa (www.picasa.com), free

NOTE Don't confuse the affordable Adobe Photoshop Elements with the much higher-priced (and more sophisticated) Adobe Photoshop CC, which is used by most professional photographers.

You can also find photo-editing programs in the Windows Store, in the Photo category.

Printing Your Photos

After you touch up (or otherwise manipulate) your photos, it's time to print them.

Choosing the Right Printer and Paper

If you have a color printer, you can make good-quality prints of your image files. Even a low-priced color inkjet can make surprisingly good prints; although, the better your printer, the better the results.

Some manufacturers sell printers specifically designed for photographic prints. These printers use special photo print paper and output prints that are almost indistinguishable from those you get from a professional photo processor. If you take a lot of digital photos, one of these printers might be a good investment.

The quality of your prints is also affected by the type of paper you use. Printing on standard laser or inkjet paper is okay for making proofs, but you'll want to use a thicker, waxier paper for those prints you want to keep. Check with your printer's manufacturer to see what type of paper it recommends for the best quality photo prints.

Making the Print

You can print photos directly from the Windows Photos app. Here's how to do it:

1. From within the Photos app, navigate to and display the photo you want to print.

2. Click the Options (three dot) button at the top of the window; then select Print.

3. When the Print window appears, as shown in Figure 22.7, select the printer you want to use.

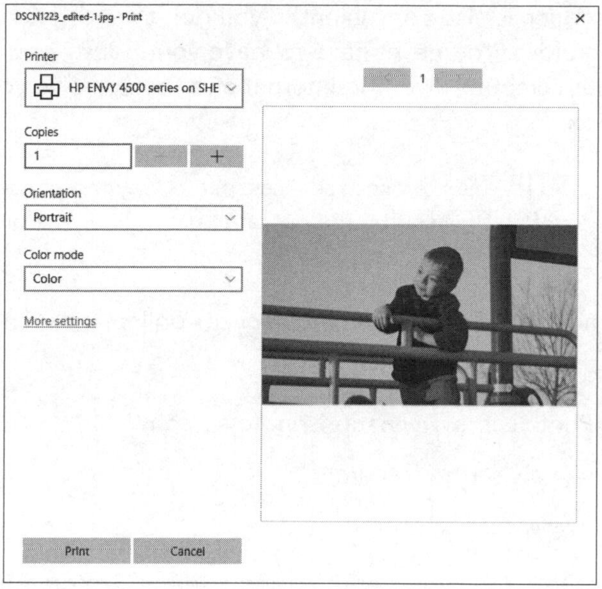

FIGURE 22.7

Printing a photo from the Photos app.

4. Select how many copies to print.

5. Pull down the Orientation list and select either Portrait (vertical) or Landscape (horizontal).

6. Click the Print button to print the photo.

Printing Photos Professionally

If you don't have your own photo-quality printer, you can use a professional photo-processing service to print your photos. You can create prints from your digital photos in two primary ways:

- Copy your image files to a CD, memory card, or USB drive and deliver the device by hand to your local photo finisher.

- Go to the website of an online photo-finishing service, and transfer your image files over the Internet.

The first option is convenient for many people, especially because numerous drugstores, supermarkets, and discount stores (including Target and Walmart) offer onsite photo-printing services. Often the printing service is via a self-serve kiosk; just insert your device, follow the onscreen instructions, and come back one-half hour later for your finished prints.

The second option is also convenient, if you don't mind waiting a few days for your prints to arrive. You never have to leave your house; you upload your photo files from your computer over the Internet and then receive your prints in your postal mailbox.

 TIP Some photo services, particularly those associated with retail chains, offer the option of picking up your prints at a local store—often with same-day service!

There are a number of photo-printing services online, including the following:

- dotPhoto (www.dotphoto.com)
- Nations Photo Lab (www.nationsphotolab.com)
- Shutterfly (www.shutterfly.com)
- Snapfish (www.snapfish.com)

To print a photo online, you start by using Internet Explorer or another browser to go to the site and sign up for a free account. After you create your account, choose which photos on your PC you want to print. After the photos are selected, the site automatically uploads them from your PC to the website. You can then select how many and what size prints you want. Enter your shipping information and credit card number, and you're good to go.

For example, Shutterfly makes it easy to order prints at a variety of sizes, from 4"×6" to 20"×30", in either matte or glossy finish. Choose the size and quantity you want for each print, and then enter your payment and shipping information.

Most sites ship within a day or two of receiving your order; add shipping time, and you should receive your prints in less than a week. Shipping is typically via the U.S. Postal Service or some similar shipping service.

Sharing Photos at an Online Photo Site

You don't have to print your photos to share them with friends. There are a number of photo-sharing websites that enable you to upload your photos and then share them with the people you love.

These photo-sharing sites let you store your photos in online photo albums, which can then be viewed by any number of visitors via their web browsers—for free. Some of these sites also offer photo-printing services, and some sell photo-related items, such as picture T-shirts, calendars, and mugs. Most of these sites are free to use; they make their money by selling prints and other merchandise.

To use a photo-sharing site, you start by signing up for a free account. After your account is created, choose which photos on your PC you want to share. After you select the photos, the site automatically uploads them from your PC to the website. You then organize the photos into photo albums, each of which has its own unique URL. You can then email the URL to your friends and family; when they access the photo site, they view your photos on their computer screens.

The most popular of these photo-sharing sites include

- DropShots (www.dropshots.com)

- Flickr (www.flickr.com)

- Photobucket (www.photobucket.com)

- Picturetrail (www.picturetrail.com)

- Webshots (www.webshots.com)

Emailing Digital Photos

There's another way to share your digital photos that doesn't involve uploads or websites. I'm talking about sharing via email; all you have to do is attach your photos to an email message you create in your regular email program and then send that message to as many recipients as you want.

You learned how to attach files to email messages in Chapter 15, "Sending and Receiving Email." Because a digital photo is just another type of computer file, the process is the same when you want to send a photo. Create a new message in your email program or web mail service, click the Attach button, and then select those photos you want to attach. Click the Send button, and your message is sent on its way, complete with the photos you selected.

As easy as this process is, you need to be aware of one issue before you start emailing your photos far and wide—the size of the photo files you're emailing.

If you're emailing photos pretty much as they were shot with your camera, you're probably emailing some large files. This can be a problem because some email services cap the size of messages users can send and receive. If you have a big photo, in the 5MB or larger range, you may not be able to send it to some or all recipients.

 NOTE   You can use most third-party photo-editing programs (but not the Windows Photos app) to resize your pictures.

For this reason, you probably want to resize your photos before you email them. If your recipients will be viewing your photos only on their computer screens, you can downsize them to the resolution of a typical screen—no more than 1920 pixels wide or 1080 pixels tall. Anything larger is unnecessary.

However, if your recipients will be printing the photos, you probably don't want to resize them—or at least not that much. A photo resized to 1920×1080 pixels doesn't have enough picture resolution to create a detailed print. You should keep your photos at or near their original size if someone is going to print them; any significant resizing results in fuzzy prints.

THE ABSOLUTE MINIMUM

Here are the key points to remember from this chapter:

- You can transfer photos from your digital camera to your PC via a USB connection or by using your camera's memory card.

- The Windows Photos app enables you to view and edit digital photos stored on your computer.

- You can also use the Photos app to print photos on your home printer.

- You can order photo prints from a variety of online printing services or from your local drugstore, supermarket, or department store.

- You can share your photos with multiple people by uploading them to an online photo-sharing website.

- You can also send photos as email attachments—as long as the files aren't too big.

23

WATCHING MOVIES, TV SHOWS, AND OTHER VIDEOS

How people watch TV shows and movies is changing. In the old days, your living room TV was tethered to your cable company's cable and you watched whatever it was they had available. Or maybe you stuck a DVD into your DVD player to watch movies on your TV set.

Today, more and more people are cutting the cable cord and ditching their DVD players to watch streaming video over the Internet, on their personal computers. The Internet is home to Netflix and Hulu and other streaming video services that enable you to watch pretty much whatever movies and TV shows you want, at your convenience. Why bother with cable at all when a whole world of viewing is available online?

Online streaming video will change your viewing habits. Just fire up your PC, connect to the Internet, and watch that episode of *Arrow* or *Chopped* that you missed last week. Or you can go on a binge and watch the last eight seasons of *Doctor Who* in a single (long) sitting. Or you can purchase or rent the latest fresh-from-the-theaters blockbuster and watch it at your own convenience in your own home.

It's all a matter of knowing where to look for the videos you want—and launching the right app for viewing them.

Watching Streaming Video Online

There's a ton of programming on the Web that you don't have to purchase or download separately to your computer. This programming is available via a technology called *streaming video*. The movie or TV show you pick is streamed over the Internet in real time to your computer. You watch the programming in your web browser or in a dedicated app. Assuming you have a fast enough Internet connection, you can find tens of thousands of free and paid videos to watch at dozens of different websites.

Viewing Movies and TV Shows on Netflix

When it comes to watching movies and TV shows online, you can't beat Netflix, a streaming video service with more than 53 million subscribers. Netflix enables you to watch all the movies and TV shows you want, all for a low $7.99/month subscription. It's tough to beat that price.

As to what you can watch, Netflix offers a mix of both classic and newer movies, as well as a surprising number of classic and newer television programming. There's a wide range of TV shows, from *The Dick Van Dyke Show* to *Marvel's Agents of Shield*, and movies old and new (and domestic and foreign, too).

 NOTE Netflix also offers a separate DVD-by-mail rental service, with a separate subscription fee. That's not what we're talking about here, however.

You can watch Netflix in its own Universal-style app or from its website. The Netflix app is my preferred way to go because it provides a more seamless full-screen experience. You can download the app (for free) from the Windows Store.

The first time you open the Netflix app, you're prompted to either create a new Netflix account or log into an existing one. Each subsequent time you open the app, it automatically logs in to this account and displays the appropriate content tailored exclusively to your viewing habits.

After you open the app and sign into your Netflix account, you then choose who is watching right now. (Netflix enables you to create profiles for up to five different viewers.) You can then browse or search for movies and TV shows to watch.

The Netflix home screen, shown in Figure 23.1, is personalized based on your viewing habits. Scroll right to view Netflix's Instant Queue, your personal Top 10, Popular movies, and more. There are also links to your top 10 shows (Top 10 for You) and New Releases.

FIGURE 23.1

Stream movies and TV series from Netflix.

To view programming by type, click the Genres (three bars) button or just right-click anywhere on the screen. You can then click a genre to view all items within that category.

If you have a specific movie or TV series in mind, click the Search (magnifying glass) icon to display the Search panel. Enter the name of the movie or show into the search box, and then press Enter.

When you find a movie or show you want to watch, click it. You now see the detail page for that show, like the one in Figure 23.2.

FIGURE 23.2

Getting ready to watch a TV show on Netflix.

If it's a movie you want to watch, just click the Play button on the movie image to start playback. If you choose to watch a TV show, you typically can choose from different episodes in different seasons. Select a season to see all episodes from that season, and then click the episode you want to watch.

When Netflix begins playing the movie or show you selected, right-click anywhere on the screen to display the Options bar, shown in Figure 23.3. Click the Pause button to pause playback; the Pause button then changes to a Play button, which you can click again to resume playback. You can also click and drag the slider control to move directly to another part of the program.

FIGURE 23.3

Viewing a program on Netflix.

Viewing TV Shows on Hulu

As good as Netflix is, it isn't the best place to find recent television programming. If you want to watch the current season of most TV shows, your best bet is Hulu, which is a streaming service similar to Netflix but with slightly different programming.

Hulu offers episodes from a number of major-network TV shows, as well as some new and classic feature films. (There are also a fair number of programs from Canada, England, and other countries.) The standard free membership offers access to a limited number of videos; the subscription plan ($7.99/month) offers a larger selection of newer shows. A paid subscription is necessary to use the Hulu app—which happens to be the best way to watch Hulu on your PC.

The Hulu app is available from the Windows Store for free. The app runs full screen in Windows, which is the way you want to watch your shows anyway.

After you install the Hulu app, you can create a new Hulu account or log in to an existing one. When you launch the app and log in, Hulu displays a series of featured programs on its main screen, as shown in Figure 23.4. Scroll right to view recommended programming by type, and then click TV to view available TV shows.

FIGURE 23.4

Selected TV programs available on Hulu.

To search for specific shows, click the Search (magnifying glass icon) to display the Search pane. Enter the name of the program into the Search box and press Enter. When the search results appear, click the show you want to watch.

You now see a detailed program page for your selection, like the one in Figure 23.5. Scroll right to view episodes by season, and then click the episode you want to watch.

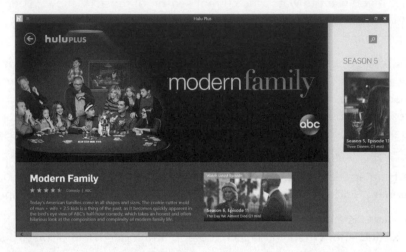

FIGURE 23.5

A detailed program page on Hulu.

Hulu begins playing the program you selected, as shown in Figure 23.6. Move your mouse over the screen (or tap the screen on a touchscreen) to display the playback controls. Click the Pause button to pause playback; the Pause button changes to a Play button, which you can click again to resume playback. Click and drag the slider control to move directly to another part of the program.

FIGURE 23.6

Viewing a program on Hulu.

Viewing Videos on Network Websites

Unfortunately, not all television programming is available from Netflix or Hulu. Some programs are available only on their networks' websites, which you can view in the Internet Explorer web browser.

For example, you can go to the CBS website (www.cbs.com) to view episodes of your favorite daytime, prime-time, and late-night series. Missed this week's episode of *The Big Bang Theory* or yesterday's *The Price is Right*? They're available online, for free, as you can see in Figure 23.7.

FIGURE 23.7

Watch CBS shows on the CBS website.

 NOTE   CBS offers some episodes for free, with a larger selection (6,500 episodes of current and classic shows) available with its All Access subscription, at $5.99/month.

Most of the other major networks have programs available for viewing on their websites. Most are free; some (such as HBO GO) are not. Check them out:

- ABC (abc.go.com)
- AMC (www.amc.com)
- CBS (www.cbs.com)
- Comedy Central (www.comedycentral.com)
- CW (www.cwtv.com)

- Fox (www.fox.com)
- HBO (www.hbogo.com)
- MeTV (www.metvnetwork.com)
- NBC (www.nbc.com)
- Nick (www.nick.com)
- Showtime (www.sho.com)
- TCM (www.tcm.com)
- TNT (www.tntdrama.com)
- USA Network (www.usanetwork.com)

In addition, you can get your daily sports fix via the streaming videos offered on the ESPN website (espn.go.com).

Downloading Videos from the iTunes Store

Netflix, Hulu, and the like are great, but they don't always offer the most recent hit movies. (You wouldn't expect them to, at their low monthly subscription prices.) If you want to see a flick fresh from the movie theater, you need to purchase it or rent it—which you can do online from Apple's iTunes Store.

To access the iTunes Store, you need to install the iTunes software on your computer. You can do this, for free, from www.apple.com/itunes/.

When you have the iTunes software installed, launch the program, and click iTunes Store at the top of the window. From within the Store, click either the Movies or TV Shows icons in the topleft corner. You can then navigate to and click the movie or show you want to purchase.

If a program is available for purchase, you'll see a Buy button with the price listed. If a program is available for rental, you'll see a Rent button with the price listed. (Figure 23.8 shows a movie with both purchase and rental options.) Some programs are available in both standard definition (SD) and high definition (HD) video; HD obviously has the better picture quality but often has a higher purchase/rental price, as well.

When you purchase a movie or TV show, it downloads to your computer and you're free to watch it as often and as long as you like; it's yours, you bought it. When you rent a program, however, it's only available to you for a limited time. With most rentals, you have 30 days to start watching the program and then must finish watching it within 24 hours of first clicking the Play button.

FIGURE 23.8

A movie available for both purchase and rental from the iTunes Store.

You watch any program you purchase or rent from within the iTunes software. Just navigate to and click the item you want to watch; iTunes will now download that item to your computer. Downloading large video files takes longer than the immediate gratification you get from streaming video, but then you can watch it whenever you want, without needing to be connected to the Internet.

FIGURE 23.9

Watching a movie in the iTunes app.

To pause or fast forward or rewind a program, mouse over the window to display the playback controls. To view a program full-screen, click the Fullscreen button in the playback controls; press Esc to return to the normal iTunes window.

Viewing Videos on YouTube

Then there's YouTube (www.youtube.com), which is the biggest video site on the Web. What's cool about YouTube is that the majority of the videos are uploaded by other users, so you get a real mix of professional-quality and amateur clips, as you can see in Figure 23.10.

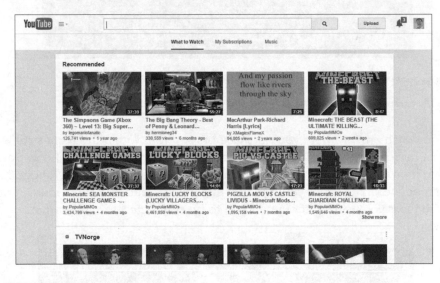

FIGURE 23.10

View professional and user-uploaded videos at YouTube.

Searching for Videos

Looking for an early performance clip of the Beatles? Or a classic toy commercial from the 1970s? Or a walk-through of the latest, greatest videogame? Or something to do with dancing monkeys? What you're looking for is probably somewhere on YouTube; all you have to do is search for it, using the top-of-page search box.

The results of your search are shown on a separate page. Each matching video is listed with a representative thumbnail image, the length of the video, a short description (and descriptive tags), the name of the user who uploaded the video, and a viewer rating (from zero to five stars).

Viewing Videos

When you find a video you like, click the image or title, and a new page appears. As you can see in Figure 23.11, this page includes an embedded video player, which starts playing the video automatically. Use the Pause and Play controls as necessary.

FIGURE 23.11

Watching a video on YouTube.

Sharing Videos

Videos become viral when they're shared between hundreds and thousands of users—and the easiest way to share a YouTube video is via email. YouTube enables you to send an email containing a link to the video you like to your friends. When a friend receives this email, he can click the link in the message to go to YouTube and play the video.

When you want to share a video, go to that video's page, and click the Share button underneath the YouTube video player. When the Share tab expands, click the Email button, and then enter the email addresses of the intended recipients into the To box. (Separate multiple addresses with commas.) Enter a personal message if you want, and then click the Send button. In a few minutes your recipients will receive the message, complete with a link to the selected video.

You can also share a given video via Facebook, Twitter, Pinterest, and other social media. Click the Share button and then the button for your social network of choice.

Uploading Your Own Videos to YouTube

Anyone can upload a movie or video to the YouTube site. After the video is uploaded, users can view the video—and if you're lucky, the video will go viral!

You can shoot YouTube videos with any computer webcam or consumer camcorder. YouTube accepts videos in just about any file format.

Uploading is easy. Just follow these steps:

1. Click the Upload button at the top of any YouTube page.

2. When the next page appears, click Select Files to Upload.

3. When the Open dialog box appears, navigate to and select the file to upload and then click the Open button.

4. While the video uploads, you're prompted to enter information about the video, including title, description, tags, category, and privacy level. Do so, and then click the Save Changes button.

That's it. After the video uploads, YouTube converts it to the proper viewing format and creates a viewing page for the video. To view your video, click the My Videos link on any YouTube page, and then click the thumbnail for your new video.

Making Your Own Home Movies

If you have a video camcorder or smartphone with built-in video camera, it's easy to download movies from your device to your PC and then edit them into professional-looking videos. The movies you shoot are actually video files that can be transferred to your Windows PC with File Explorer and stored on your computer's hard disk.

You can then edit the raw video files into more professional-looking productions. You might, for example, want to cut out some boring footage, combine two or more clips, insert transitions between clips, and even add titles and credits to your movie.

You can do all these things—and more—with a PC-based video-editing program. These programs perform many of the same functions as the professional editing consoles you might find at your local television station. Today's video-editing programs are surprisingly easy to use—and the results are amazing!

The most popular Windows-compatible video-editing programs are quite affordable—typically $100 or less. The most popular of these include the following:

- Adobe Premiere Elements (www.adobe.com, $99.99)

- Pinnacle Studio (www.pinnaclesys.com, $59.95)

- Sony Movie Studio (www.sonycreativesoftware.com, $49.95)

- VideoStudio Pro (www.corel.com, $79.99)

- Windows Movie Maker (windows.microsoft.com/en-us/windows-live/movie-maker, free)

Playing DVD Movies on Your PC

What about watching old-fashioned DVD movies on your PC? Well, older versions of Windows included the necessary technology to play DVDs, but Windows 10 does not. This means that you can't use Windows itself to play DVDs on your computer—although DVD playback is still possible.

If you want to watch DVDs on a Windows 10 computer, you need to use a third-party media player program. You might already have such a program installed; many PC manufacturers include DVD or media player programs as part of the package with new computers. Look on the Start screen for a tile labeled "movies," "movie player," "media player," or something like that.

If your computer did not come with a movie player app, you can easily install such a program to play DVD movies. There are a number of popular programs out there, including the following:

- BlazeDVD (www.blazevideo.com, $49.95)

- PowerDVD (www.cyberlink.com, $59.95)

- WinDVD (www.corel.com, $49.99)

- Zoom Player (www.inmatrix.com, free)

Watching Online Videos on Your Living Room TV

Watching movies and other online videos on your PC is fine if you're on the go, but it's not the same as watching programming on the flat screen TV you have in your living room. Some newer TVs (sometimes called "smart" TVs) have built-in Internet, so you can watch Netflix and Hulu directly from the TV itself. Older TVs, however, don't have Internet connections, which means you're limited to over-the-air and cable/satellite programming.

You can, however, connect many PCs to your TV to watch Internet-based programming. All you need is the right connections on your PC and the right connecting cable.

If your computer has an HDMI connector, it's an easy task. HDMI is the cable technology used to connect high-definition Blu-ray players, cable boxes, and other equipment to flatscreen TVs; the HDMI cable carries both audio and video signals. Just connect an HDMI cable from your PC to a similar HDMI input on your TV, and you're ready to go. Start Netflix, Hulu, or YouTube on your PC, as you would normally, and then switch your TV to the corresponding HDMI input. The programming you're playing on your PC is displayed on your TV. Sit back and start watching.

THE ABSOLUTE MINIMUM

Here are the key points to remember from this chapter:

- If you want to watch movies and classic TV programming, subscribe to either Netflix or Hulu Plus.

- If you want to watch recent Hollywood movies, you need to purchase or rent from an online video store, such as the iTunes Store, which you access from the iTunes app.

- If you want to watch videos uploaded by other users, check out YouTube.

- If you want to play DVD movies on your PC, you need to purchase a separate DVD-player application.

- To watch streaming video from your PC on your living room TV, connect an HDMI cable from your PC to your TV.

PLAYING MUSIC

Your personal computer is a full-featured digital music machine. You can use your PC to stream music from Pandora and other online services, download music from the iTunes Store and other online music stores, create your own digital music library, and even play music from CDs. There's a whole world of great music ahead!

Listening to Streaming Music Online

The music industry has changed a lot in the past 10–15 years. In the late 1990s everybody was listening to music on compact discs—which themselves had supplanted vinyl records and cassettes in the 1980s. In the early 2000s, however, we all learned to love digital music downloads from the Internet, first from unauthorized download sites, such as Napster, and later from legal online music stores, such as Apple's iTunes Store.

Digital downloading (and ripping digital music from purchased CDs) was the big thing for a while, but within the past few years we've seen another significant change in the way we get our music. We're now in the decade of streaming music, where an increasing number of music lovers listen to music online, without purchasing a single song. It's kind of like a highly personalized type of radio, delivered to our computers (and smartphones and tablets) over the Internet.

These online music services don't download music files to your computer or other device; instead, music is streamed in real time. You need an Internet connection to stream music in this fashion, of course, but there always seems to be some sort of connection nearby. (If there isn't, you can't listen to your streaming music.)

There are two primary types of delivery services for streaming audio over the Internet. The first model, typified by Spotify, enables you to specify which songs you want to listen to; we call these *on-demand services*. The second model, typified by Pandora, is more like traditional radio in that you can't dial up specific tunes; you have to listen to whatever the service beams out, but in the form of personalized playlists or virtual radio stations. There are also traditional radio stations online, which offer less personalized listening.

Listening to Spotify and Other On-Demand Streaming Services

The first type of streaming music service is the on-demand service. With these services, you can search for and play specific tracks by specific artists. You can also play entire albums or multiple-song playlists either you or other users create. Some services also let you create virtual "radio stations" based on criteria you select—that is, you specify a song or artist or genre, and let the service pick which tracks to play.

Some of these services are free, but play commercials every few songs. Others offer monthly subscription plans and do away with the commercials; most plans run $5–$10 per month. (Some services, like Spotify, offer both free and subscription plans, with the subscription plans being commercial-free.)

You access most streaming music services either from Internet Explorer or another web browser or from a free app. In most instances, listening is as easy as going to the music service's website, searching for the music you want, and clicking the Play button.

What kind of music can you find on these on-demand music services? Pretty much anything you want! Most of these services offer tens of millions of tracks in a variety of genres for your listening pleasure. Although there are some notable holdouts in the artist community (you won't find any Beatles songs streaming online), I think you'll be pleasantly surprised at what you get for a low (or non-existent) monthly fee.

Table 24.1 compares the most popular on-demand streaming music services today.

TABLE 24.1 On-Demand Streaming Music Services

Service	URL	Price	Selection (Number of Tracks Available)
Apple Music	www.apple.com/music/	Subscription ($9.99/month)	30 million
Google Play Music All Access	play.google.com/about/music/	Subscription ($9.99/month)	22 million
Rdio	www.rdio.com	Free (ad supported) Subscription ($4.99–$9.99/month)	22 million
Rhapsody Premier	www.rhapsody.com	Subscription ($9.99/month)	32 million
Slacker Premium	www.slacker.com	Free (ad supported) Subscription ($9.99/month)	13 million
Spotify	www.spotify.com	Free (ad supported) Subscription ($4.99–$9.99/month)	30 million
Xbox Music Pass	music.xbox.com	Subscription ($9.99/month)	30 million

Of these on-demand services, Spotify is far and away the most popular. You can listen to Spotify from the service's website (using its Web player), or via its traditional desktop application.

Spotify's basic membership is free, but you're subjected to commercials every few songs. If you want to get rid of the commercials (and get on-demand music on your mobile devices), you need to pay for a $9.99/month subscription.

Most listeners use the Spotify app on their computers. As you can see in Figure 24.1, you can browse for music by genre or use the search box to search for specific songs, albums, or artists. You can also listen to lists compiled by Spotify or by other users.

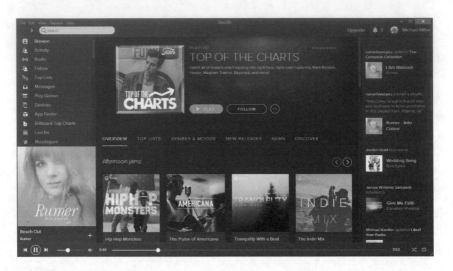

FIGURE 24.1

Listening to on-demand streaming music with the Spotify app.

When you choose a track or album, the album cover appears in the lower-left corner, along with the traditional playback controls. Click Pause to pause playback and Play to resume playback. You can also use the "scrub" control at the bottom to move to a specific point within the current song.

Listening to Pandora and Other Personalized Playlist Services

In contrast to on-demand streaming music services, the second type of service doesn't let you call up specific songs. Instead, you create your own personalized music station based on a song or artist you specify.

So, for example, if you like James Taylor, these services enable you to create a station based on the music of James Taylor. You'll get some James Taylor tunes and additional tracks by artists who are similar to Mr. Taylor.

Similarly, you can create stations based on specific tracks or broader genres. It's kind of like listening to traditional radio, in that you have no control over what track plays next—save being able to skip songs you don't like. And, just like radio, you can't rewind or repeat a given track; you have to listen to songs in the order presented.

Table 24.2 details the most popular of these personalized playlist streaming music services.

TABLE 24.2 Personalized Playlist Streaming Music Services

Service	URL	Price	Selection (Number of Tracks Available)
Pandora Radio	www.pandora.com	Free (ad supported)	1 million+
		Subscription ($4.99/month)	
Rhapsody unRadio	www.rhapsody.com	Subscription ($4.99/month)	32 million
Slacker Radio	www.slacker.com	Free (ad supported)	13 million
		Subscription ($3.99/month)	

Although there are services with larger music libraries, the most popular of these personalized playlist services is Pandora. That's probably because Pandora does such a good job at identifying music you like. Using the Music Genome Project as its base, Pandora considers more than 400 different musical attributes, such as syncopation and tonality, when selecting the next song to play. You can then give a track a thumbs up or thumbs down, further fine-tuning the current station.

Most listeners use Pandora for free and put up with the commercials. If you want to get rid of the commercials, pay $4.99/month for a Pandora One subscription.

As you can see in Figure 24.2, Pandora runs in your web browser. The "stations" you've created appear in a list on the left side of the window, with information about the currently playing track and artist in the middle. Playback controls are on top, along with the name of the current track.

FIGURE 24.2

Listening to a personalized radio station in Pandora.

To create a new station, simply enter the name of a song, artist, or type of music into the Create Station box at the top left. Pandora then creates the station and adds it to your list.

Listening to Traditional Radio Stations Online

In addition to all the personalized stations you can create with Pandora and similar services, you can also listen to traditional AM and FM radio over your computer. You don't need to have a radio handy to listen to your favorite stations; just tune in over the Internet using your web browser. (These services are also great if you want to listen to your hometown radio stations when you're on vacation, or if you've moved away.)

There are two main services for listening to AM/FM radio online: iHeartRadio (www.iheart.com) and TuneIn Radio (www.tunein.com). Both let you browse or search for local stations by location and genre. TuneIn Radio also lets you listen in to local police and fire bands, whereas iHeartRadio offers a selection of web-only and user-created custom stations. Both services are free. (Figure 24.3 shows the TuneIn Radio website playing a local Minneapolis radio station.)

FIGURE 24.3

Listening to a local FM station with TuneIn Radio.

NOTE If you listen to Sirius or XM satellite radio in your car, you can also listen to Sirius/XM Radio online, at www.siriusxm. com/player/. This is a subscription-only service with more than 130 channels of music, news, and talk—including several web-only channels that aren't available via normal satellite radio.

Purchasing and Downloading Digital Music

Streaming music services enables you to listen to all the music you want, which is great. The only bad thing about this is that you don't actually own any of this music; you have to be connected to the Internet and the service to get access to the music they offer.

If you're of a certain age, you're more used to compiling your own personal music collection. Although compact discs are fast becoming old tech, you can still create your own music library—via digital music you purchase and download from the Internet.

There are a number of digital music stores online. The oldest and largest of these is Apple's iTunes Store, with more than 37 million tracks available for purchase. Also popular are the Amazon Digital Music Store and Google Play Music; the former with more than 18 million tracks available, the latter with more than 22 million tracks.

TIP The iTunes Store is the store of choice if you have an Apple iPhone, iPod, or iPad; it fits in seamlessly with the Apple infrastructure and offers music in Apple's popular AAC file format. The Amazon and Google stores are more universal (and preferred if you have an Android smartphone or tablet), offering music in the ubiquitous MP3 file format.

Purchasing Music from the iTunes Store

To access Apple's iTunes Store (and to play back any music you've downloaded) you need to install the iTunes software. It's free; download it at www.apple.com/itunes/.

When you launch the iTunes software, click the iTunes Store button at the top of the window. This connects you to the Internet and displays the Store's home page. To view only music items, as shown in Figure 24.4, click the Music icon at the top-left corner of the window.

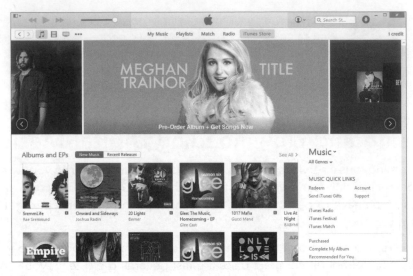

FIGURE 24.4

Shopping for music in the iTunes Store.

To browse music by category, click All Genres on the right and select a category. Alternatively, you can search for a given song, album, or artist by entering the appropriate query into the search box at the top of the iTunes window.

After you see a list of albums, click an album cover to view all the tracks in that album, as shown in Figure 24.5. To purchase an individual track, click the Buy (price) button for that track; to purchase an entire album, click the Buy button for that album.

FIGURE 24.5

Purchasing music from the iTunes Store.

Individual tracks in the iTunes Store range from 69 cents to $1.29 each. You can also purchase and download complete albums.

 NOTE The iTunes Store offers more than just music for download. iTunes also sells (or rents) movies, TV shows, music videos, podcasts, audiobooks, and eBooks (in the ePub format). You even get access to iTunes U, which offers all manner of textbooks, courses, and educational materials, and Apple's App Store for the iPhone and iPad.

Purchasing Music from the Amazon Digital Music Store

Amazon's Digital Music Store offers individual songs and complete albums in the Universal MP3 digital music file format. Songs start at 69 cents each, with album prices running $5 and up. You can access the store at www.amazon.com/mp3/.

As you can see in Figure 24.6, you can browse for music by genre (click a category in the left column) or search for specific songs, albums, and artists, using the top-of-page search box. When you open a product page for a given album, you have the option of purchasing the entire album or individual tracks. The songs you purchase are then downloaded to your PC.

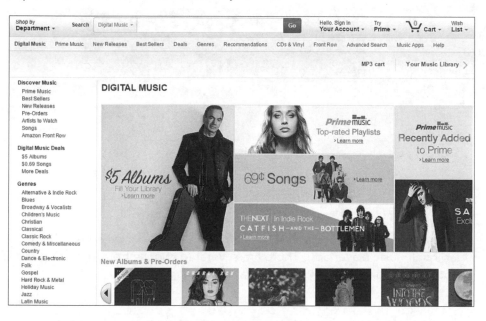

FIGURE 24.6

Shopping for music from Amazon's Digital Music Store.

Purchasing Music from Google Play Music

The Google Play Music Store, like the Amazon store, offers individual tracks and complete albums for purchase and download in the MP3 file format. You access the Google store from your web browser, at play.google.com/store/music/.

As you can see in Figure 24.7, you can display music by genre, Top Charts, and New Releases. Navigate to an album page and you have the option of purchasing the complete album (typically in the $9.99 range) or individual tracks (most at $1.29). Items you purchased are automatically downloaded to your PC.

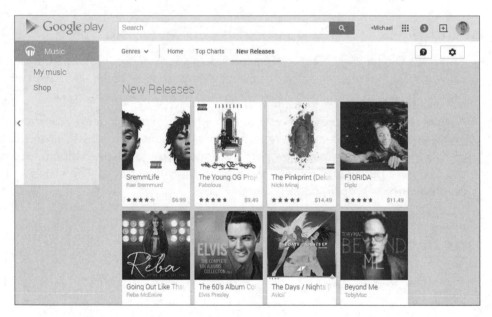

FIGURE 24.7

Shopping for music from the Google Play Music Store.

Playing Digital Music on Your PC

To play the digital music you download or rip from your personal CDs, you need a digital music player app. There are several to choose from, including the iTunes, Xbox Music, and Windows Media Player apps.

Playing Music with the iTunes App

You use the iTunes software to play any music you've purchased from the iTunes Store. (The software is kind of a one-stop-shop for music in the Apple ecosystem.) As you recall, iTunes is a free app you can download from www.apple.com/itunes/.

To display all the music stored on your PC, click the My Music button at the top of the iTunes window. As you can see in Figure 24.8, iTunes displays the album view by default. To view your music by song, recording artist, or genre, click the down arrow at the top right and make a new selection.

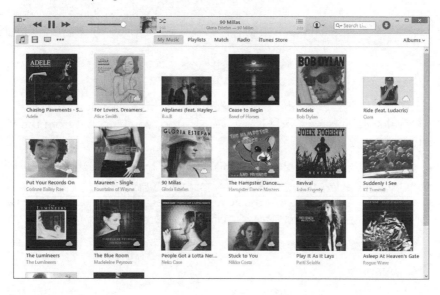

FIGURE 24.8

Viewing and playing digital music in the iTunes player.

To play an individual track or album, double-click that item. A mini-player displays at the top of the iTunes window, along with a set of playback controls. Click the Pause button to pause playback; click the Play button to resume playback.

> **NOTE** If you have an iPhone, iPod, or iPad, you can also use the iTunes software to synchronize ("sync") music from your computer to your portable device. If you've downloaded or ripped new music to your PC, it will be automatically copied to your portable device the next time you connect your device to your computer.

The iTunes program also enables you to combine multiple songs into a single playlist. To create a new playlist, start by clicking the Playlists button to display the Playlists pane. Click the + button at the bottom of the Playlists pane and then click New Playlist. When the new Playlists pane appears on the right side of the window, enter a title for this playlist into the first text box. To add a song to this playlist, drag it from the Content pane into the Playlists pane. Repeat this step to add multiple songs to the playlist and, when you finish adding tracks to the playlist, click the Done button.

To play a playlist, click the Playlists button to display the Playlists pane, and then click that playlist. The contents of the selected playlist display in the Content pane; click the Play button to begin playback.

 TIP To play the tracks in the playlist in random order, click the Shuffle icon in the mini-player. (When activated, the Shuffle icon turns blue.)

Playing Music with the Groove Music App

Microsoft includes two different music player apps in Windows 10. The newer Universal-style app is called Groove Music App; you launch it from the Windows Start menu.

As you can see in Figure 24.9, you display your music collection by clicking Collection in the left navigation pane. You can then display your music by album, artist, or song—and sort your music alphabetically, by date added, by release year, by genre, or by artist. Double-click an album to display its contents.

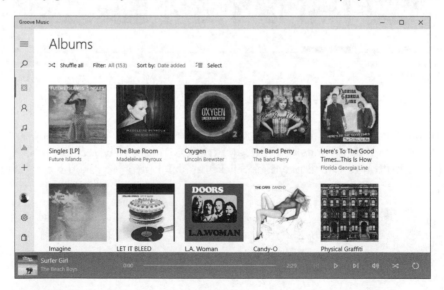

FIGURE 24.9

Browsing albums with the Groove Music app.

As you can see in Figure 24.10, all the tracks of an album display on the album page. To play back an entire album, click the Play button. To play a specific track, double-click that track. Playback controls are located at the bottom of the window.

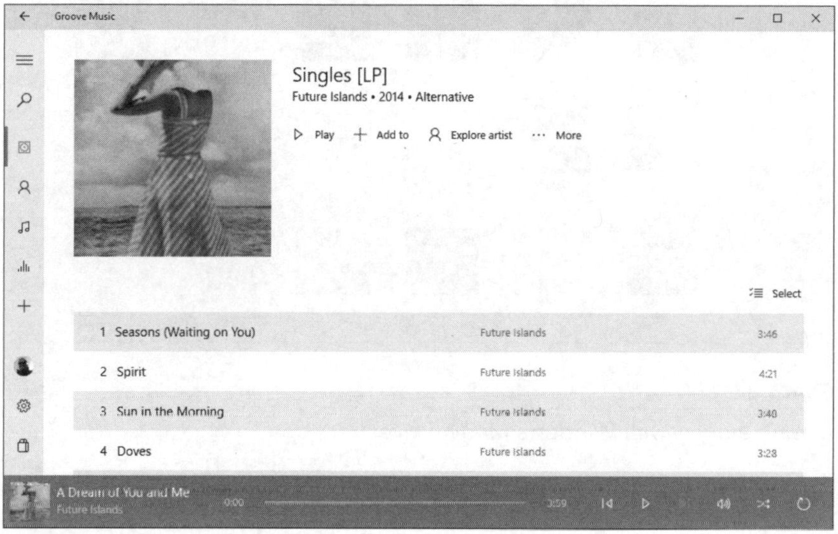

FIGURE 24.10

Playing an album with the Groove Music app.

You can create a new playlist by clicking New Playlist in the navigation pane and then giving the playlist a name. To add a song to a playlist, drag the track from the content pane to the playlist in the navigation pane. To play a playlist, double-click it in the navigation pane.

Playing Music with Windows Media Player

The Groove Music app is nice, but there are some things it can't do, such as play, burn, or rip CDs. Some users prefer the versatility of Microsoft's Windows Media Player, a more traditional desktop app that's been around for a decade or more now.

You launch Windows Media Player (WMP) from the Windows Start menu. Use the navigation pane on the left to display your music by artist, album, or genre, as shown in Figure 24.11. Double-click an album to open it and begin playback; double-click an individual track to play it. Playback controls are at the bottom of the window.

FIGURE 24.11

Browsing albums with Windows Media Player.

To view all your existing playlists, click Playlists in the navigation pane. Click the Create Playlist button to create a new playlist; to add a song to a playlist, drag it from the contents pane to the name of the playlist in the navigation pane.

Listening to CDs on Your PC

If your PC has a CD/DVD drive, it's easy to play CDs on your PC. You can also use your PC to rip music from a CD to store digitally on your computer or to burn a new CD from digital music stored on your PC.

You can use either iTunes or Windows Media Player to play, rip, and burn CDs. We'll use WMP for our examples next.

 NOTE   The process of copying music from a CD to a computer's hard drive, in digital format, is called *ripping*. The reverse process, copying music from your PC to a blank CD, is called *burning*.

Playing a CD

To play a CD with WMP, open the program and then insert your music CD into your PC's CD/DVD drive. The CD should automatically appear in the WMP window, with all the tracks listed, as shown in Figure 24.12. Click the Play button to begin playback; click Pause to pause playback. You can also click the Forward arrow to skip to the next track on the CD or the Back arrow to skip to the previous track. Double-click a specific track to jump directly to that track.

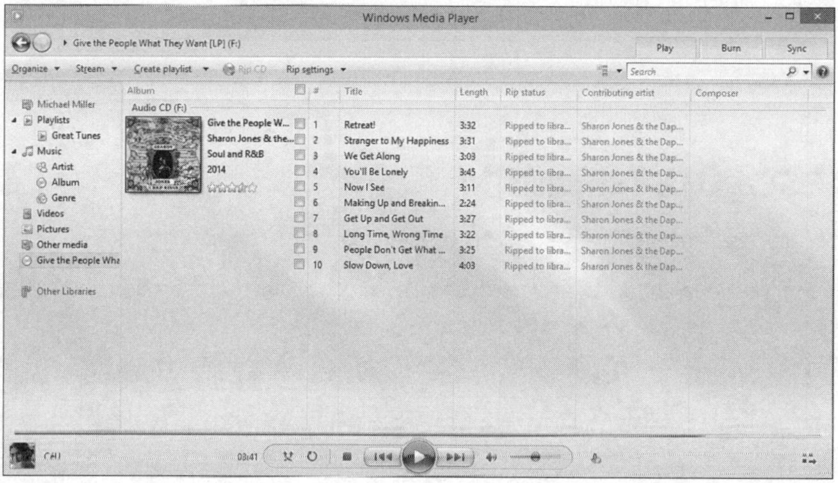

FIGURE 24.12

Viewing a track list with Windows Media Player.

Ripping a CD to Your PC

You can also use WMP to copy songs from any CD to your PC's hard drive for future listening on your computer. Start by launching WMP and then inserting the music CD into your PC's CD/DVD drive.

The CD should automatically appear in the WMP window. Check those tracks you want to copy to your computer, and uncheck those you don't want to copy.

Next, click the Rip CD button. The selected tracks are now copied to your PC's hard disk and automatically added to the Music library.

Burning Your Own CDs

You might prefer to take CDs with you to play in your car or on the go. Did you know that you can use WMP to create your own "mix" CDs, with tracks from multiple artists and albums? It's called *burning* a CD, and it's relatively easy to do.

From within WMP, click the Burn tab in the right pane. Now navigate to the albums and tracks you want to include on the CD, and drag the tracks you want onto the Burn pane. Make sure that the running time of the songs you select is less than 80 minutes long because that's the maximum length you can put on a CD.

Next, insert a blank CD into your PC's CD drive. Click the Start Burn button at the top of the Burn pane. WMP copies the selected tracks to the blank CD and ejects the disc when it's done.

THE ABSOLUTE MINIMUM

Here are the key points to remember from this chapter:

- You can listen to music over the Internet with streaming music services such as Spotify and Pandora.

- You can purchase and download digital music from online music stores, such as the iTunes Store, Amazon Digital Music Store, and Google Play Store.

- To play digital music stored on your PC, use a music player app, such as iTunes, Groove Music, or Windows Music Player.

- Use Windows Music Player or iTunes to play, rip, and burn CDs on your PC.

PROTECTING YOUR PC FROM COMPUTER ATTACKS, MALWARE, AND SPAM

As you've seen, a lot of what you'll do on your computer revolves around the Internet. Unfortunately, when you connect your computer to the Internet, you open a whole new can of worms—literally. Computer worms, viruses, spyware, spam, and the like can attack your computer and cause it to run slowly or not at all. In addition to these malicious software programs (called *malware*) that can infect your computer, you're likely to come across all manner of inappropriate content that you'd probably rather avoid. It can be a nasty world online if you let it be.

Fortunately, it's **easy** to protect your computer and your family from these dangers. All you need are a few software utilities—and a lot of common sense!

Safeguarding Your System from Computer Viruses

A *computer virus* is a malicious software program designed to do damage to your computer system by deleting files or even taking over your PC to launch attacks on other systems. A virus attacks your computer when you launch an infected software program, launching a "payload" that oftentimes is catastrophic.

Watching for Signs of Infection

How do you know whether your computer system has been infected with a virus?

In general, whenever your computer starts acting different from normal, it's possible that you have a virus. You might see strange messages or graphics displayed on your computer screen or find that normally well-behaved programs are acting erratically. You might discover that certain files have gone missing from your hard disk or that your system is acting sluggish—or failing to start at all. You might even find that your friends are receiving emails from you (that you never sent) that have suspicious files attached.

If your computer exhibits one or more of these symptoms—especially if you've just downloaded a file from the Internet or received a suspicious email message—the prognosis is not good. Your computer is probably infected.

 NOTE   Many computer attacks today are executed using personal computers compromised by a computer virus. These so-called *zombie computers* are operated via remote control in an ad hoc attack network called a *botnet*. A firewall program protects against incoming attacks and botnet controllers.

Catching a Virus

Whenever you share data with another computer or computer user (which you do all the time when you're connected to the Internet), you risk exposing your computer to potential viruses. There are many ways you can share data and transmit a virus:

- Opening an infected file attached to an email message or instant message or sent to you from within a social network
- Launching an infected program file downloaded from the Internet
- Sharing a USB memory drive or data CD that contains an infected file
- Sharing over a network a computer file that contains an infection

Of all these methods, the most common means of virus infection is via email. Whenever you open a file attached to an email message, you stand a good chance of infecting your computer system with a virus—even if the file was sent by someone you know and trust. That's because many viruses "spoof" the sender's name, thus making you think the file is from a friend or colleague. The bottom line is that no email or instant message attachment is safe unless you were expressly expecting it.

Practicing Safe Computing

Because you're not going to completely quit doing any of these activities, you'll never be 100% safe from the threat of computer viruses. There are, however, some steps you can take to reduce your risk:

- Don't open email attachments from people you don't know—or even from people you do know, if you aren't expecting them. That's because some viruses can hijack the address book on an infected PC, thus sending out infected email that the owner isn't even aware of. Just looking at an email message won't harm anything; the damage comes when you open a file attached to the email. A good rule of thumb is that if you weren't expecting the file, don't open it.

- Don't accept files sent to you via instant messaging or social networking chat; like email attachments, files sent via messaging and chat can be easily infected with viruses and spyware.

- Download files only from reliable file archive websites, such as Download. com (www.download.com) and Tucows (www.tucows.com/downloads), or from legitimate online stores, such as the Windows Store.

- Don't access or download files from music and video file-sharing networks, which are notoriously virus and spyware-ridden. Instead, download music and movies from legitimate sites, such as the iTunes Store and Amazon Digital Music Store.

- Don't execute programs you find posted to web message boards or blogs.

- Don't click links sent to you from strangers via instant messaging or in a chat room.

- Share USB drives, CDs, and files only with users you know and trust.

- Use antivirus software—and keep it up-to-date with the most recent virus definitions.

These precautions—especially the first one about not opening email attachments—should provide good insurance against the threat of computer viruses.

 CAUTION   If you remember nothing else from this chapter, remember this: Never open an unexpected file attachment. Period!

Disinfecting Your System with Antivirus Software

Antivirus software programs can detect known viruses and protect your system against new, unknown viruses. These programs check your system for viruses each time your system is booted and can be configured to check any programs you download from the Internet. They're also used to disinfect your system if it becomes infected with a virus.

Fortunately, Windows 10 comes with its own built-in antivirus utility. It's called Windows Defender, and you can see it in action by clicking the Windows Defender item in the Windows System folder on the Start menu.

 NOTE   Windows Defender may or may not be activated on your new PC. Some computer manufacturers prefer to include third-party antivirus software and thus disable Windows Defender by default.

As you can see in Figure 25.1, Windows Defender runs in the background, monitoring your computer against all sorts of malware, including both viruses and spyware. Although Defender automatically scans your system on its own schedule, you can opt to perform a manual scan at any time by clicking the Scan Now button.

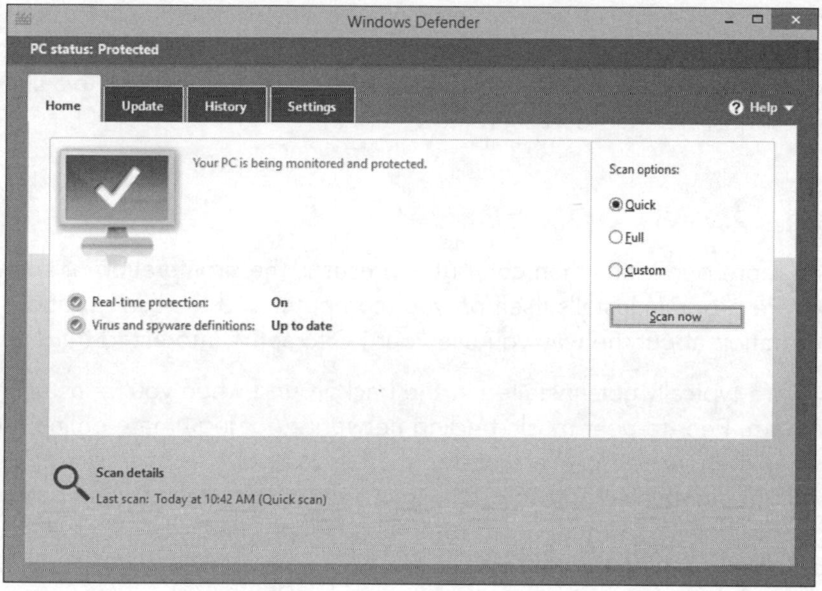

FIGURE 25.1

Windows Defender—the built-in antimalware utility for Windows.

Of course, you're not locked into using Microsoft's antimalware solution. There are a lot of third-party antivirus programs available, including the following:

- AVG Anti-Virus (www.avg.com)

- Avira Antivirus (www.avira.com)

- Kaspersky Anti-Virus (www.kaspersky.com)

- McAfee AntiVirus Plus (www.mcafee.com)

- Malwarebytes Anti-Malware (www.malwarebytes.org)

- Norton Security (http://us.norton.com)

- Webroot AntiVirus (www.webroot.com)

- Trend Micro Antivirus + Security (www.trendmicro.com)

CAUTION   Your antivirus software is next to useless if you don't update it at least weekly. An outdated antivirus program won't recognize—and protect against—the latest computer viruses.

Whichever antivirus program you choose, you need to configure it to go online periodically to update the virus definition database the program uses to look for known virus files. Because new viruses are created every week, this file of known viruses must be updated accordingly.

Hunting Down Spyware

Even more pernicious than computer viruses is the proliferation of *spyware*. A spyware program installs itself on your computer and then surreptitiously sends information about the way you use your PC to some interested third party.

Spyware typically gets installed in the background when you're installing another program. Peer-to-peer music-trading networks (*not* legitimate online music stores, such as the iTunes Store) are one of the biggest sources of spyware; when you install the file-trading software, the spyware is also installed. Also bad are fly-by-night file download sites, which often trick you into installing spyware as part of the software download process.

Having spyware on your system is nasty—almost as bad as being infected with a computer virus. Some spyware programs even hijack your computer and launch pop-up windows and advertisements when you visit certain web pages. If there's spyware on your computer, you definitely want to get rid of it.

Unfortunately, many antivirus programs won't catch spyware because spyware isn't a virus. To track down and uninstall these programs, then, you might need to run a separate antispyware utility.

 NOTE   Windows Defender, included free in Windows 10, guards against both viruses and spyware.

Here are some of the best of these spyware fighters:

- Ad-Aware (www.lavasoftusa.com)
- Spybot Search & Destroy (www.safer-networking.org)

In addition, some of the major Internet security suites include antispyware modules. Check the program's feature list before you buy.

Defending Against Computer Attacks

Connecting to the Internet is a two-way street—not only can your PC access other computers online, but other computers can also access *your* PC. This means that, unless you take proper precautions, malicious hackers can read your private data, damage your system hardware and software, and even use your system (via remote control) to cause damage to other computers.

You protect your system against an outside attack by blocking the path of attack with a *firewall*. A firewall is a software program that forms a virtual barrier between your computer and the Internet. The firewall selectively filters the data that is passed between both ends of the connection and protects your system against an outside attack.

Using the Windows Firewall

Fortunately for all of us, Microsoft builds a firewall utility into Windows. The Windows Firewall is activated by default; although, you can always check to make sure that it's up and working properly. You do this by opening the Windows Control Panel, clicking System and Security, and then clicking Windows Firewall.

Using Third-Party Firewall Software

For most users, the Windows Firewall is more than enough protection against computer attacks. That said, a number of third-party firewall programs also are available, most of which are more robust and offer more protection than the Windows built-in firewall. The best of these programs include

- Comodo Firewall (personalfirewall.comodo.com)
- ZoneAlarm Free Firewall (www.zonealarm.com/software/free-firewall/)

 NOTE   If you're running a third-party firewall program, you might need to turn off the Windows Firewall so that the two don't interfere with each other.

Fighting Email Spam

If you're like most users, you get a fair amount of unsolicited, unauthorized, and unwanted email messages in your inbox—in other words, *spam*. These spam messages are the online equivalent of the junk mail you receive in your postal mailbox and are a huge problem.

Although it's probably impossible to do away with 100% of the spam you receive (you can't completely stop junk mail, either), there are steps you can take to reduce the amount of spam you have to deal with. The heavier your spam load, the more steps you can take.

Protecting Your Email Address

Spammers accumulate email addresses via a variety of methods. Some use high-tech methods to harvest email addresses listed on public web pages and message board postings. Others use the tried-and-true approach of buying names from list brokers. Still others automatically generate addresses using a "dictionary" of common names and email domains.

One way to reduce the amount of spam you receive is to limit the public use of your email address. It's a simple fact: The more you expose your email address, the more likely it is that a spammer will find it—and use it.

To this end, you should avoid putting your email address on your web page or your company's web page. You should also avoid including your email address in postings you make to web-based message boards or Usenet newsgroups. In addition, you should most definitely not include your email address in any of the conversations you have in chat rooms or via instant messaging.

Another strategy is to actually use *two* email addresses. Take your main email address (the one you get from your ISP) and hand it out only to a close circle of friends and family; do *not* use this address to post public messages or to register at websites. Then obtain a second email address (you can get a free one at Outlook.com or Gmail) and use that one for all your public activity. When you post on a message board or newsgroup, use the second address. When you order something from an online merchant, use the second address. When you register for website access, use the second address. Over time, the second address will attract the spam; your first email address will remain private and relatively spam-free.

 TIP If you do have to leave your email address in a public forum, you can insert a spamblock into your address—an unexpected word or phrase that, although easily removed, will confuse the software spammers use to harvest addresses. For example, if your email address is johnjones@myisp.com, you might change the address to read johnSPAMBLOCKjones@myisp.com. Other users will know to remove the SPAMBLOCK from the address before emailing you, but the spam harvesting software will be foiled.

Blocking Spammers in Your Email Programs

Most email software and web-based email services include some sort of spam filtering. You should always enable the antispam features in your email program or service. Doing so should block most of the unwanted messages you might otherwise receive.

 TIP   It's a good idea to review messages in your spam folder periodically to make sure no legitimate messages have been accidentally sent there.

Resisting Phishing Scams

Phishing is a technique used by online scam artists to steal your identity by tricking you into disclosing valuable personal information, such as passwords, credit card numbers, and other financial data. If you're not careful, you can mistake a phishing email for a real one—and open yourself up to identity theft.

A phishing scam typically starts with a phony email message that appears to be from a legitimate source, such as your bank, eBay, PayPal, or another official institution. When you click the link in the phishing email, you're taken to a fake website masquerading as the real site, complete with logos and official-looking text. You're encouraged to enter your personal information into the forms on the web page; when you do so, your information is sent to the scammer, and you're now a victim of identity theft. When your data falls into the hands of criminals, it can be used to hack into your online accounts, make unauthorized charges on your credit card, and maybe even drain your bank account.

Until recently, the only guard against phishing scams was common sense. That is, you were advised never to click through a link in an email message that asks for any type of personal information—whether that be your bank account number or eBay password. Even if the email *looks* official, it probably isn't; legitimate institutions and websites never include this kind of link in their official messages. Instead, access your personal information only by using your web browser to go directly to the website in question. Don't link there!

Fortunately, Windows now offers some protection against phishing scams, in the form of a SmartScreen Filter that alerts you to potential phishing sites. When you attempt to visit a known or suspected phishing site, the browser displays a warning message. Do not enter information into these suspected phishing sites—return to your home page instead! But even with these protections, you still need to use your head. Don't click through suspicious email links, and don't give out your personal information and passwords unless you're sure you're dealing with an official (and not just an official-looking) site!

Shielding Your Children from Inappropriate Content

The Internet contains an almost limitless supply of information on its tens of billions of web pages. Although most of these pages contain useful information, it's a sad fact that the content of some pages can be quite offensive to some people—and that there are some Internet users who prey on unsuspecting youths.

As a responsible parent, you want to protect your children from any of the bad stuff (and bad people) online, while still allowing access to all the good stuff. How do you do this?

Using Content-Filtering Software

If you can't trust your children to always click away from inappropriate web content, you can choose to install software on your computer that performs filtering functions for all your online sessions. These safe-surfing programs guard against either a preselected list of inappropriate sites or a preselected list of topics—and then block access to sites that meet the selected criteria. After you have the software installed, your kids won't be able to access the really bad sites on the Web.

The most popular filtering programs include the following:

- CyberPatrol (www.cyberpatrol.com)
- CYBERsitter (www.cybersitter.com)
- Net Nanny (www.netnanny.com)

In addition, many of the big Internet security suites (such as those from McAfee and Norton/Symantec) offer built-in content-filtering modules.

Encouraging Safe Computing

Although using content-filtering software is a good first step, the most important thing you can do, as a parent, is to create an environment that encourages appropriate use of the Internet. Nothing replaces traditional parental supervision, and at the end of the day, you have to take responsibility for your children's online activities. Provide the guidance they need to make the Internet a fun and educational place to visit—and your entire family will be better for it.

Here are some guidelines you can follow to ensure a safer surfing experience for your family:

- Make sure that your children know never to give out identifying information (home address, school name, telephone number, and so on) or to send their photos to other users online. This includes not putting overly personal information (and photos!) on their Facebook or Twitter pages.

- Provide each of your children with an online pseudonym so they don't have to use their real names online.

- Don't let your children arrange face-to-face meetings with other computer users without parental permission and supervision. If a meeting is arranged, make the first one in a public place, and be sure to accompany your child.

- Teach your children that people online might not always be who they seem; just because someone says that she's a 10-year-old girl doesn't necessarily mean that she really is 10 years old, or a girl.

- Consider making Internet surfing an activity you do together with your younger children—or turn it into a family activity by putting your kids' PC in a public room (such as a living room or den) rather than in a private bedroom.

- Set reasonable rules and guidelines for your kids' computer use. Consider limiting the number of minutes/hours they can spend online each day.

- Monitor your children's Internet activities. Ask them to keep a log of all websites they visit or check their browser history; oversee any chat sessions they participate in; check out any files they download; even consider sharing an email account (especially with younger children) so that you can oversee their messages.

- Don't let your children respond to messages that are suggestive, obscene, belligerent, or threatening—or that make them feel uncomfortable in any way. Encourage your children to tell you if they receive any such messages, and then report the senders to your ISP.

- Install content-filtering software on your PC, and set up one of the kid-safe search sites (discussed earlier in this section) as your browser's start page.

Teach your children that Internet access is not a right; it should be a privilege earned by your children and kept only when their use of it matches your expectations.

THE ABSOLUTE MINIMUM

Here are the key points to remember from this chapter:

- Avoid computer viruses by not opening unsolicited email attachments and by using an antivirus software program.

- Use antispyware tools to track down and remove spyware programs from your computer.

- Windows 10 has its own Windows Defender antimalware utility that guards against computer viruses and spyware.

- Protect your computer from an Internet-based attack by turning on the Windows Firewall or using a third-party firewall program.

- Fight email spam by keeping your email address as private as possible and utilizing your email program's spam filter.

- Avoid falling for phishing scams characterized by fake—but official-looking—email messages.

- To protect against inappropriate content on the Internet, install content-filtering software—and make sure you monitor your children's online activities.

26

PERFORMING PREVENTIVE MAINTENANCE AND DEALING WITH COMMON PROBLEMS

"An ounce of prevention is worth a pound of cure."

That old adage might seem trite and clichéd, but it's also true—especially when it comes to your computer system. Spending a few minutes a week on preventive maintenance can save you from costly computer problems in the future.

To make this chore a little easier, Windows includes several utilities to help you keep your system running smoothly. You should use these tools as part of your regular maintenance routine—or if you experience specific problems with your computer system.

And if you experience more serious problems—well, try not to panic. There are ways to fix most issues you encounter, without necessarily calling in the tech support guys.

Maintaining Your Computer

Most computers these days, especially those running Windows 10, don't require a lot of handholding to keep them up and running. That said, there's a little bit of routine maintenance you might want to undertake—just to make sure your system remains in its optimal operating condition.

Cleaning Up Unused Files

Most desktop and notebook computers have pretty big hard disks; ultrabooks and tablets do not. But even if your computer has a tremendous amount of storage, it's still easy to end up with too many useless files and programs taking up too much disk space.

Fortunately, Windows includes a utility that identifies and deletes unused files. The Disk Cleanup tool is what you want to use when you need to free up extra hard disk space for more frequently used files.

To use Disk Cleanup, follow these steps:

1. Open File Explorer.

2. Navigate to the This PC section, right-click the drive you want to clean up— usually the C: drive (Local Disk)— and click Properties to open the Properties dialog box.

3. Select the General tab (displayed by default), and then click the Disk Cleanup button.

TIP You can also access drive tools from File Explorer's Manage tab on the Ribbon.

4. Disk Cleanup automatically analyzes the contents of your hard disk drive. When it's finished analyzing, it presents its results in the Disk Cleanup dialog box, shown in Figure 26.1.

5. You have the option of permanently deleting various types of files: downloaded program files, temporary Internet files, offline web pages, deleted files in the Recycle Bin, and so forth. Select which files you want to delete.

6. Click OK to begin deleting.

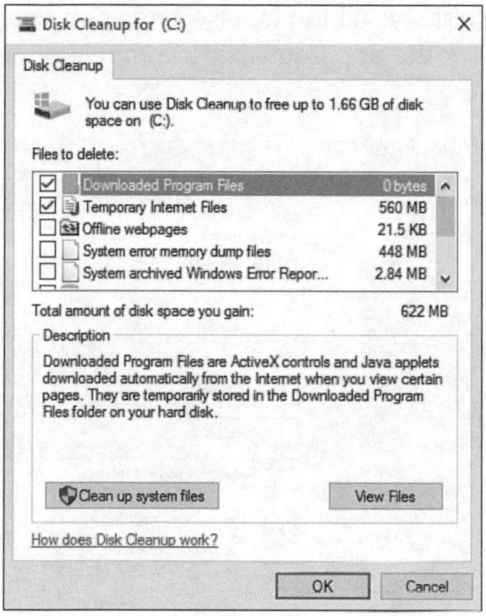

FIGURE 26.1

Use Disk Cleanup to delete unused files from your hard disk.

NOTE   You can safely choose to delete all the files found by Disk Cleanup except the setup log files, which the Windows operating system sometimes needs.

Removing Unused Programs

Another way to free up valuable hard disk space is to delete those programs you never use. This is accomplished using the Uninstall or Change a Program utilities in Windows. Use the following steps.

TIP   Most brand-new PCs come with unwanted programs and trial versions installed at the factory. Many users choose to delete these "bloatware" programs when they first run their PCs.

1. Click the Start button and select Settings to open the Settings window.

2. Click System to open the System settings.

3. Click to select the Apps & Features tab.

4. Windows now displays all the installed apps on your system, as shown in Figure 26.2. Click the app you want to remove; then click the Uninstall button for that app.

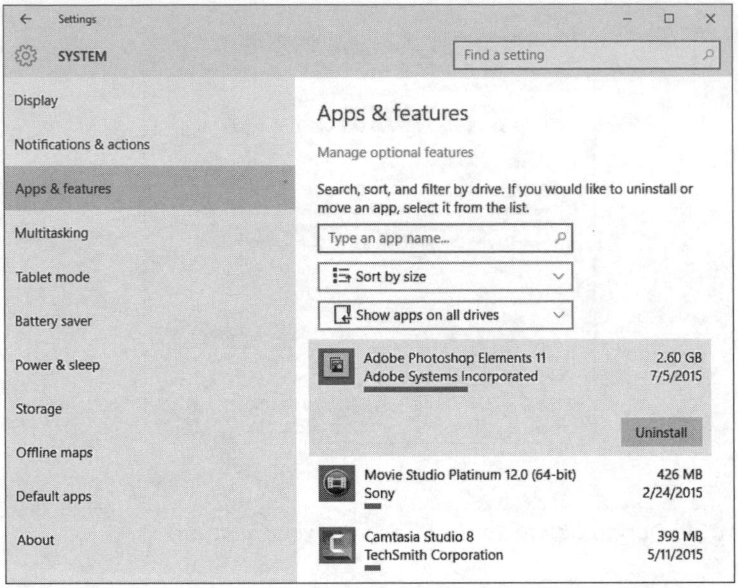

FIGURE 26.2

Uninstall any program you're no longer using.

Performing a Hard Disk Checkup with ScanDisk

Any time you run an application, move or delete a file, or accidentally turn the power off while the system is running, you run the risk of introducing errors to your hard disk. These errors can make it harder to open files, slow down your hard disk, or cause your system to freeze when you open or save a file or an application.

Fortunately, you can find and fix most of these errors directly from within Windows. All you have to do is run the built-in ScanDisk utility.

To find and fix errors on your hard drive, follow these steps:

1. Open File Explorer.

2. Navigate to the This PC section, right-click the drive you want to scan (usually the C: drive), and click Properties to open the Properties dialog box.

3. Select the Tools tab.

4. Click the Check button in the Error-Checking section.

5. When the Error Checking dialog box appears, click Scan Drive.

Windows now scans your hard disk and attempts to fix any errors it encounters. Note that you might be prompted to reboot your PC if you're checking your computer's C: drive.

Keeping Your Hardware in Tip-Top Condition

There's also a fair amount of preventive maintenance you can physically perform on your computer hardware. It's simple stuff, but it can really extend the life of your PC.

System Unit

The system unit on a traditional desktop PC—or the entire unit of an all-in-one, notebook, or tablet computer—has a lot of sensitive electronics inside, from memory chips to disk drives to power supplies. Check out these maintenance tips to keep your system unit from flaking out on you:

- Position your computer in a clean, dust-free environment. Keep it away from direct sunlight and strong magnetic fields. In addition, make sure that your system unit and your monitor have plenty of air flow around them to keep them from overheating.

- Hook up your system unit to a surge suppressor to avoid damaging power spikes.

- Avoid turning on and off your system unit too often; it's better to leave it on all the time than incur frequent "power on" stress to all those delicate components.

- However, turn off your system unit if you're going to be away for an extended period—anything longer than a few days.

- Check all your cable connections periodically. Make sure that all the connectors are firmly connected and all the screws properly screwed—and make sure that your cables aren't stretched too tight or bent in ways that could damage the wires inside.

Keyboard

Even something as simple as your computer keyboard requires a little preventive maintenance from time to time. Check out these tips:

- Keep your keyboard away from young children and pets—they can get dirt and hair and Play-Doh all over the place, and they have a tendency to put way too much pressure on the keys.

- Keep your keyboard away from dust, dirt, smoke, direct sunlight, and other harmful environmental stuff. You might even consider putting a dust cover on your keyboard when it's not in use.

- Use a small vacuum cleaner to periodically sweep the dirt from your keyboard. (Alternatively, you can use compressed air to *blow* the dirt away.) Use a cotton swab or soft cloth to clean between the keys. If necessary, remove the keycaps to clean the switches underneath.

- If you spill something on your keyboard, disconnect it immediately and wipe up the spill. Use a soft cloth to get between the keys; if necessary, use a screwdriver to pop off the keycaps and wipe up any seepage underneath. Let the keyboard dry thoroughly before trying to use it again.

Display

If you think of your computer display as a little television set, you're on the right track. Just treat your screen as you do your TV, and you'll be okay. That said, look at these preventive maintenance tips:

- As with all other important system components, keep your monitor away from direct sunlight, dust, and smoke. Make sure that it has plenty of ventilation, especially around the back; don't cover the rear cooling vents with paper or any other object, and don't set anything bigger than a small plush toy on top of the cabinet.

- With your monitor turned off, periodically clean the monitor screen. Use water to dampen a lint-free cloth, and then wipe the screen; do not spray liquid directly on the screen. Do not use any cleaner that contains alcohol or ammonia; these chemicals may damage an LCD screen. (You can, however, use commercial cleaning wipes specially formulated for LCD screens.)

- Don't forget to adjust the brightness and contrast controls on your monitor every now and then. Any controls can get out of whack—plus, your monitor's performance will change as it ages, and simple adjustments can often keep it looking as good as new.

Printer

Your printer is a complex device with a lot of moving parts. Follow these tips to keep your printouts in good shape:

- Use a soft cloth, mini-vacuum cleaner, or compressed air to clean the inside and outside of your printer on a periodic basis. In particular, make sure that you clean the paper path of all paper shavings and dust.

- If you have an inkjet printer, periodically clean the inkjets. Run your printer's cartridge cleaning utility, or use a small pin to make sure they don't get clogged.

- If you have a laser printer, replace the toner cartridge as needed. When you replace the cartridge, remember to clean the printer cleaning bar and other related parts, per the manufacturer's instructions.

- Don't use alcohol or other solvents to clean rubber or plastic parts—you'll do more harm than good!

Maintaining a Notebook PC

All the previous tips hold for both desktop and notebook PCs. If you have a notebook PC, however, there are additional steps you need to take to keep everything working in prime condition.

Using the Windows Mobility Center

Let's start with all the various settings that are unique to a notebook PC—power plan, display brightness, presentation settings, and so forth. Windows puts all these settings into a single control panel called the Windows Mobility Center. As you can see in Figure 26.3, you can use the Mobility Center to configure and manage just about everything that makes your notebook run better.

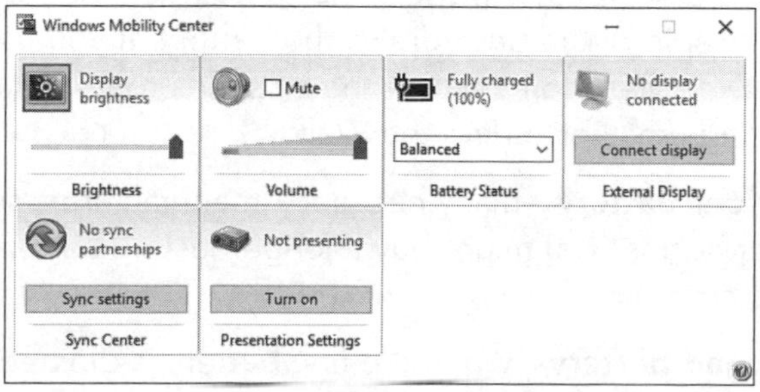

FIGURE 26.3

Manage key notebook PC settings with the Windows Mobility Center.

To access the Windows Mobility Center, right-click the Start button and then click Mobility Center. Click or tap the button or adjust the slider for whichever option you need to change.

 NOTE Some notebook manufacturers add their own mobile configuration settings to the Windows Mobility Center.

Conserving Battery Life

One of the key issues with a notebook PC is battery life. It's especially important if you use your notebook a lot on the road.

Any notebook, even a desktop replacement model, gives you at least an hour of operation before the battery powers down. If you need more battery life than that, here are some things you can try:

- **Change your power scheme**—Windows includes several built-in power schemes that manage key functions to provide either longer battery life or better performance. (It's always a trade-off between the two.) You can switch power schemes from the Windows Mobility Center (in the Battery Status section) or by clicking the Power icon in the notification area of the Windows taskbar.

- **Dim your screen**—The brighter your screen, the more power your PC uses. Conserve on power usage by dialing down the brightness level of your notebook's screen.

- **Turn it off when you're not using it**—A PC sitting idle is still using power. If you're going to be away from the keyboard for more than a few minutes, turn off the notebook to conserve power—or put the PC into sleep mode, which also cuts power use.

- **Don't do anything taxing**—Anytime you write or read a file from your notebook's hard disk, you use power. The same goes with using the CD or DVD drive; every spin of the drive drains the battery. If you use your notebook to watch DVD movies, don't expect the batteries to last as long as if you were just checking email or surfing the Web.

- **Buy a bigger battery**—Many notebook manufacturers sell batteries that have various capacities. You might buy a longer-lasting battery than the one that came in the box.

- **Buy a second battery**—When the first battery is drained, remove it and plug in a fresh one.

- **Buy a smaller notebook**—Ultrabook models use less power and have longer battery life than do traditional notebooks, which in turn are less power-hungry than desktop replacement models. The smaller the screen and the less powerful the CPU, the longer the notebook's battery life.

If worse comes to worst, keep an eye out for an available power outlet. Most coffee shops and airport lounges have at least one seat next to a power outlet; just carry your notebook's AC adapter with you and be ready to plug in when you can.

Securing Your Notebook

One of the great things about a notebook PC is that it's small and easily portable. One of the bad things about a notebook PC is that's it's small and easily portable—which makes it attractive to thieves. Take care to protect your notebook when you use it in public, which may mean investing in a notebook lock or some similar sort of antitheft device. Of course, just being vigilant helps; never leave your notebook unattended in a coffee shop or airport terminal.

In addition, be careful about transmitting private data over a public Wi-Fi network. Avoid the temptation to do your online shopping (and transmit your credit card number) from your local coffee shop; wait until you're safely connected to your home network before you send your private data over the Wi-Fi airwaves.

Troubleshooting Computer Problems

Computers aren't perfect. It's possible—although unlikely—that at some point in time, something will go wrong with your PC. It might refuse to start, it might freeze up, and it might crash and go dead. Yikes!

When something goes wrong with your computer, there's no need to panic (even though that's what you'll probably feel like doing). Most PC problems have easy-to-find causes and simple solutions. The key thing is to keep your wits about you and attack the situation calmly and logically—following the advice you'll find in this chapter.

No matter what kind of computer-related problem you're experiencing, there are six basic steps you should take to track down the cause of the problem. Work through these steps calmly and deliberately, and you're likely to find what's causing the current problem—and then be in a good position to fix it yourself:

1. **Don't panic!**—Just because there's something wrong with your PC is no reason to fly off the handle. Chances are there's nothing seriously wrong. Besides, getting all panicky won't solve anything. Keep your wits about you and proceed logically, and you can probably find what's causing your problem and get it fixed.

2. **Check for operator errors**—In other words, *you* might have done something wrong. Maybe you clicked the wrong button, pressed the wrong key, or plugged something into the wrong jack or port. Retrace your steps and try to duplicate your problem. Chances are the problem won't recur if you don't make the same mistake twice.

3. **Check that everything is plugged into the proper place and that the system unit itself is getting power**—Take special care to ensure that all your cables are *securely* connected—loose connections can cause all sorts of strange results.

4. **Make sure you have the latest versions of all the software installed on your system**—While you're at it, make sure you have the latest versions of device drivers installed for all the peripherals on your system. (Conversely, if you've just installed a new program or update, you might try removing it. Chances are it may have caused a problem.)

5. **Try to isolate the problem by when and how it occurs**—Walk through each step of the process to see if you can identify a particular program or driver that might be causing the problem. If you've just installed a new app (or updated an old one), consider that that might be the cause of your problem.

6. **When all else fails, call in professional help**—If you think it's a Windows-related problem, contact Microsoft's technical support department. If you think it's a problem with a particular program, contact the tech support department of the program's manufacturer. If you think it's a hardware-related problem, contact the manufacturer of your PC or the dealer you bought it from. The pros are there for a reason—when you need technical support, go and get it.

 CAUTION Not all tech support is free. Unless you have a brand new PC or brand new software, expect to pay a fee for technical support.

Troubleshooting in Safe Mode

If you're having trouble getting Windows to start, it's probably because some setting is wrong or some driver is malfunctioning. The problem is, how do you get into Windows to fix what's wrong when you can't even start Windows?

The solution is to hijack your computer before Windows gets hold of it and force it to start *without* whatever is causing the problem. You do this by watching the screen as your computer boots up and pressing the F8 key just before Windows starts to load. This displays the Windows startup menu, where you select Safe mode.

Safe mode is a special mode of operation that loads Windows in a simple configuration. When in Safe mode, you can look for device conflicts, restore incorrect or corrupted device drivers, or restore your system to a prior working configuration (using the System Restore utility, discussed later in this chapter).

 NOTE   Depending on the severity of your system problem, Windows might start in Safe mode automatically.

Reacting When Windows Freezes or Crashes

Probably the most common computer trouble is the freeze-up. That's what happens when your PC just stops dead in its tracks. The screen looks normal, but nothing works—you can't type onscreen, you can't click any buttons, nothing's happening. Even worse is when Windows crashes on you—just shuts down with no warning.

If your system freezes or crashes, the good news is that there's probably nothing wrong with your computer hardware. The bad news is that there's probably something funky happening with your operating system.

This doesn't mean your system is broken. It's just a glitch. And you can recover from glitches. Just remember not to panic and to approach the situation calmly and rationally.

What Causes Windows to Freeze?

If Windows up and freezes, what's the likely cause? There can be many different causes of a Windows freeze, including the following:

- You might be running an older software program or game that isn't compatible with your version of Windows. If so, upgrade the program.

- A memory conflict might exist between applications or between an application and Windows. Try running fewer programs at once or running problematic programs one at a time to avoid potential memory conflicts.

- You might not have enough memory installed on your system. Upgrade the amount of memory in your PC.

- You might not have enough free hard disk space on your computer. Delete any unnecessary files from your hard drive.

- Your hard disk might be developing errors or bad sectors. Check your hard disk for errors, as described in the "Performing a Hard Disk Checkup with ScanDisk" section earlier in this chapter.

Dealing with Frozen Windows

When Windows freezes, you need to get it unfrozen and up and running again. The way to do this is to shut down your computer.

In older versions of Windows, you could force a shutdown by holding down the Ctrl+Alt+Del keys. That doesn't work in Windows 10; instead, you need to press the Windows key and your PC's power button simultaneously. If that doesn't work, just press and hold the power button until the PC shuts down.

If your system crashes or freezes frequently, however, you should call in a pro. These kinds of problems can be tough to track down by yourself when you're dealing with Windows.

Dealing with a Frozen Program

Sometimes Windows works fine but an individual software program freezes. Fortunately, recent versions of Windows present an exceptionally safe environment; when an individual application crashes or freezes, it seldom messes up your entire system. You can use a utility called the Windows Task Manager to close the problem application without affecting other Windows programs.

When a Windows application freezes or crashes, press Ctrl+Alt+Del, and when the next screen appears, click or tap Task Manager; this opens the Windows Task Manager. To display everything there is to display, click More Details; you now see a series of tabs, as shown in Figure 26.4. Select the Processes tab, go to the Apps section, and click the task that's frozen. Click the End Task button and wait for the app to close.

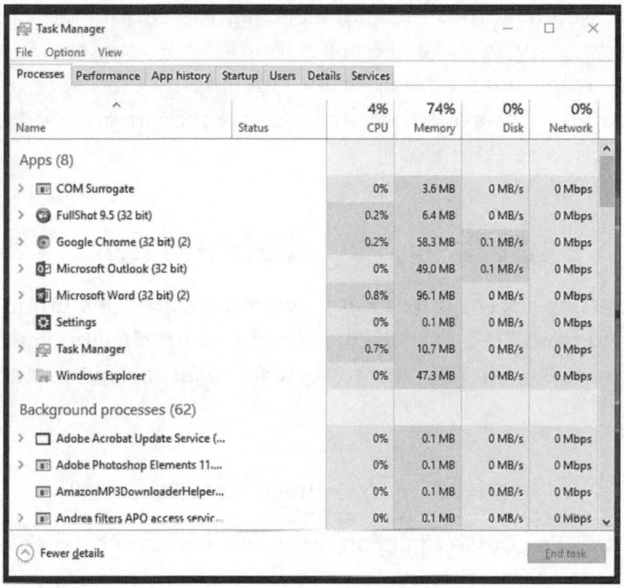

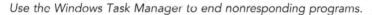

FIGURE 26.4

Use the Windows Task Manager to end nonresponding programs.

If you have multiple applications that crash on a regular basis, the situation can often be attributed to insufficient memory. See your computer dealer about adding more RAM to your system.

Dealing with a Major Crash

Perhaps the worst thing that can happen to your computer system is that it crashes—completely shuts down—without warning. If this happens to you, start by not panicking. Stay calm, take a few deep breaths, and then get ready to get going again.

You should always wait about 60 seconds after a computer crashes before you try to turn on your system again. This gives all the components time to settle down and—in some cases—reset themselves. Just sit back and count to 60 (slowly); then press your system unit's "on" button.

Nine times out of ten, your system will boot up normally, as if nothing unusual has happened. If this is what happens for you, great! If, however, your system doesn't come back up normally, you need to start troubleshooting the underlying problem, as discussed previously.

Even if your system comes back up as usual, the sudden crash might have done some damage. A system crash can sometimes damage any software program that was running at the time, as well as any documents that were open when the crash occurred. You might have to reinstall a damaged program or recover a damaged document from a backup file.

Restoring, Resetting, or Refreshing Your System

If you experience severe or recurring system crashes, it's time to take serious action. In Windows 10, there are three options for dealing with serious problems. In terms of severity, you can opt to restore, reset, or completely refresh your system.

Restoring Your System to a Previous State

The least intrusive course of action when your system crashes is to use Microsoft's System Restore utility. This utility can automatically restore your system to the state it was in before the crash occurred—and save you the trouble of reinstalling any damaged software programs. It's a great safety net for when things go wrong.

System Restore works by monitoring your system and noting any changes that are made when you install new applications. Each time it notes a change, it automatically creates what it calls a *restore point*. A restore point is basically a "snapshot" of key system files (including the Windows Registry) just before the new application is installed.

If something in your system goes bad, you can run System Restore to set things right. Pick a restore point before the problem occurred (such as right before a new installation), and System Restore will undo any changes made to monitored files since the restore point was created. This restores your system to its preinstallation—that is, *working*—condition.

To restore your system from a restore point, follow these steps:

1. Right-click the Start button and then click System to display the System window.

2. Click System Protection in the Navigation pane to open the System Properties dialog box.

3. Make sure the System Protection tab is selected (see Figure 26.5).

4. Click the System Restore button to display the System Restore window.

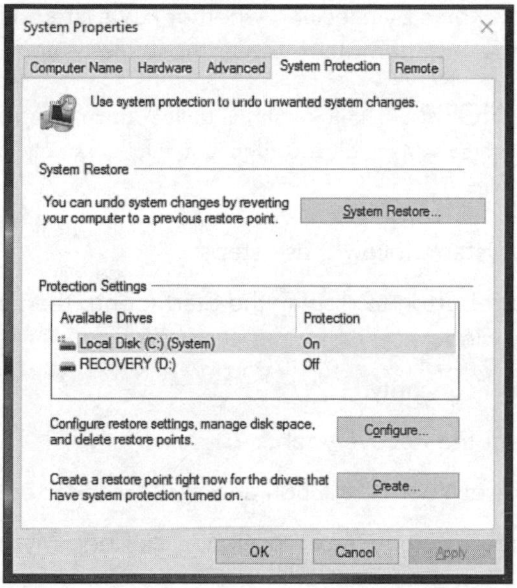

FIGURE 26.5

Use the System Restore utility to restore damaged programs or system files.

5. Click the Next button.

6. Click the restore point you want to return to, and then click the Next button.

7. When the confirmation screen appears, click the Finish button.

 CAUTION System Restore helps you recover any damaged programs and system files, but it doesn't help you recover damaged documents or data files.

Windows now starts to restore your system. You should make sure that all open programs are closed because Windows needs to be restarted during this process.

When the process is complete, your system should be back in decent working shape. Note, however, that it might take one-half hour or more to complete a system restore—so you'll have time to order a pizza and eat dinner before the operation is done!

Refreshing System Files

When a system file gets corrupted or deleted, Windows 10 provides the ability to "refresh" your system with the current versions of important system files. The

Refresh PC utility works by checking whether key system files are working properly. If it finds any issues, it attempts to repair those files—and only those files.

 NOTE The Refresh PC utility doesn't remove any of your personal files or documents. It refreshes only Windows system files.

To refresh your system, follow these steps:

1. Click the Start button to display the Start menu, then select Settings to display the Settings window.

2. Click Update & Security.

3. Click to select the Recovery tab.

4. Go to the Reset Your PC section and click Get Started.

5. When prompted to choose an option, click Keep My Files.

Windows prepares your system for the refresh, which might take a few minutes. Your computer eventually restarts. When you see the Start screen, your system is refreshed.

Resetting Your System to Its Original Condition

Resetting your system is more drastic than simply refreshing it. The Reset PC utility wipes your hard disk clean and reinstalls Windows from scratch. That leaves you with a completely reset system—but without any of the apps you've installed or the files you created.

 CAUTION The Reset PC utility completely deletes any files, documents, and programs you have on your system. Back up your files before taking this extreme step, and then restore your files from the backup and reinstall all the apps you use.

To reset your system, follow these steps:

1. Click the Start button to display the Start menu; then select Settings to display the Settings window.

2. Click Update & Security.

3. Click to select the Recovery tab.

4. Go to the Reset This PC section and click Get Started.

5. When prompted to choose an option, click Remove Everything, then follow the onscreen instructions.

Windows begins resetting your system by deleting everything on your hard drive and reinstalling the Windows operating system. This might take some time. When the process is complete, you need to re-enter your Windows product key and other personal information—but you'll have a like-new system, ready to start using again.

THE ABSOLUTE MINIMUM

Here are the key points to remember from this chapter:

- Dedicating a few minutes a week to PC maintenance can prevent serious problems from occurring in the future.

- Windows includes a number of utilities you can use to keep your hard drive in tip-top shape.

- Make sure that you keep all your computer hardware away from direct sunlight, dust, and smoke, and make sure that your system unit has plenty of ventilation.

- If you have a notebook PC, take appropriate steps to conserve battery life—and keep your PC safe from thieves!

- You can shut down frozen programs from the Windows Task Manager, which you display by pressing Ctrl+Alt+Del.

- Some problems can be fixed from Windows Safe mode; to enter Safe mode, restart your computer and press F8 before the Windows Start screen appears.

- If your system has serious problems, you can opt to restore, refresh, or completely reset Windows to its original factory condition.

Index

B

C

D

J

K

P

W

35674055724810